DIMENSIONS MATH 8B
Common Core

a Singapore Math® Program

STAR PUBLISHING PTE LTD

 Singapore Math Inc®

STAR PUBLISHING PTE LTD

Star Publishing Pte Ltd
115A Commonwealth Drive #05-12
Singapore 149596
Tel: (65) 64796800
Website: www.starpub.com.sg
Email: contactus@starpub.com.sg

in association with

SM Singapore Math Inc®

Singapore Math Inc
19535 SW 129th Avenue
Tualatin, OR 97062
Website: www.SingaporeMath.com
Email: customerservice@singaporemath.com

Based on the original series entitled
Discovering Mathematics, approved by
Ministry of Education, Singapore.

© 2013 **Star Publishing Pte Ltd**

ISBN 978-981-4250-63-4
ISBN 978-981-4250-67-2 (Hardcase)

PREFACE

DIMENSIONS MATH COMMON CORE is a series of textbooks designed for students in middle schools. Developed in collaboration between Star Publishing Pte Ltd and Singapore Math Inc., this series follows the Singapore Mathematics Framework and also covers the topics in the Common Core State Standards.

The emphasis of this series is on empowering students to learn mathematics effectively. Depending on the topics covered, different approaches are adopted for the presentation of concepts to facilitate understanding and internalization of concepts by students and to instill in them an interest to explore the topics further.

Each book includes appropriate examples, class activities, and diagrams to understand the concepts and apply them. Information technology skills are incorporated as appropriate.

With this comprehensive series, we hope that students will find learning mathematics an interesting and fun experience so that they will be motivated to study the subject, discover mathematical features and apply them in real-life situations.

Our special thanks to Richard Askey, Professor Emeritus (University of Wisconsin-Madison) for his indispensable advice and suggestions in the production of Dimensions Math Common Core series.

We wish to express our sincere thanks to all those who have provided valuable feedback and great assistance in the production of this series.

The Writing Team
Dimensions Math Common Core

TEXTBOOK FEATURES

The textbooks provide a solid well-balanced, comprehensive, and systematic approach to the teaching of mathematics. A combination of different approaches has been adopted in the presentation of mathematical concepts to motivate students and empower them to become independent learners. Examples and questions have been carefully designed to ensure that students not only understand the concepts, but are also able to apply them.

Example
Helps students understand and master a concept through a worked example

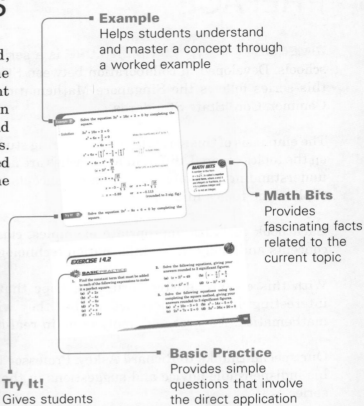

Math Bits
Provides fascinating facts related to the current topic

Basic Practice
Provides simple questions that involve the direct application of concepts

Try It!
Gives students an opportunity to answer a similar question to check how well they have grasped the concept

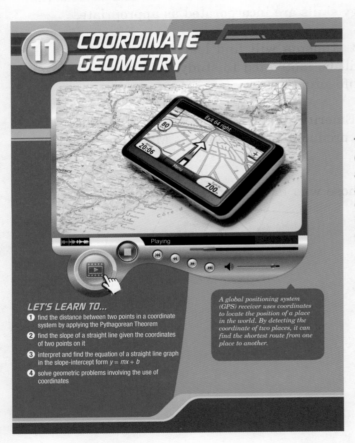

11 COORDINATE GEOMETRY

LET'S LEARN TO...
1. find the distance between two points in a coordinate system by applying the Pythagorean Theorem
2. find the slope of a straight line given the coordinates of two points on it
3. interpret and find the equation of a straight line graph in the slope-intercept form $y = mx + b$
4. solve geometric problems involving the use of coordinates

A global positioning system (GPS) receiver uses coordinates to locate the position of a place in the world. By detecting the coordinate of two places, it can find the shortest route from one place to another.

Chapter Opener
Introduces the topic through real-life applications and identifies the chapter's learning outcomes

In A Nutshell
Consolidates important rules and concepts for quick and easy review

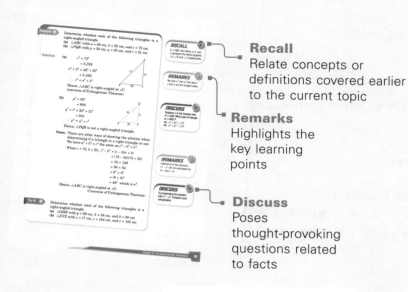

Class Activities
Introduces new mathematical concepts through cooperative learning methods

Recall
Relate concepts or definitions covered earlier to the current topic

Remarks
Highlights the key learning points

Discuss
Poses thought-provoking questions related to facts

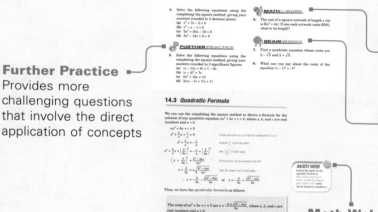

Further Practice
Provides more challenging questions that involve the direct application of concepts

Math@Work
Provides questions that involve the application of integrated concepts to practical situations

Brainworks
Provides higher-order thinking questions that involve an open-ended approach to problem solving

Math Web
Provides website links for additional information

Review Exercise
Gives students the opportunity to apply the concepts learned in the chapter through a variety of integrated questions

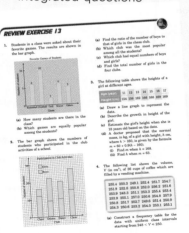

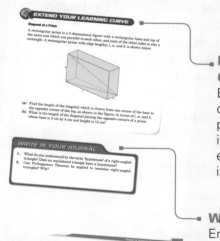

Extend Your Learning Curve
Extends and applies concepts learned to problems that are investigative in nature and engages the students in independent research

Write In Your Journal
Encourages reflective learning

CONTENTS

Contents

Chapter 8   Graphs of Linear and Quadratic Functions   1
    8.1   Linear Function   2
        A. Idea of Functions   2
        B. Linear Functions   5
        C. Rate of Change   9
    8.2   Graphs of Quadratic Functions   18
        A. Graph of $y = ax^2 + bx + c$, where $a > 0$ 18
        B. Graph of $y = ax^2 + bx + c$, where $a < 0$ 23
    In a Nutshell   28
    Review Exercise 8   29
    Extend Your Learning Curve   31
    Write in Your Journal   31

Chapter 9   Graphs in Practical Situations   32
    9.1   Tables, Charts and Graphs   33
    9.2   Distance-Time Graphs   38
    In a Nutshell   48
    Review Exercise 9   49
    Extend Your Learning Curve   51
    Write in Your Journal   51

Chapter 10   Pythagorean Theorem   52
    10.1 Pythagorean Theorem   53
    10.2 The Converse of Pythagorean Theorem   60
        A. Definition   60
        B. Determination of Right-Angled Triangles   60
    10.3 Applications of Pythagoras Theorem   65
    In a Nutshell   72
    Review Exercise 10   73
    Extend Your Learning Curve   75
    Write in Your Journal   75

Chapter 11   Coordinate Geometry   **76**
      11.1   Distance Between Two Points   77
      11.2   Slope of a Straight Line   83
      11.3   Equation of a Straight Line   90
      In a Nutshell   96
      Review Exercise 11   97
      Extend Your Learning Curve   99
      Write in Your Journal   99

Chapter 12   Mensuration of Pyramids, Cylinders, Cones and Spheres   **100**
      12.1   Pyramids   101
         A.   Introducing Pyramids   101
         B.   Nets and Surface Areas of Pyramids   103
         C.   Volumes of Pyramids   106
      12.2   Cylinders   113
         A.   Volume and Surface Area of a Cylinder   113
      12.3   Cones   120
         A.   Introducing Cones   120
         B.   Net and Surface Area of a Cone   121
         C.   Volume of a Cone   124
      12.4   Spheres   129
         A.   Introducing Spheres   129
         B.   Volume of a Sphere   130
         C.   Surface Area of a Sphere   131
      In a Nutshell   138
      Review Exercise 12   130
      Extend Your Learning Curve   142
      Write in Your Journal   142

Chapter 13   Data Analysis   **143**
      13.1   Organizing Data in Frequency Tables   144
      13.2   Bar Graphs and Histograms   154
         A.   Bar Graphs   154
         B.   Histograms   159
      13.3   Line Graphs and Scatter Plots   165
         A.   Line Graphs   165
         B.   Scatter Plots   169
      In a Nutshell   179
      Review Exercise 13   180
      Extend Your Learning Curve   182
      Write in Your Journal   182

Chapter 14 More About Quadratic Equations   **183**

    14.1   Solving Quadratic Equations by Factorization   184

    14.2   Completing the Square Method   187

    14.3   Quadratic Formula   192

    14.4   Graphical Method   196

    14.5   Applications of Quadratic Equations   200

    In a Nutshell   205

    Review Exercise 14   206

    Extend Your Learning Curve   207

    Write in Your Journal   207

Answers   **208**

8 GRAPHS OF LINEAR AND QUADRATIC FUNCTIONS

Playing

LET'S LEARN TO...

1. understand the idea of functions
2. draw the graph of a linear function
3. state the properties of the graphs of linear functions
4. draw the graph of a quadratic function
5. state the properties of the graphs of quadratic functions

Do you know that a stream of water that is projected into the air forms a beautiful symmetrical curve? The curve is the graph of a quadratic function.

8.1 *Linear Functions*

A Idea of Functions

In our daily life, we often come across two quantities that have certain relations between them. Let us see how we can represent some relations.

CLASS ACTIVITY 1

Objective: To represent a relation between two quantities.

Questions

1. A department store holds a clearance sale. All items are sold at 20% discount. To help customers work out the selling prices, the store manager considers using a table of marked prices (x) and their corresponding selling prices (y). However, he needs your help to complete such a table as shown below.

Marked price (x)	50	100	150	200	250
Selling price (y)		80			

(a) Copy and complete the above table.

(b) Represent each pair of values of x and y as an ordered pair such as (100, 80).

(c) Plot the ordered pairs in (b) in a copy of the given coordinate plane.

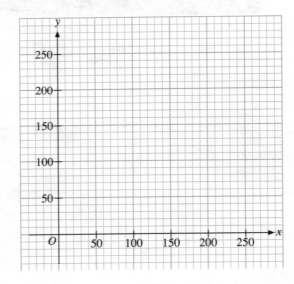

(d) Suggest an equation that represents the relation between x and y.

2. There are thirty tablets of vitamin C in a bottle. Benny consumes two tablets per day. Let y be the number of remaining tablets in the bottle after the xth day.

(a) Copy and complete the following table.

x	0	2	5	10	15
y	30				

(b) Represent each pair of values of x and y as an ordered pair.

(c) Plot the ordered pairs in **(b)** in a copy of the given coordinate plane.

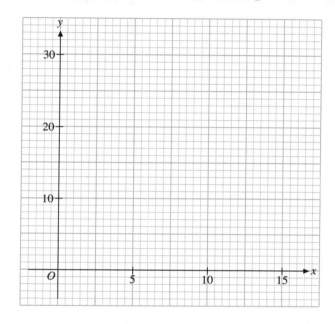

(d) Write down an equation that represents the relation between x and y.

In each case in Class Activity 1, we see that there is a value of y corresponding to every value of x. In mathematics, this type of relation is called a **function**.

> A variable y is a function of another variable x if for each x, there is to exactly one value of y which is determined by x.

To get a better idea of functions, we can compare a function to a number-processing machine.

Let us consider how the number-processing machine on the right works.

For each input value of x, the machine yields an output value of y. For instance, in Question 1 of Class Activity 1, when the input values are $x = 50$, 100, and 150, the output values are $y = 40$, 80, and 120 respectively.

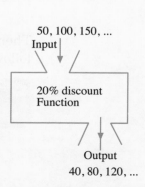

50, 100, 150, ...
Input

20% discount Function

Output
40, 80, 120, ...

A function can be represented in different ways. From Class Activity 1, we see that:

> A function can be represented by
> - a table of values,
> - ordered pairs,
> - a graph, or
> - an equation.

Example 1

The initial temperature of some water in a kettle is 20 °C. Upon heating, the temperature of the water increases by 10 °C per minute. Let y °C be the temperature of the water after x minutes.

(a) Complete the following table.

x	0	2	4	6	8
y					

(b) Draw the graph of y against x for $0 \leqslant x \leqslant 8$.
(c) Express y as a function of x.

Solution

(a) The initial temperature is 20 °C, that is when $x = 0$, temperature of water $y = 20$ °C.
The temperature increases by 10 °C every minute.

When $x = 2$, increase in temperature $= 10 \times 2$
$$= 20 \text{ °C}$$

∴ temperature of water after 2 minutes $= 20 + 20$
$$= 40 \text{ °C}.$$

Similarly,

when $x = 4$, temperature of water $= 20 + 10 \times 4$
$$= 60 \text{ °C};$$

when $x = 6$, temperature of water $= 20 + 10 \times 6$
$$= 80 \text{ °C};$$

when $x = 8$, temperature of water $= 20 + 10 \times 8$
$$= 100 \text{ °C}.$$

Therefore, the corresponding values of x and y are as follows:

x	0	2	4	6	8
y	20	40	60	80	100

(b) By plotting the ordered pairs $(0, 20)$, $(2, 40)$, ..., $(8, 100)$, and drawing a straight line through the points, we obtain the graph of y against x as shown below.

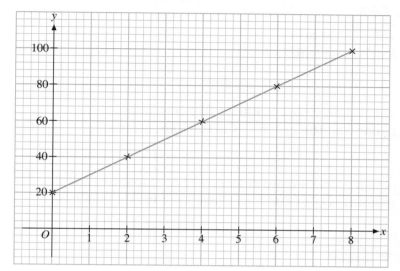

(c) Using the reasoning in **(a)**,
temperature of water after x minutes $= (20 + 10x)$ °C.
$\therefore$ the required function is $y = 20 + 10x$.

DISCUSS
In this case, is the function $y = 20 + 10x$ valid for
(a) $x = -1$?
(b) $x = 9$?

Try It! **1**

The initial depth of some water in a burette is 24 cm. The water level decreases by 4 cm per minute. Let y cm be the depth of the water after x minutes.
(a) Copy and complete the following table.

x	0	2	4	6
y				

(b) Draw the graph of y against x for $0 \leqslant x \leqslant 6$.
(c) Express y as a function of x.

B Linear Functions

In Class Activity 1, the equations of the functions of the two cases are respectively

$$y = \frac{4}{5}x \quad \text{and} \quad y = 30 - 2x.$$

The graph of each of these two functions is a straight line. Such functions are called **linear functions**.

In general, we have the following definition.

> A linear function y of x is a function that can be written in the form
> $$y = mx + b,$$
> where m and b are constants.

Note that the function $y = mx + b$ is called a linear function because the powers of x and y are equal to one and the graph of the function is a straight line.

The features of the linear function $y = mx + b$ are determined by the constants m and b. Let us explore the meanings of m and b in Class Activities 2 and 3.

Objective: To explore the meaning of m in the linear equation, $y = mx + b$.

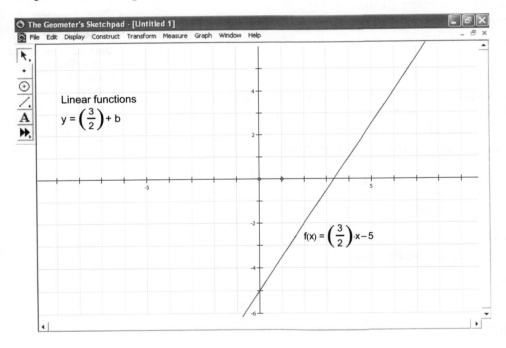

Task

(a) Choose **Graph | Plot New Function** command. A New Function window will appear.

(b) Enter the expression $\left(\dfrac{3}{2}\right)x - 5$ in the New Function window and click OK. The graph of the function $y = \left(\dfrac{3}{2}\right)x - 5$ will appear on the screen as shown above.

REMARKS
In Sketchpad, functions of x are denoted by f(x), g(x), etc. For instance, the function

$y = \dfrac{3}{2}x - 5$ is denoted by

$f(x) = \dfrac{3}{2}x - 5$.

(c) Use the above method to draw each of the following graphs on the same screen.

(i) $y = \left(\dfrac{3}{2}\right)x - 3$

(ii) $y = \left(\dfrac{3}{2}\right)x$

(iii) $y = \left(\dfrac{3}{2}\right)x + 2$

Questions

1. What is the common feature of the above linear graphs?

2. Find the slope of each graph.

3. Find the y-intercept of each graph.

4. Suggest the features of the graph of $y = \left(\dfrac{3}{2}\right)x + b$, where b is a constant.

In Grade 7, we have learned about the slope of linear graphs. **Slope** of a straight line is a measure of its steepness, that is how much it rises vertically for per unit length horizontally.

$$\text{Slope of a line} = \frac{\text{rise}}{\text{run}} = \frac{\text{vertical change}}{\text{horizontal change}}$$

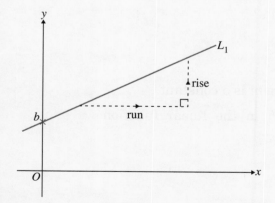

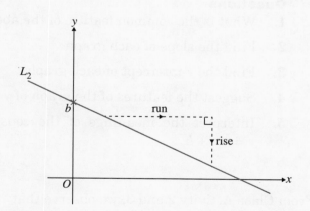

$$\text{Slope of } L_1 = \frac{\text{rise}}{\text{run}} > 0 \qquad\qquad \text{Slope of } L_2 = \frac{\text{rise}}{\text{run}} < 0$$

The y-coordinate of the point of intersection of the linear graph with the y-axis is called the **y-intercept** of the graph.

Objective: To explore the meaning of b in the linear equation, $y = mx + b$.

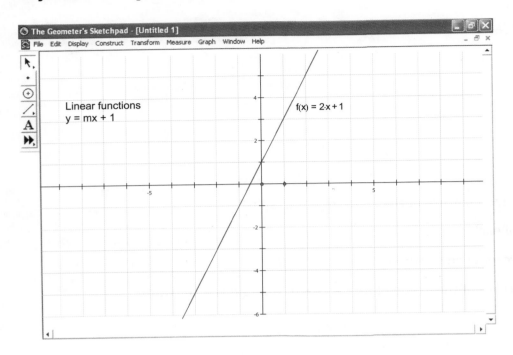

Tasks

(a) On a Sketchpad screen, draw the graph of $y = 2x + 1$ as shown above.

(b) Draw the graph of each of the following functions on the same screen.

  (i) $y = 3x + 1$ **(ii)** $y = 1$
  (iii) $y = -x + 1$ **(iv)** $y = -2.5x + 1$

Questions

1. What is the common feature of the above linear graphs?

2. Find the slope of each graph.

3. Find the y-intercept of each graph.

4. Suggest the features of the graph of $y = mx + 1$, where m is a constant.

5. Interpret the meanings of the constants m and b in the linear function $y = mx + b$.

From Class Activity 2 and 3, we observe that:

> The graph of the linear function $y = mx + b$ is a straight line with slope $= m$ and y-intercept $= b$.

For instance, the graph of $y = -7x + 6$ is a straight line with slope $= -7$ and y-intercept $= 6$.

C Rate of Change

In Grade 7, we have learned to use ratios to compare the rates at which two quantities change. For instance, price rate of per fluid ounce of juice, weekly wage rate and rate of running. These comparisons are called **rates of change**.

Slope measures the steepness of a line by comparing how much the y-variable changes, its *rise*, to how much the x-variable changes, its *run*, by using a ratio. The slope of a line is thus a rate of change. It is the rate of change of the linear function defining the line. The value of y that corresponds to $x = 0$, that is the y-intercept, is also referred to as the **initial value** of the linear function.

In the following activity, we shall see how we can be determine the rates of change and initial values of some linear functions.

CLASS ACTIVITY 4

Objective: To determine the rate of change and initial value of a linear function.

Questions

1. Reagan opens a savings account. She deposits an equal amount every month and makes no withdrawals. After 2 months, she has $310 in her account. After 5 months, she has $550. After 10 months, she has $950.
    (a) Find the rate of change of the balance in Reagan's account while she is saving.
    (b) What is the unit of measure for your answer?
    (c) Find the initial amount which Reagan has deposited when she opened the savings account.

2. Gardener Peter has some fertilizer which he applies to the lawn. The table shows the mass y grams of fertilizer remaining after he has applied a certain amount of the fertilizer to x square meters of lawn.

Area of lawn ($x\,\mathrm{m}^2$)	Mass of fertilizer (y g)
20	1,600
30	1,350
50	850
80	100

    (a) Determine if the application of fertilizer to the lawn in this case is a linear function,
    (b) Using the information in the table, find the rate of change in mass per square meter if the function is a linear.

3. **(a)** Graph the data of Questions 1 and 2 each on a sheet of graph paper.
    (b) Find the slope of each line. What can you say about the relationship between the slope of each line and the respective rate of change found in part **1(a)** and **2(b)**.
    (c) From the graph of Question 2, find the initial amount of fertilizer which the gardener has.

4. After Olivia had her coffee at a café near her home, she decided to walk to her favorite bookstore which is located 3,000 meters from her home. The graph below shows the distance y meters from home she travelled in x minutes.

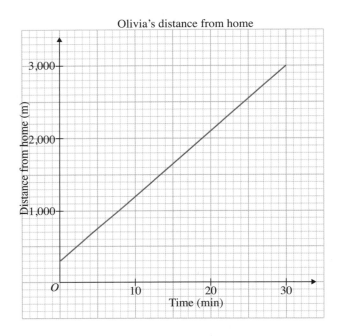

Olivia's distance from home

    (a) Find the rate of change of this linear relationship.
    (b) What is the initial value? What does this value represent?
    (c) Express y as a function of x.

Using linear functions to describe or approximate relationships in the real world is referred to as **linear modeling**. If $y = mx + b$ is a linear model of changing quantities x and y, then the slope m is the rate at which y is changing per unit increase in x, while the y-intercept b is the **initial value** of y that corresponds to $x = 0$. The slope m is measured in units of y per unit of x, while the y-intercept, b is measured in units of y.

Example 2

The table shows the distance y km traveled while driving on a highway.

Time (x hr)	1	2	3	3.5
Distance (y km)	90	180	270	315

(a) Draw the graph of y against x for $0 \leqslant x \leqslant 3.5$.
(b) Find the slope of the graph and explain what the slope represents.
(c) Find the initial value of y.
(d) Express y as a function of x.

Solution

(a) By plotting the ordered pairs (1, 90), (2, 180), (3, 270), and (3.5, 315), and drawing a straight line through the points, we obtain the graph of y against x as shown below.

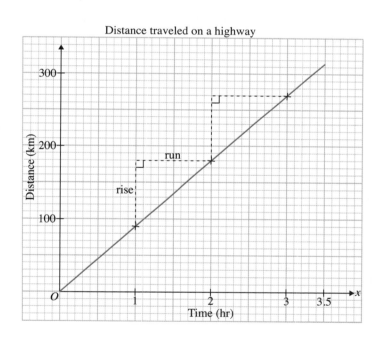

Distance traveled on a highway

REMARKS
For straight lines, the slope between any two points on the line is the same. That is, the rate of change is constant.

(b) To find the slope, pick any two points on the line such as (1, 90) and (2, 180).

$$\text{Slope} = \frac{\text{rise}}{\text{run}} \qquad \text{Definition of slope}$$

$$= \frac{180 - 90}{2 - 1}$$

$$= \frac{90}{1} \quad \longleftarrow \text{change in km} \\ \longleftarrow \text{change in hour}$$

A distance of 90 km is traveled in every 1 hour. Thus, the rate of traveling on a highway is 90 km/hr.

REMARKS
The rate of traveling is better referred to as speed.

(c) The straight line graph in **(a)** passes through $y = 0$ when $x = 0$.

Thus, the initial value of y is 0 km.

(d) Since the initial value is 0 and for every 1 hour, the distance increases by 90,

$\therefore$ the required function is $y = 90x$.

 Try It! 2 The table shows the distance y km traveled while driving in the city.

Time (x hr)	1.5	2	3	4
Distance (y km)	75	100	150	200

(a) Draw the graph of y against x for $0 \leqslant x \leqslant 4$.

(b) Find the slope of the graph and explain what the slope represents.

(c) Find the initial value of y.

(d) Express y as a function of x.

Example 3

Knox had some gasoline in his truck. After driving 100 miles, he had 11 gallons left. The graph below shows part of Knox's journey.

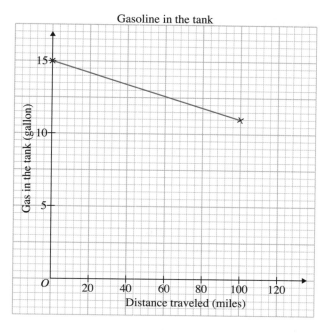

Gasoline in the tank

(a) Find the rate of change of this linear relationship. Explain what this rate represents.

(b) What is the *mpg* of Knox's truck?

(c) What is the meaning of the value 15 on the vertical axis?

(d) Assuming the rate you found in part (b) remains constant throughout Knox's journey, what will be the maximum distance Knox can travel before he runs out of gasoline?

REMARKS

For linear functions, the rate of change is constant.

Solution

(a) Slope of the line $= \dfrac{\text{rise}}{\text{run}}$

$= \dfrac{11 - 15}{100 - 0}$ ← change in gallons
← change in miles

$= \dfrac{-1}{25}$

$= -0.04$

Thus, the rate of change is −0.04 gal/mi and it indicates that Knox's truck is using 0.04 gallons of gasoline for every mile that he travels.

DISCUSS

What do you think the negative value of the slope means? What can you say about the amount of gasoline in the tank?

(b) The slope $\frac{-1}{25}$ also tells us that Knox can drive 25 miles on one gallon of gasoline. Thus, the mpg of Knox's truck is 25 miles per gallon.

Note: *mpg* (miles per gallon) refers to the number of miles that can be traveled on one gallon of gasoline.

(c) The value 15 on the vertical axis is the initial value of y; this means Knox initially had 15 gallons of gasoline in the tank before he started driving.

(d) Knox can drive 25 miles on one gallon of gasoline. Thus with 15 gallons of gasoline, the maximum distance Knox can travel will be 25 × 15 = 375 miles.

Try It! **3**

There is a small crack in a water container and water is leaking from it. The graph below shows the amount of water, y liters, that remained in the container after x hours.

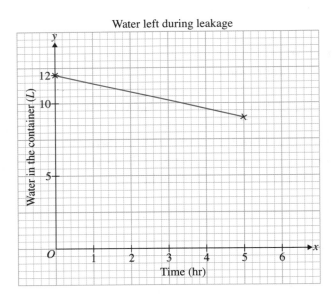

Water left during leakage

(a) Find the rate of change of this relationship. What does this rate show?
(b) What is the meaning of the value 12 on the vertical axis?
(c) How much water remained in the container after 24 hours?

The slope of a straight line is the same throughout the line for all its points, therefore the rate of change is constant. A linear function has a constant rate of increase or decrease. This constant rate of change is the slope of the straight line.

REMARKS

Graphs of non-linear functions are not linear and do not have a constant rate of change.

The rate of change of a function y of x indicates whether it is increasing or decreasing. A function is said to be **increasing** when y increases as x increases and y decreases as x decreases. The functions in Example 2 and Try It 2 are increasing functions.

A function y of x is said to be **decreasing** when y decreases as x increases and y increases as x decreases. The functions in Example 3 and Try It 3 are decreasing functions. If the slope of a linear function is 0, then the function is neither increasing nor decreasing, but is constant. The graph of a constant function is a horizontal line.

EXERCISE 8.1

 BASIC PRACTICE

1. A function y of x has the following table of values.

x	0	2	4	6
y	3	5	7	9

   Represent the function by
   (a) ordered pairs,
   (b) a graph,
   (c) an equation.

2. A function y of x is given by the following ordered pairs:

   $$(0, 0), (1, 2), (3, 6), (5, 10).$$

   Represent the function by
   (a) a table of values,
   (b) a graph,
   (c) an equation.

3. The diagram shows the graph of a function. Represent the function by
   (a) a table of values,
   (b) ordered pairs,
   (c) an equation.

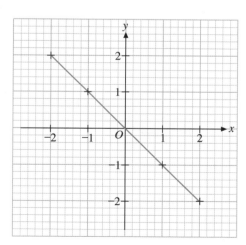

4. The equation of a function is $y = 2x - 1$.
   (a) Construct a table of values of the function for $x = -3, -1, 0,$ and 3.
   (b) Write down the ordered pairs of the function for $x = -3, -1, 0,$ and 3.
   (c) Draw the graph of the function for $-3 \leqslant x \leqslant 3$.

5. Determine which of the following is a linear function. If so, find the constant rate of change. If not, explain your reasoning.
   (a) (i) The Fast Car Rental Company charges $50 per day plus a $10 service charge to rent one of its cars.
       (ii) Barry loans $120 to Kelly who pays it back in equal amounts over 8 weeks.
   (b) (i)

Number of days	Overdue charge ($)
1	1.20
2	2.40
3	4.80
4	9.60

   (ii)

Number of hours worked	Wages ($)
2	30
4	60
6	90
8	120

6. (a) Copy and complete the following table of values for the linear function $y = -\frac{1}{2}x + 3$.

x	−4	−2	0	2
$y = -\frac{1}{2}x + 3$				

   (b) Draw the graph of the function.
   (c) State the slope and y-intercept of the graph.
   (d) Is this function an increasing or decreasing function?

7. (a) Write a function for the perimeter P of a square with sides x cm. Is the perimeter of a square a linear or non-linear function of the length of its sides? Explain briefly.
   (b) Write a function for the area A of a square with sides x cm. Is the area of a square a linear or non-linear function of the length of its sides? Explain briefly.

8. A function y of x is given by the following table.

x	0	1	1.5	2	2.5	3
y	1	2	3.25	5	7.25	10

   (a) Represent the function by a graph on a coordinate plane.
   (b) Is the function a linear function? Why?

9. The table shows the amount of money raised by Martin who collected pledges to run in a charity race.

Distance (x km)	2	4	8	10
Money ($$y$)	8	16	32	40

   (a) Draw the graph of y against x for $0 \leqslant x \leqslant 10$.
   (b) Find the rate of change of this function and explain what it represents.
   (c) Is this function an increasing or decreasing function?
   (d) Find the initial value of y.
   (e) Express y as a function of x.

10. The table shows the temperature of a cup of hot tea that is left on the table over a period of 9 hours.

Time (hr)	0	3	6	9
Temperature (°C)	96	69	42	15

   (a) Draw a graph to represent the data.
   (b) Find the rate of change of this function and explain what it represents.
   (c) Is this function an increasing or decreasing function?
   (d) Find the initial value of y.
   (e) Express y as a function of x.

11. (a) Draw the graphs of the functions

$$y = 3x - 2 \quad \text{and} \quad y = -\frac{5}{2}x - 2$$

on the same coordinate plane for $-3 \leqslant x \leqslant 3$.

(b) State the common feature of the above two graphs.

12. (a) Draw the graphs of the functions

$$y = -2x + 4 \quad \text{and} \quad y = -2x$$

on the same diagram for $-4 \leqslant x \leqslant 4$.

(b) State the common feature of the above two graphs.

 **MATH @ WORK**

13. For an on-site repair job, a computer technician charges $40 per visit and $30 per hour of service. Let $\$y$ be the total charge for an on-site job that requires x hours of work.

(a) Copy and complete the following table.

x	1	2	3	4
y				

(b) Express y as a function of x.
(c) Draw the graph of the function y of x.
(d) Find the total charge for an on-site job of 2.5 hours.

14. Jean earns $2,000 a month. She spends $\$x$ and saves $\$y$ each month.

(a) Copy and complete the following table.

x	1,000	1,300	1,600	2,000
y				

(b) Express y as a function of x.
(c) Is y an increasing or decreasing function of x?
(d) Draw the graph of the function y of x.

15. The price of a new mobile phone is $400. Its value decreases by $80 each year. Let $\$y$ be the value of the mobile phone after x years.

(a) Copy and complete the following table.

x	0	1	3	5
y				

(b) Draw the graph of y against x.
(c) Express y as a function of x.
(d) In which year will this phone have no resale value?

 **BRAIN WORKS**

16. Alex opens a small café. The set-up cost for equipment and renovation is $20,000. The operating cost is $6,000 a month. Let $\$y$ be the total cost to start and operate the café for x months.

(a) Copy and complete the following table.

x	1	3	5	10
y				

(b) Express y as a function of x.
(c) Draw the graph of y against x for $0 \leqslant x \leqslant 15$.
(d) Assume that the monthly gross income of the café is $\$k$, where k is a constant. Alex hopes to break even (i.e., making neither a gain nor a loss) within 10 to 15 months in his business. Find a possible value of k.

17. Make a table of four values for each of the following cases where
(a) the rate of change is $2 per liter,
(b) the initial value is 7 pounds and the rate of change is 1.5 pounds per month.

18. Write a problem to represent a rate of change of 1 inch for every foot.

8.2 *Graphs of Quadratic Functions*

In an earlier section, we have learned that the graph of the linear function $y = mx + b$, where the highest power of x is 1, is a straight line.

What would the shape of the graph of the function $y = x^2 - 3$ be, where the highest power of x is 2?

In general, the function $y = ax^2 + bx + c$, where a, b, and c are constants and $a \neq 0$, is called a **quadratic function**. For instance, $y = 2x^2 + 3x + 4$, $y = x^2 - 3$, and $y = -x^2 - 6x + 1$ are quadratic functions y of x.

Let us first explore the graph of the quadratic function $y = ax^2 + bx + c$, where the coefficient of x^2 is positive, i.e. $a > 0$. The graph of a quadratic function is called a **quadratic graph**.

A Graph of $y = ax^2 + bx + c$, where $a > 0$

The simplest quadratic function is $y = x^2$. We can draw its graph as follows.

STEP ❶ Set up a table of values.

x	-3	-2	-1	0	1	2	3
$y = x^2$	9	4	1	0	1	4	9

STEP ❷ Plot the points on a Cartesian plane.

STEP ❸ Join the points to form a smooth curve. The curve is the graph of $y = x^2$.

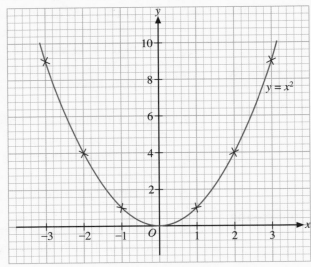

The graph of $y = x^2$ is a curve that is symmetrical about the y-axis. We say that it opens upwards. Do all quadratic graphs have the same shape as the above curve? Let us draw more quadratic graphs and investigate their properties.

CLASS ACTIVITY 5

Objective: To investigate the properties of the graph of a quadratic function $y = ax^2 + bx + c$ for $a > 0$.

Questions

1. (a) Copy and complete the following tables.

(a) (i)

x	−4	−3	−2	−1	0	2	3	4
$y = \frac{1}{2}x^2$	9	4	1	0	1	4	9	

(ii)

x	−2	−1.5	−1	0	1	1.5	2
$y = 2x^2$	9	4	1	0	1	4	9

(iii)

x	−2	−1.5	−1	0	1	1.5	2
$y = 2x^2 + 1$							

(iv)

x	−2	−1.5	−1	0	1	1.5	2
$y = 2x^2 - 3$							

(v)

x	−3	−2	−1	0	1	2	3
$y = x^2$							

(vi)

x	−4	−3	−2	−1	0	1	2
$y = (x + 1)^2$							

(vii)

x	−2	−1	0	1	2	3	4
$y = (x - 1)^2$							

(viii)

x	−2	−1	0	1	2	3	4
$y = (x - 1)^2 - 2$							

(b) Draw the graphs of the equations in **(i)**, **(ii)**, **(iii)**, and **(iv)** on a sheet of graph paper using the same scales as shown below.

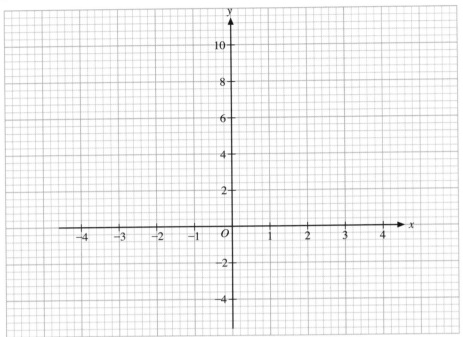

(c) Draw the graphs of the equations in **(v)**, **(vi)**, **(vii)**, and **(viii)** on another sheet of graph paper using the same scales as that in **(b)**.

(d) (i) Describe the graphs in **(b)** and **(c)**.

(ii) Write down the coordinates of the lowest point of each graph.

(iii) Which graph has the widest shape?

(iv) At how many points does each graph meet the x-axis?

(v) At how many points does each graph meet the y-axis?

(vi) Study the shapes of the graphs. Are they symmetrical? If they are, state the equation of the line about which each graph is symmetrical.

In Class Activity 5, we generalized the equation $y = x^2$ in three ways. One was to multiply x^2 by a positive number such that $y = ax^2$. The numbers 2 and $\frac{1}{2}$ were used in the activity but it could be other positive numbers.

When the number is larger than 1, the graph becomes narrower. The graph becomes broader when the number is between 0 and 1.

Next, we added or subtracted a number such that $y = ax^2 + c$, as in (iii) and (iv). This either raised or lowered the graph $y = ax^2$ in the Cartesian plane.

Finally, we added or subtracted a constant from the variable x, such that $y = (x + 1)^2$ and $y = (x - 1)^2$, as in (vi) and (vii). The original graph $y = x^2$ is shifted to the left or right along the x-axis. In all cases, the shape and size of the original graph remains the same. These three operations can be combined to get the general function $y = ax^2 + bx + c$.

DISCUSS

What are the expanded forms of the quadratic functions $y = (x + 1)^2$, $y = (x - 1)^2$ and $y = (x - 1)^2 - 2$?

The graphs of quadratic functions $y = ax^2 + bx + c$, for $a > 0$, have the following properties which were illustrated in Class Activity 5.

1. When $a > 0$, the graph opens upward. It is sometimes called a **parabola**.

2. The graph has a lowest point. This point is called the **minimum point** of the parabola.

3. The vertical line through the minimum point is the **line of symmetry** of the graph.

4. The smaller the numerical value of a, the wider the graph opens upward.

5. The graph may meet the x-axis at 0, 1 or 2 points. However, it meets the y-axis at only 1 point.

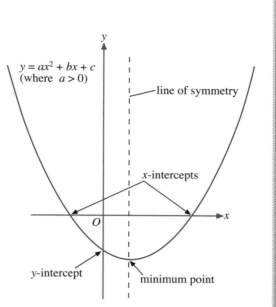

MATH WEB

You can look up 'parabola' on the Internet to read about some of its properties. Most of these will be treated in later courses.

REMARKS

The x-coordinate of a point of intersection of a graph and the x-axis is called an **x-intercept** of the graph.

Example 4

A horizontal bridge is 20 m long and it is supported by a suspension cable. The height, y m, of the cable over the bridge at a distance, x m, from one end of the bridge is given by

$$y = 0.03x^2 - 0.6x + 5, \quad \text{for } 0 \leqslant x \leqslant 20.$$

(a) Draw the graph of $y = 0.03x^2 - 0.6x + 5$ for $0 \leqslant x \leqslant 20$.
(b) Find the height of the cable at one end.
(c) State the line of symmetry of the graph.
(d) Find the minimum height of the cable above the bridge.

Solution

(a) We set up a table of values for the function.

$$y = 0.03x^2 - 0.6x + 5$$

x	0	4	8	10	12	16	20
y	5	3.08	2.12	2	2.12	3.08	5

The diagram below shows the graph of $y = 0.03x^2 - 0.6x + 5$.

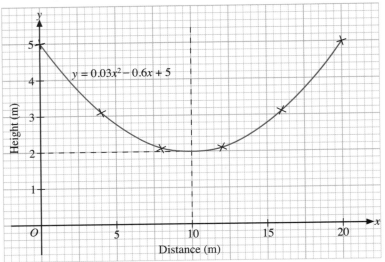

REMARKS

The shape of the graph drawn depends on the scales on both axes. In this example, if both axes are in the same scale, the shape of the parabola would be much wider.

(b) When $x = 0$, we have $y = 5$.
The height of the cable at one end is 5 m.

(c) The line of symmetry is $x = 10$, since $x = 10$ is the same distance from $x = 0$ and $x = 20$, where y has the same value 5, and also between $x = 8$ and $x = 12$ where y has the same value 2.12.

(d) The minimum point of the graph is at $(10, 2)$.
The minimum height of the cable is 2 m when the cable is 10 m from one end.

DISCUSS

How can you check if the point $(3, 3.3)$ lies on the graph of $y = 0.03x^2 - 0.6x + 5$, or above or below this graph?

Try It! 4

The diagram shows a partial cross-section of a hand torch. The curve AED is a reflector surface and its equation is given by

$$y = \frac{2}{9}x^2 - \frac{4}{3}x + 3 \quad \text{for } 0 \leqslant x \leqslant 6,$$

where y cm is the vertical distance of a point on the surface from the base BC when the point is x cm from the wall AB. On a Cartesian plane, the coordinates of B and C are $(0, 0)$ and $(6, 0)$ respectively.

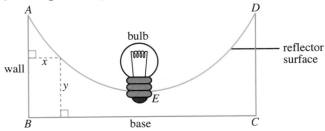

(a) Draw the graph of $y = \frac{2}{9}x^2 - \frac{4}{3}x + 3$ for $0 \leqslant x \leqslant 6$.
(b) Find the distance AB.
(c) State the line of symmetry of the graph.
(d) Find the minimum distance of the reflector surface from the base.

Graph of $y = ax^2 + bx + c$, where $a < 0$

The graph of the quadratic function $y = ax^2 + bx + c$ for $a < 0$ is drawn in the same way as the case for $a > 0$. Let us learn how to draw such graphs.

CLASS ACTIVITY 6

Objective: To investigate the properties of the graph of a quadratic function $y = ax^2 + bx + c$ for $a < 0$.

Questions

(a) Copy and complete the following tables.

(i)

x	−3	−2	−1	0	1	2	3
$y = -x^2$							

(ii)

x	−2	−1.5	−1	0	1	1.5	2
$y = -3x^2$							

(iii)

x	−3	−2	−1	0	1	2	3
$y = -x^2 - 2$							

(iv)

x	−4	−3	−2	−1	0	1	2
$y = -(x+1)^2 + 2$ $= -x^2 - 2x + 1$							

(b) Draw the graphs of the equations above on a sheet of graph paper using the same scales as shown below.

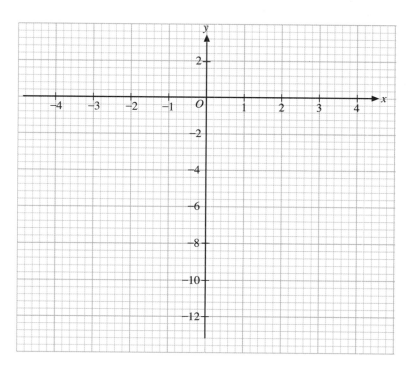

(c) (i) Describe the graphs in **(b)**.
　　(ii) Write down the coordinates of the highest point of each graph.
　　(iii) Which graph has the narrowest shape?
　　(iv) At how many points does each graph meet the x-axis?
　　(v) At how many points does each graph meet the y-axis?
　　(vi) Write down the equation of the line of symmetry of each graph.

(d) Work with a classmate to write a summary of the properties of the graphs of quadratic functions $y = ax + bx + c$, for $a < 0$, which were illustrated in Class Activity 6.

Example 5

When a stone is thrown upwards from the top of a building, its height h m from the ground at time t s is given by

$$h = -5t^2 + 10t + 40.$$

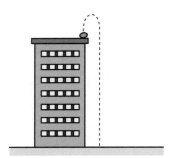

(a) Draw the graph of $h = -5t^2 + 10t + 40$ for $0 \leqslant t \leqslant 4.5$.
(b) Find the height of the building.
(c) Find the time of flight of the stone.
(d) When is the stone 20 m from the ground?
(e) State the line of symmetry of the graph in **(a)**.
(f) Find the maximum height of the stone from the ground.

Solution　**(a)** $h = -5t^2 + 10t + 40$

t	0	1	2	3	4	4.5
h	40	45	40	25	0	−16.25

The diagram below shows the graph of $h = -5t^2 + 10t + 40$.

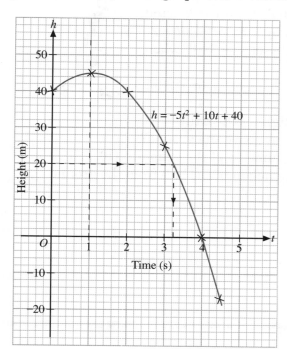

(b) When $t = 0$, the stone is right at the top of the building.
From the graph, when $t = 0$, $h = 40$.
The height of the building is 40 m.

(c) When the stone hits the ground, $h = 0$.
From the graph, $h = 0$ occurs when $t = 4$.
The time of flight is 4 s.

(d) Draw the horizontal line at $h = 20$ to intersect the graph.
The t-coordinate of the point of intersection is the required time.
The stone will be 20 m from the ground after about 3.2 s.

(e) The line of symmetry is $t = 1$.

(f) The maximum point of the graph is (1, 45).
The maximum height is 45 m.

Note: We can draw the graph of $h = -5t^2 + 10t + 40$ for all real values of t. However, as we can see from the graph, the value h is negative for $t > 4$. Therefore, the graph is only applicable to this problem for $0 \le t \le 4$.

When David hits a football with his head, the height h m of the ball from the ground after t seconds is given by $h = -5t^2 + 6t + 2$.

(a) What is the height of the ball when David hits it?

(b) Draw the graph of $h = -5t^2 + 6t + 2$ for $0 \leqslant t \leqslant 1.5$.

(c) Find the time of flight of the ball.

(d) When is the ball 3 m above the ground?

(e) State the line of symmetry of the graph in (b).

(f) Find the maximum height of the ball from the ground.

EXERCISE 8.2

BASIC PRACTICE

1. (a) Copy and complete the following table.

x	−3	−2	−1	0	1	2	3
$y = x^2 - 4$							

(b) Taking 2 cm to represent 1 unit on the x-axis and 2 cm to represent 2 units on the y-axis, draw the graph of $y = x^2 - 4$ for $-3 \leqslant x \leqslant 3$.

(c) State the line of symmetry and the minimum point of the graph.

2. (a) Copy and complete the following table.

x	−4	−3	−2	−1	0	1	2
$y = x^2 + 2x + 1$							

(b) Taking 2 cm to represent 1 unit on the x-axis and 2 cm to represent 2 units on the y-axis, draw the graph of $y = x^2 + 2x + 1$ for $-4 \leqslant x \leqslant 2$.

(c) State the line of symmetry and the minimum point of the graph.

(d) State the coordinates of the point(s) where the graph meets the x-axis. What is/are the point(s) called?

3. (a) Copy and complete the following table.

x	−1	0	1	2	3	4	5
$y = -\frac{1}{2}x^2 + 2x$							

(b) Taking 2 cm to represent 1 unit on both axes, draw the graph of $y = -\frac{1}{2}x^2 + 2x$ for $-1 \leqslant x \leqslant 5$.

(c) State the line of symmetry and the maximum point of the graph.

(d) What are the coordinates of the points of intersection of the graph and the x-axis?

4. **(a)** Copy and complete the following table.

x	–5	–4	–3	–2	–1	0	1
$y = -3x^2 - 18x - 32$							

(b) Taking 2 cm to represent 1 unit on the x-axis and 2 cm to represent 10 units on the y-axis, draw the graph of $y = -3x^2 - 18x - 32$ for $-5 \leqslant x \leqslant 1$.

(c) State the line of symmetry and the maximum point of the graph.

(d) Find the y-intercept of the graph.

(e) At how many points does the graph cut the x-axis?

 FURTHER PRACTICE

5. Draw the graph of each of the following equations for the indicated values of x.

(a) $y = \dfrac{1}{4}x^2 + x$ for $-5 \leq x \leq 1$

(b) $y = 2x^2 - 6x + 7$ for $-1 \leqslant x \leqslant 4$

(c) $y = 6 - x - x^2$ for $-4 \leqslant x \leqslant 3$

(d) $y = -2x^2 + 3x - 3$ for $-2 \leqslant x \leqslant 3$

For each graph, state its

(i) line of symmetry,

(ii) minimum or maximum point,

(iii) x-intercept(s),

(iv) y-intercept.

6. For the graph of equation **5(d)**, are the points $\left(\dfrac{1}{2}, -1\right)$ and $\left(\dfrac{3}{2}, -3\right)$ on or above or below the graph of $y = -2x^2 + 3x - 3$?

 MATH@WORK

7. A store has a rectangular signboard of dimensions 7 m by 3 m. The store manager changes the dimensions by decreasing the length by x m, while increasing the width by x m. The area of the signboard is A m² after the changes.

(a) Express A in terms of x.

(b) Draw the graph of A against x for $0 \leqslant x \leqslant 7$.

(c) Find the value of x that gives the greatest area of the signboard. What is this area?

8. The height, h m, of a golf ball at time, t s, from the ground is given by $h = -5t^2 + 15t$.

(a) Find the time of flight of the golf ball.

(b) Draw the graph of $h = -5t^2 + 15t$ during the time of flight.

(c) Find the maximum height of the golf ball from the ground.

(d) When is the golf ball 8 m above the ground?

9. An arch ABC is a parabola with equation $y = -3x^2 + 6x$ for $0 \leqslant x \leqslant 2$, where x is the horizontal distance and y is the vertical distance, in meters, of a point, P, on the arch from the foot, A, of the arch (refer to the diagram).

(a) Draw the graph of the arch, taking 2 cm to represent 0.5 m on both axes.

(b) How wide is the bottom, AC, of the arch?

(c) Find the maximum height of the arch.

(d) State the line of symmetry of the arch.

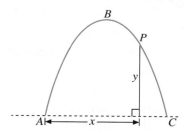

10. When x chairs are made in a day, the cost $\$y$ for each chair is given by

$$y = x^2 - 20x + 150 \quad \text{for } 0 \leqslant x \leqslant 15.$$

(a) Draw the graph of $y = x^2 - 20x + 150$ for $0 \leqslant x \leqslant 15$.

(b) How many chairs have to be made in a day so that the cost per chair is a minimum?

(c) What are the possible numbers of chairs to be made in a day so as to keep the cost per chair less than $60?

11. Quadratic graphs can be drawn using the command **Graph-Plot New Function** in Sketchpad software. Use the software to explore the following.

(a) Draw the graphs of $y = ax^2$ for several values of a $\left(\text{such as } a = -3, -2, -1, -\dfrac{1}{2}, \dfrac{1}{2}, 1, 2, 3\right)$ on the same diagram. Discuss the effect of a on the shapes and positions of the graphs.

(b) Draw the graphs of $y = x^2 + bx + 4$ for several values of b on the same diagram. Discuss the effect of b on the shapes and positions of the graphs.

(c) Draw the graphs of $y = -x^2 - 2x + c$ for several values of c on the same diagram. Discuss the effect of c on the shapes and positions of the graphs.

IN A NUTSHELL

Idea of Functions

- y is a function of x if for each x, there is exactly one value of y which is determined by x.

- A function can be represented by
  (i) a table of values,
  (ii) ordered pairs,
  (iii) a graph, or
  (iv) an equation.

Linear Function

- A linear function y of x is a function of the form $y = mx + b$, where m and b are constants.

- The graph of a linear function $y = mx + b$ is a straight line where m is the slope and b is the y-intercept of the line.

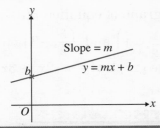

Properties of the Graph of the Quadratic Function
$y = ax^2 + bx + c$, where $a \neq 0$

- It is in the shape of a parabola.

- It opens upward and has a minimum point when $a > 0$. It opens downward and has a maximum point when $a < 0$.

- It has a vertical line of symmetry through its minimum point or maximum point.

- It meets the x-axis at zero, one or two points.

- It meets the y-axis at only one point.

1. A linear function y of x is given by the following table.

x	1	3	5	7	9
y	1	5	9	13	17

  (a) Represent the function by
     (i) ordered pairs,
     (ii) an equation.
  (b) State the slope and the y-intercept of the linear graph as defined by the equation.
  (c) Draw the graph of the function for $-1 \leqslant x \leqslant 9$.

2. The table shows the distance y miles a cyclist covered in x minutes.

Time (min)	Distance (miles)
30	8
60	16
90	24
120	32

  (a) Draw a graph to represent the given data.
  (b) Find the rate of change of this function.
  (c) What does the rate of change represent?
  (d) Express y as a function of x.

3. The number of minutes, x, provided under different cell phone plans and the costs, y, are shown in the table below.

Minutes	300	500	700	900	1100
Cost ($)	24	31	38	45	52

  (a) Draw a graph to represent the given data.
  (b) Find the rate of change of this function and explain what it represents.
  (c) Find the initial value of this function. What does it represent?
  (d) Express y as a function of x.

4. The value of a new car is $80,000. In 5 years' time, the car will be worth $20,000. Assume that the value of the car decreases at a constant rate of $$m$ per year, and the value of the car is $$y$ after x years.
  (a) Find the value of m.
  (b) Copy and complete the following table.

x	0	1	2	3	4	5
y						

  (c) Express y as a function of x.
  (d) Draw the graph of the function.

5. A pottery will supply 100 pots if the price of each pot is $80. It will supply 175 such pots if the price is $110. Assume that the supply quantity (y) is related to the price ($$x$) of each pot by the function $y = mx + b$, where m and b are constants.
  (a) Find the values of m and b.
  (b) Draw the graph of the function $y = mx + b$ for $0 \leqslant x \leqslant 150$.
  (c) What is the minimum price of each pot at which the pottery is willing to supply the pots?

6. **(a)** Draw the graph of $y = x^2 - 6x + 7$ for $0 \leqslant x \leqslant 6$.
  (b) State the coordinates of the minimum point of the graph.
  (c) Find the x-intercepts of the graph, rounding your values to 1 decimal place.

7. **(a)** Draw the graph of $y = 2x^2 + 6x + 5$ for $-5 \leqslant x \leqslant 1$.
  (b) State the line of symmetry and the minimum point of the graph.
  (c) Determine if each of the points $(-2.5, 2.5)$ and $(0.5, 9.5)$ lies on the graph of $y = 2x^2 + 6y + 5$, or above or below this graph.

8. A cannon ball is fired from a cliff into the sea. Its vertical distance, h m, above sea-level at time, t seconds, is given by $h = -5t^2 + 20t + 60$, for $t \geqslant 0$ and $h \geqslant 0$.
   (a) Draw the graph of $h = -5t^2 + 20t + 60$ for $0 \leqslant t \leqslant 7$.
   (b) Using the graph, find
       (i) the height of the cliff,
       (ii) the maximum height of the cannon ball above sea-level,
       (iii) the time of flight of the cannon ball.

9. The quadratic graph $y = x^2 + bx + c$ passes through the points $P(-1, -6)$ and $Q(2, 6)$.
   (a) Find the values of the constants b and c.
   (b) With the values of b and c obtained in (a), draw the graph of $y = x^2 + bx + c$ for $-5 \leqslant x \leqslant 2$.
   (c) From the graph, find
       (i) its line of symmetry,
       (ii) its minimum point.

10. Jane makes and sells handmade bags. If x bags are made where $1 \leqslant x \leqslant 8$, the cost of each bag $\$y$ is given by $y = x^2 - 8x + 65$.
   (a) Using 2 cm to represent 1 unit on the x-axis and 2 cm to represent 10 units on the y-axis, draw the graph of $y = x^2 - 8x + 65$ for $0 < x \leqslant 8$.
   (b) What is the number of bags Jane should make so that the cost per bag is the lowest?
   (c) What is the y-intercept of the graph and what does it represent?

Translation of Axes

The diagram shows the graph of the quadratic function $y = 6x - x^2$. The point M is the maximum point of the graph.

(a) State the coordinates of M.

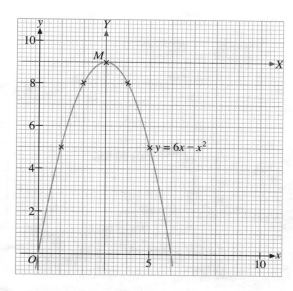

Suppose that we draw a horizontal axis, MX, and a new vertical axis, MY, at the point M.

(b) With reference to these new axes, MX and MY,
  (i) state the coordinates of the point M,
  (ii) state the coordinates of the point O,
  (iii) do you think the equation of the graph still takes the form $Y = aX^2 + bX + c$? If not, what form do you think the equation of the graph should be?
  (iv) find the equation of the graph.

WRITE IN YOUR JOURNAL

Describe the properties of
(a) a linear graph $y = mx + b$,
(b) a quadratic graph $y = ax^2 + bx + c$

that you have learned in this chapter.

9 GRAPHS IN PRACTICAL SITUATIONS

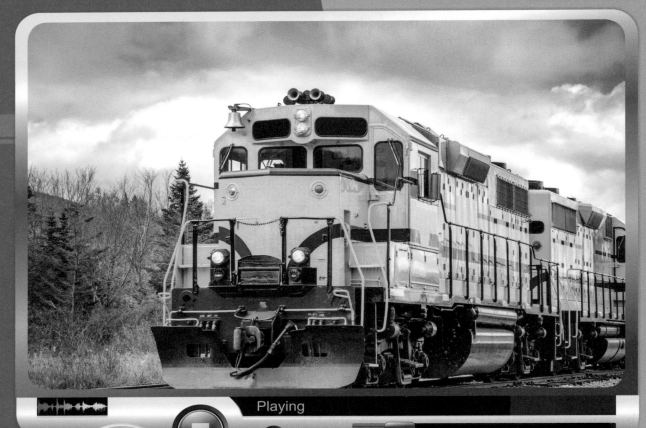

Playing

LET'S LEARN TO...

1. interpret and utilize data from tables and charts
2. draw graphs from given data
3. represent motion of moving objects using distance-time graphs
4. interpret distance-time graphs

The motion of a USA train can be described using a graph, such as a distance-time graph.

9.1 Tables, Charts, and Graphs

In our daily life, information such as schedules, fares, and charges, are presented concisely using tables, charts, and graphs. To extract useful information from them in order to help us plan and make decisions, it is important for us to know how to read and interpret them.

Example 1

The following table shows the flying distance (in miles) between some cities in the USA.

From/To	ATL	DLS	LAS	MIA	PHX	SAN
Atlanta (ATL)	0	729	1,740	596	1,580	1,890
Dallas (DFW)	729	0	1,050	1,120	865	1,170
Las Vegas (LAS)	1,740	1,050	0	2,170	255	259
Miami (MIA)	596	1,120	2,170	0	1,970	2,260
Phoenix (PHX)	1,580	865	255	1,970	0	304
San Diego (SAN)	1,890	1,170	259	2,260	304	0

Source: www.webflyer.com

(a) Read, from the table, the flying distance between
   (i) Las Vegas and Dallas,
   (ii) Atlanta and Miami.
(b) Mr. Carter travels from Phoenix to Miami via Dallas. How much longer is the distance traveled compared to that if he goes on a direct flight from Phoenix to Miami?

Solution

(a) (i) The required distance is the value at the cell where the row Las Vegas and the column Dallas meet. Thus, the distance between Las Vegas and Dallas is 1,050 mi.

   (ii) The required distance is the value at the cell where the row Atlanta and the column Miami meet. Thus, the distance between Atlanta and Miami is 596 mi.

(b) From the table, we can read
   distance between Phoenix and Miami = 1,970 mi,
   distance between Phoenix and Dallas = 865 mi,
   distance between Dallas and Miami = 1,120 mi.
   distance from Phoenix to Miami via Dallas
   = 865 + 1,120
   = 1,985 mi
   Thus, the distance is longer by 1,985 − 1,970 = 15 mi.

REMARKS

A table cell is one grouping within a table. Cells are grouped horizontally (rows of cells) and vertically (columns of cells).

DISCUSS

Why are the values in the cells along the main diagonal of the chart all zeros?

Try It! **1**

Refer to the chart in Example 1.
(a) Find the flying distance
    (i) from Miami to Las Vegas,
    (ii) from Atlanta to San Diego.
(b) How much shorter is the distance if the journey from Atlanta to San Diego is made via Phoenix?

Example **2**

The following is a conversion table between US gallons and liters.

US gallons (x gal.)	2	4	6	8	10
Liters (y L)	7.57	15.14	22.71	30.28	37.85

(a) Draw the graph of y against x.
(b) Read from the graph,
    (i) the number of liters in 5 US gallons,
    (ii) the number of US gallons in 35 liters.
(c) Find the slope of the graph.
(d) How many liters are there in one US gallon?

Solution

(a) The diagram below shows the conversion graph of liters (y) against US gallons (x).

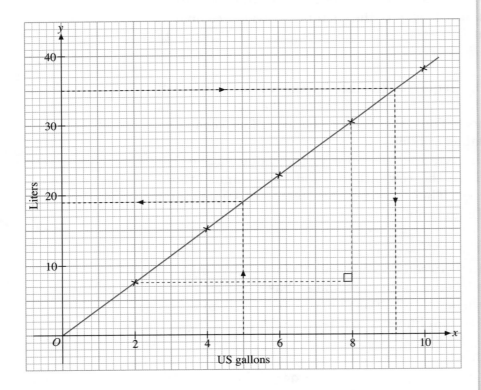

DISCUSS

1. Why does the graph pass through the origin?

2. What is the relationship between the variables x and y?

(b) (i) Draw a vertical line at $x = 5$ to meet the graph and then read the y-coordinate of the point of intersection. We have 5 US gallons $\approx$ 19 liters.

(ii) Draw a horizontal line at $y = 35$ to meet the graph and then read the x-coordinate of the point of intersection. We have 35 liters $\approx$ 9.2 US gallons.

(c) Take two points (2, 7.57) and (8, 30.28) on the graph, and draw the right-angled triangle to find the slope of the graph.

$$\text{Slope of the line} = \frac{30.28 - 7.57}{8 - 2}$$
$$= 3.785$$

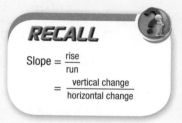

RECALL

$$\text{Slope} = \frac{\text{rise}}{\text{run}}$$
$$= \frac{\text{vertical change}}{\text{horizontal change}}$$

(d) Hence, there are 3.785 liters in one US gallon.

Try It! 2 The following is a conversion table between miles and kilometers.

Miles (x mi)	2	4	6	8	10
Kilometers (y km)	3.22	6.44	9.66	12.88	16.10

(a) Draw the graph of y against x.
(b) Read from the graph,
    (i) the number of kilometers in 9 miles,
    (ii) the number of miles in 5 kilometers.
(c) Find the slope of the graph.
(d) Express y in terms of x.

EXERCISE 9.1

⚙ BASIC PRACTICE

1. The following is a conversion table between kilograms and pounds.

Kilograms (x kg)	2	4	6	8	10
Pounds (y lb)	4.4	8.8	13.2	17.6	22.0

(a) Draw the graph of y against x.
(b) Find, from the graph,
    (i) the number of pounds in 5 kg,
    (ii) the number of kilograms in 15 lb.

2. The following table shows the driving distance (in kilometers) between four towns.

From/To	CY	NP	SB	WL
Clayton (CY)		46	120	69
Newport (NP)	46		72	83
Sunbury (SB)	120	72		114
William (WL)	69	83	114	

(a) Complete the chart by filling in the missing values. Explain your answers.

(b) What is the driving distance between each of the following pairs of towns?
    (i) Newport and William
    (ii) William and Sunbury
    (iii) Clayton and Newport
    (iv) Sunbury and Clayton

3. An ice cream parlor has the following menu.

Items	Classic flavors	Premium flavors
Single scoop – cone or cup	$1.99	$2.49
Double scoop – cone or cup	$3.49	$3.99
Triple scoop – cone or cup	$4.99	$5.49
Freshly made waffle cone	add $1.50	
Toppings – sauce, fruits – nuts	$0.89 each $0.59 each	

Mrs. Ford's four children, Anne, Bella, Cliff, and David, made the following ice cream orders.

Anne: a double scoop ice cream of classic flavors in a freshly made waffle cone topped with strawberry sauce and almond bits

Bella: a double scoop ice cream of premium flavors in a freshly made waffle cone topped with fruits

Cliff: a triple scoop ice cream of classic flavors in a freshly made waffle cone

David: a triple scoop ice cream of premium flavors topped with chocolate sauce

(a) What is the price of each of their orders?
(b) Whose order costs the most?

 FURTHER PRACTICE

4. The following is a conversion table between temperature in degrees Celsius (°C) and temperature in degrees Fahrenheit (°F).

Celsius (x °C)	20	40	60	80	100
Fahrenheit (y °F)	68	104	140	176	212

(a) Draw the graph of y against x.
(b) Read from the graph,
    (i) the corresponding value in °F for 0 °C,
    (ii) the corresponding value in °F for 10 °C,
    (iii) the corresponding value in °C for 80 °F.
(c) Find an equation connecting x and y.

5. The following table tabulates the cost of a journey, $\$y$, of x miles on the taxi.

Distance (x miles)	2	4	6	8	10
Cost of journey ($\$y$)	7	11	15	19	23

(a) Draw the graph of y against x.
(b) Use your graph to find
    (i) how much a taxi journey of 6.5 miles would cost,
    (ii) the boarding charge,
    (iii) the cost for each mile travelled.
(c) Hence, find the equation that represents the rate charged by this cab company.

6. The graph shows the expected depreciation in the value of a particular model of car in the first five years after its purchase.
   (a) From the graph, write down
      (i) the purchase price of this car,
      (ii) when its value will depreciate to $10,000.
   (b) Find the nearest whole percentage drop in the value of this car
      (i) in the first year,
      (ii) in the second year.
   (c) What is the nearest total percentage of depreciation in the value of the car within the first 5 years?

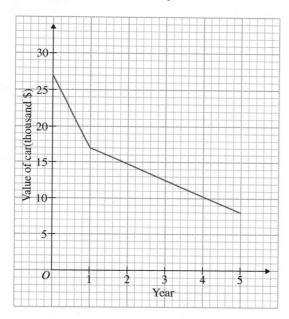

MATH@WORK

7. The table below shows some equivalent amounts of euros and US dollars (US$).

Euros (x)	16	25	40	50
US$ (y)	20.22	31.60	50.55	63.19

   (a) Draw a graph to show the conversion between euros and US dollars.
   (b) Use your graph to convert
      (i) 35 euros to US dollars,
      (ii) US$35 to euros.

   (c) Determine the exchange rate of euros to US dollars. Express your answer as 1 euro = US$y.

8. A mobile phone pricing scheme charges $20 per month with 80 minutes of free connection time. The connection charge after the first 80 minutes is 16 cents per minute.
   (a) Find the monthly charge if the connection time in a month is
      (i) 60 minutes,
      (ii) 80 minutes,
      (iii) 100 minutes.
   (b) Let $y be the monthly charge when the connection time is x minutes. Draw the graph of y against x for $0 \leqslant x \leqslant 120$.

BRAIN WORKS

9. A hardware store kept hammers, chisels, saws, and pliers on racks A, B, and C. During a routine check of the stock, the store manager found that there were 23 pieces of these tools on rack A, of which 4 were hammers and 5 were saws. On rack B, there were 34 pieces of these tools, of which 6 were chisels and 8 were saws. On rack C, there were 7 chisels, 14 saws and 12 pairs of pliers. There were a total of 23 hammers, 25 chisels and 25 pairs of pliers.
   (a) Represent the above data in a table.
   (b) Find the total number of tools on all the three racks.

9.2 *Distance-Time Graphs*

We can also construct graphs to model real situations of motion of objects. In this unit, we shall learn about distance-time graphs. A distance-time graph depicts the distance of an object from a reference point at time t.

A **distance-time graph** is drawn on a rectangular plane with distance from a reference point shown on the vertical axis and the time taken on the horizontal axis.

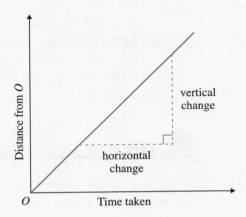

A distance-time graph can be a straight line or a curved line. In this chapter, we will focus mainly on the straight line graphs. By definition, slope of a straight line = $\dfrac{\text{vertical change}}{\text{horizontal change}}$. Thus, the **slope of a distance-time graph** may be defined as

$$\frac{\text{Distance traveled}}{\text{Time taken}}$$

which is the **speed of a moving object**.

A straight line in a distance-time graph indicates constant speed.

The steeper the line is, the faster the speed. However, a curved line indicates non-uniform or varying speeds.

Example 3

Michael rode a bicycle from home to his destination which was 60 km away. The diagram below shows the distance-time graph of his journey.

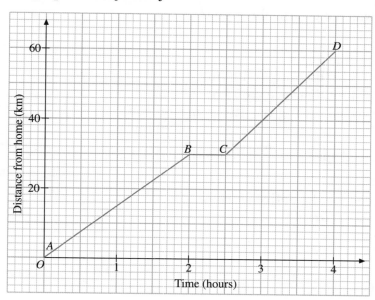

Use the graph to answer the following questions.
(a) Find the speed at which Michael was traveling during the first 2 hours.
(b) What is the state of motion during the part BC on the graph?
(c) Find the speed at which Michael was traveling during the 4th hour.
(d) Find the average speed for the entire journey.

Solution **(a)** The coordinates of B are (2, 30).
This means that the distance Michael traveled in the first 2 hours was 30 km.

$$\therefore \text{ the required speed} = \frac{\text{Distance traveled}}{\text{Time taken}}$$

$$= \frac{30}{2}$$

$$= 15 \text{ km/hr}$$

Note: Since the line segment AB is a straight line, it means that Michael traveled equal distances in equal time intervals. In other words, he traveled at a uniform speed in the part of the journey AB, and this speed is given by the slope of the line segment AB, which is 15 km/hr.

REMARKS
The speed during the first 2 hours is given by the slope of the line segment AB.

(b) The part BC is horizontal. It shows that there was no change in the distance from Michael's home from time = 2 hr to time = $2\frac{1}{2}$ hr. Hence, Michael was at rest, that is, he was not cycling for $\frac{1}{2}$ hour.

(c) Reading from the graph,
when time = 3 hr, distance = 40 km;
when time = 4 hr, distance = 60 km.
Distance traveled during the 4th hour = 60 − 40
$$= 20 \text{ km}$$

∴ the required speed = $\frac{20}{1}$ = 20 km/hr

REMARKS

Explore the relationship between distance and time in an interactive activity at http://www.mathwarehouse.com/graphs/distance-time-graph-activity.php and visit http://www.mathwarehouse.com/graphs/distance-vs-time-graph-lesson.php for more information on distance-time graphs.

(d) Average speed for the entire journey
$$= \frac{\text{Total distance traveled}}{\text{Total time taken}}$$
$$= \frac{60}{4}$$
$$= 15 \text{ km/hr}$$

Try It! ③ Jim began his journey of 60 km at 07:00 hours. The distance-time graph below represents Jim's journey.

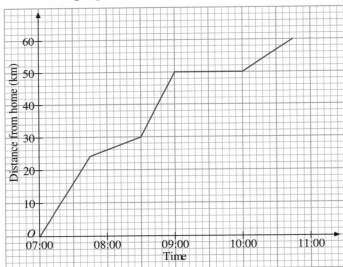

Use the graph to answer the following questions.
(a) How long did Jim take to complete the journey?
(b) At what time was Jim 20 km from his destination?
(c) How far was Jim from his destination after his rest?
(d) What is the total time he spent resting?
(e) Find Jim's average speed during the first half hour.
(f) During which time interval did Jim travel at his fastest speed? What was that speed?
(g) Find Jim's average speed for the whole journey.

Example 4

Betty walked along a track PQ that was 800 m long. The distance-time graph of her walk is shown below.

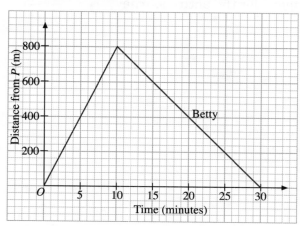

(a) Describe briefly Betty's journey as represented by the above graph.

(b) What was Betty's speed at time = 17 minutes?

(c) Find Betty's average speed in m/min for the entire journey.

(d) Jacky walked at a uniform speed of 80 m/min from Q to P along the same track. He started walking 5 minutes later than Betty.

  (i) How long did it take Jacky to reach P?

  (ii) Draw Jacky's distance-time graph on the given diagram.

  (iii) When and where did Betty meet Jacky?

Solution

(a) The speed at a specific time is the slope of the speed-time graph at that time.

During the first 10 minutes, Betty walked from P to Q, which was 800 m away, at a uniform speed

$= \dfrac{800}{10} = 80$ m/min.

Then, Betty returned to P from Q at a different uniform speed $= \dfrac{800}{20} = 40$ m/min.

(b) Slope of the graph from time = 10 min to time = 30 min is given by $-\dfrac{800}{20} = -40$

$\therefore$ at time = 17 min, slope = -40

The negative slope indicates that the direction of motion is towards the starting point P but speed is a positive quantity.

Therefore, Betty's speed was 40 m/min.

(c) The time Betty took to walk from P to Q is 10 min and that from Q to P is 20 min.

Betty's average speed for the entire journey

$$= \frac{800 + 800}{10 + 20}$$

$$= 53\frac{1}{3} \text{ m/min}$$

(d) (i) Time taken by Jacky

$$= \frac{\text{Distance traveled}}{\text{Speed}}$$

$$= \frac{800}{80}$$

$$= 10 \text{ min}$$

(ii)

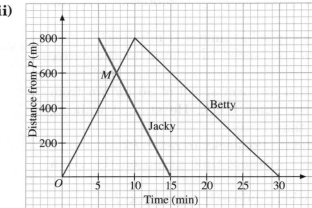

The red line segment in the diagram above shows Jacky's distance-time graph. It is obtained by joining the points (5, 800) and (15, 0) by a line segment.

(iii) Betty met Jacky at the time when their distance-time graphs intersect at the point $M(7.5, 600)$. Hence, they met 7.5 min after Betty started walking, at a point 600 m away from P.

Jane cycled from P to Q along a road and then returned to P along the same road. The distance-time graph of her journey is shown below.

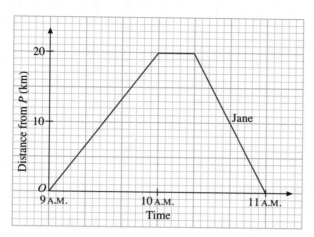

(a) Describe briefly Jane's journey as represented by the above graph.

(b) Find Jane's average speed for the entire journey.

(c) Karen started traveling from Q to P along the same road at 9:20 A.M., at a uniform speed of 15 km/h.
  (i) Draw Karen's distance-time graph on the given diagram.
  (ii) At what time did Karen arrive at P?
  (iii) When and where did Jane meet Karen?

In general, the slopes of a distance-time graph can be interpreted as follows.

❶ An upward sloping straight line indicates motion with **uniform speed** (the distance moved for each unit of time is the same).

❷ A straight line parallel to the time-axis indicates a state of **rest** (no change in distance). The time taken for the rest is recorded in the graph.

❸ A curve indicates motion with non-uniform or **varying speed**. The change in speed can be **increasing** or **decreasing**.

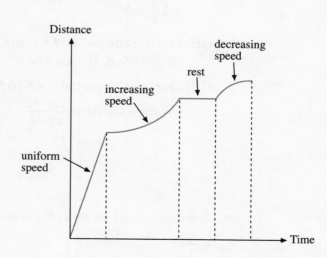

Example 5

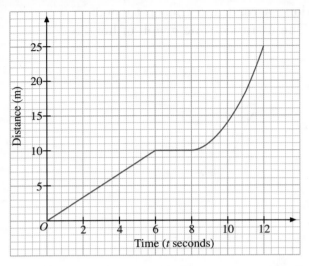

The distance-time graph for the first 12 seconds of a journey of a car is shown above.

(a) During which time interval was the speed non-uniform?

(b) Find the average speed
    (i) during the first 6 seconds,
    (ii) during the period $t = 6$ to $t = 8$,
    (iii) during the period $t = 8$ to $t = 12$.

(c) What is the average speed for the entire journey?

Solution

(a) The speed was non-uniform during the interval 8 s to 12 s.

(b) **(i)** Average speed during the first 6 seconds

$$= \frac{10}{6}$$

$$= 1\frac{2}{3} \text{ m/s}$$

    (ii) During the period $t = 6$ to $t = 8$, there is no change in distance. Hence, the average speed is 0 m/s.

    (iii) During the period $t = 8$ to $t = 12$,

$$\text{average speed} = \frac{25 - 10}{12 - 8}$$

$$= \frac{15}{4}$$

$$= 3\frac{3}{4} \text{ m/s}$$

(c) Average speed for the entire journey

$$= \frac{25}{12}$$

$$= 2\frac{1}{12} \text{ m/s}$$

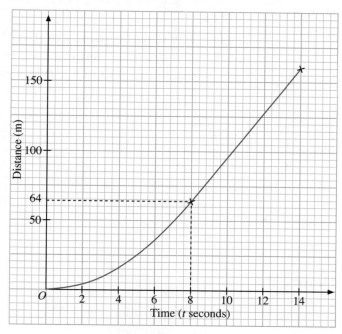

The distance-time graph for the first 14 seconds of a journey of a moving object is shown above.
  (a) What is the total distance covered in the 14 seconds?
  (b) Find the average speed
      (i) during the period $t = 0$ to $t = 8$,
      (ii) during the period $t = 8$ to $t = 14$,
      (iii) for the entire journey.

EXERCISE 9.2

 BASIC PRACTICE

1. Peter went on a cycling trip. The distance-time graph on the right shows his journey.
   (a) How far did Peter cycle on the trip?
   (b) Peter stopped to mend a puncture in the tire. At what time did that happen, and what was the time lapse before he continued with his journey?
   (c) During which time interval did Peter cycle at his fastest speed? What was that speed?

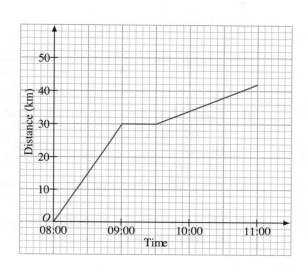

2. The diagram shows the distance-time graph of a cyclist's journey.

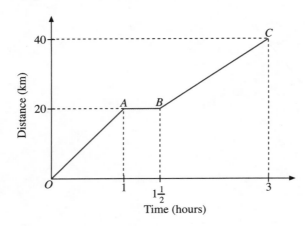

(a) Find the speed of the cyclist during the period represented by
    (i) *OA*,
    (ii) *AB*,
    (iii) *BC*.
(b) Find the average speed of the cyclist for the entire journey.

3. The diagram shows the distance-time graph of Mrs. Brown's journey.

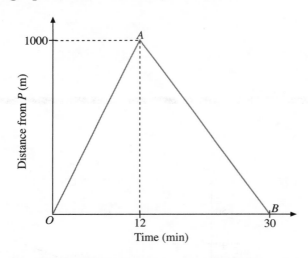

(a) Find Mrs. Brown's speed during the period represented by
    (i) *OA*,
    (ii) *AB*.
(b) Find Mrs. Brown's average speed for the entire journey.
(c) Describe briefly Mrs. Brown's journey as represented by the graph.

FURTHER PRACTICE

4. The distance-time graph of Alicia's journey along a road joining two cities, *P* and *Q*, which are 80 km apart is shown below.

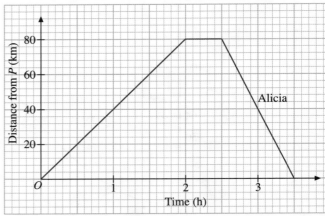

(a) How long was Alicia at rest during the journey?
(b) Find Alicia's average speed for the entire journey.
(c) John traveled at a uniform speed of 60 km/h from *Q* to *P*. He set off one hour later than Alicia.
    (i) Draw John's distance-time graph on the same diagram.
    (ii) When and where did Alicia meet John?

5. The diagram shows a simplified distance-time graph model of Jordan's and Clark's performances in a 200-m race. Jordan allowed Clark an advantage of a certain distance.

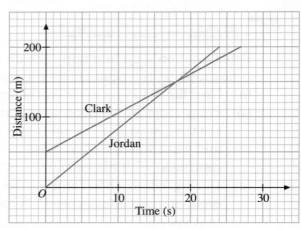

(a) What was the advantage, in terms of distance, given to Clark?

(b) Find Jordan's speed in the race.

(c) When and where did Jordan overtake Clark?

(d) Who won the race? How much faster, in seconds, was the winner?

6.

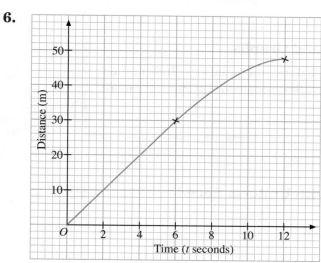

The distance-time graph for the first 12 seconds of the motion of a cart is shown above.

(a) Find the speed of the cart during the first 6 seconds.

(b) Describe the motion of the cart during the period $t = 6$ to $t = 12$. Find the average speed of the cart during this period.

(c) What is the average speed of the cart in the 12 seconds?

7. Susan drove to visit her parents who stayed 100 km away. In the first 20 km, her average speed was 60 km/h. She stopped for a 10-minute coffee break and then continued driving another 50 minutes before she reached her parents' house.

(a) Find the time taken for the first 20 km of Susan's journey.

(b) Draw a distance-time graph to represent Susan's journey to her parents' house taking a scale of 1 cm to represent 10 minutes on the horizontal axis and 1 cm to represent 20 km on the vertical axis.

(c) What is Susan's average speed for the entire journey?

MATH@WORK

8. Make up a narrative that can describe the journey represented by the distance-time graph below. Explain what is happening for each segment.

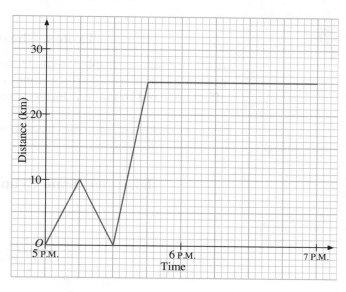

9. Peter took 10 minutes to travel from his school to the gym. The distance between the school and the gym is 1.5 km. Peter completed half of his journey at a uniform speed in 5 minutes. Then, he met a friend and stopped to chat with him between the 5th minute and the 6th minute. Peter then continued his journey to the gym at a uniform speed.

(a) Draw the distance-time graph for Peter's journey.

(b) Find Peter's speed in meters per second during

   (i) the first 5 minutes,

   (ii) the last 4 minutes

   of the journey.

BRAINWORKS

10. Create a distance-time graph of a cyclist or motorist, incorporating a horizontal line, sloping lines with positive and negative slopes, and one curved part. Write a story describing the journey represented by the graph.

Tables, Charts, and Graphs

A table, chart or graph can model real life data and situations. Information presented in tables, charts, and/or graphs allow people to communicate more effectively and to make informed decisions.

Distance-Time Graph with Uniform Speed

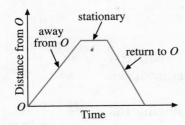

Speed = slope of a distance-time graph

The steeper the slope of the distance-time graph, the faster the object moves.

Distance-Time Graph with Non-Uniform Speed

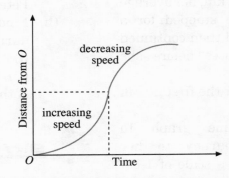

1. The graph below shows the conversion between US dollars (US$) and Singapore dollars (S$) on a particular day in May 2013.
    (a) Use the graph to convert
        (i) US$36 to S$,
        (ii) S$50 to US$.
    (b) Determine the exchange rate of Singapore dollars to one US dollar.

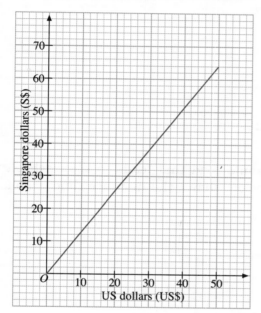

2. A mobile telecommunications company charges a connection fee of 30 cents for each call (incoming or outgoing). The call rate is 20 cents per minute for the first 6 minutes and 10 cents per minute thereafter. Let y be the total charge for a call lasting t minutes.
    (a) Copy and complete the following table.

t	2	4	6	8	10	15	20
y							

    (b) Draw the graph of y against t for $0 \leqslant t \leqslant 20$.
    (c) If the charge for a certain call is $2, find the duration of this call.

3. The chart below shows the local times in various cities around the world at the moment when it is 22:00 on Monday in New York, USA.

City	Day & Time
Auckland	Tuesday, 14:00
Boston, USA	Monday, 22:00
Chicago, USA	Monday, 21:00
Dubai	Tuesday, 06:00
Halifax, USA	Monday, 23:00
Hong Kong	Tuesday, 10:00
Honolulu, USA	Monday, 16:00
London	Tuesday, 03:00
New York, USA	**Monday, 22:00**
Seattle, USA	Monday, 19:00
Singapore	Tuesday, 10:00
Sydney	Tuesday, 12:00
Tokyo	Tuesday, 11:00
Vancouver	Monday, 19:00

http://www.timeanddate.com/worldclock

    (a) Which are the cities with times
        (i) behind New York?
        (ii) ahead of Singapore?
    (b) Find the time difference between
        (i) Halifax and New York,
        (ii) London and Sydney,
        (iii) Honolulu and Auckland.
    In each case, state whether the time of the first city of each part is ahead or behind that of the second city.
    (c) A non-stop flight from Chicago to Honolulu takes 9 hours. If the flight departs Chicago on Saturday at the local time 10 A.M., find the day and local time of arrival in Honolulu.
    (d) Paul, who is on a business trip in Singapore, wishes to make a telephone call to his family members in Seattle. His family would normally be asleep by 10:00 P.M. each night and wakes up at 7:00 A.M. the next morning. Would it be an appropriate time for Paul to call them at Singapore time 11:00 A.M. without disrupting their sleep?

4. The diagram below shows the distance-time graph for David's journey.

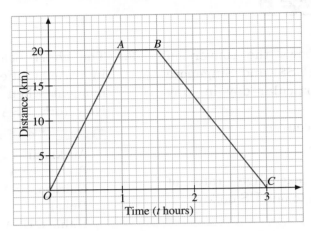

(a) Find David's speed during the period represented by
   (i) *AB*,
   (ii) *BC*.
(b) Find David's average speed for the entire journey.
(c) How far was David from his start point after 2 hours 15 minutes?

5. Peter's and Mary's homes are located along the same road that leads to their school, which is 1,000 m away from Mary's home. The diagram below shows the distance-time graphs of their journeys from home to school on a certain day.

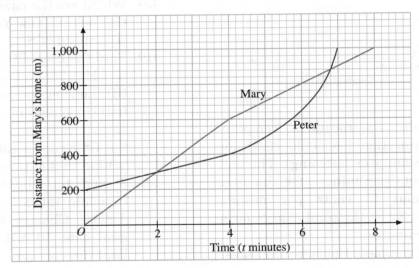

(a) Find the speed at which Mary traveled during
   (i) the first 4 minutes,
   (ii) the last 4 minutes.
(b) Find Mary's average speed for her journey from home to school.
(c) What is the distance between Peter's home and Mary's home?
(d) Who arrived at the school first?
(e) When and where did Peter and Mary meet on their way to the school?
(f) Estimate the distance between them when *t* = 4.

6. The distance-time graph of a delivery truck on its goods delivery is shown below.

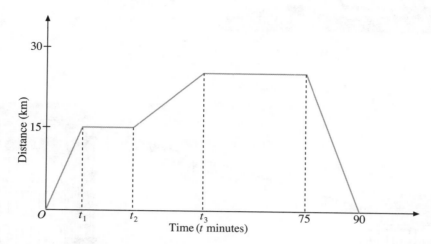

The delivery truck set off from the factory and drove 15 km at the speed of 1.5 km/min to its first destination. The workers spent 15 minutes to unload the goods and then left for the next destination. The truck traveled 20 minutes at the speed of 0.5 km/min to reach the second destination. After the goods were included at the second destination, the delivery truck then returned to its factory.

(a) Find the times t_1, t_2, and t_3.

(b) How far is the second destination from the factory?

(c) What is the total time spent to unload the goods at the two destinations?

(d) Find the speed at which the truck travels when it is returning to its factory.

EXTEND YOUR LEARNING CURVE

Graphs in Stock Markets

Graphs are also employed to present data in stock markets. Collect some graphs about stock prices from the newspapers and Internet, and try to interpret the information in those graphs.

WRITE IN YOUR JOURNAL

What are some of the data that are useful in your daily life and are presented in tables, charts, and graphs? What problems do you think will arise if these data are not presented as such? Give instances where some data can be presented better in tables, charts, and graphs to aid your understanding and interpretation.

10 PYTHAGOREAN THEOREM

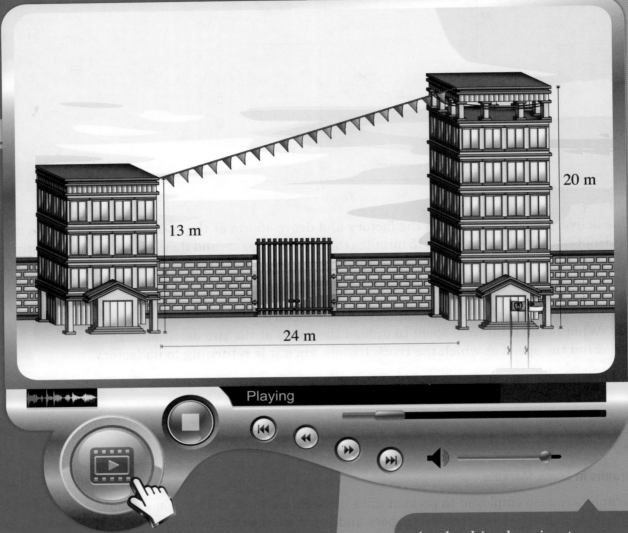

13 m

20 m

24 m

Playing

LET'S LEARN TO...

1. state Pythagorean Theorem and its converse
2. apply Pythagorean Theorem to solve problems
3. determine whether a triangle is right-angled given the lengths of its three sides
4. locate square roots of non-perfect squares on a number line diagram

A school is planning to celebrate its graduation day. The principal wants to put a banner that stretches across the tops of two school buildings. What is the length of the banner given the measurements of the buildings as shown?

10.1 Pythagorean Theorem

In a right-angled triangle, the side opposite to the right angle is called the **hypotenuse**. It is the longest side of the right-angled triangle. In the figure below, the side AB, which is opposite to $\angle C$, is the hypotenuse.

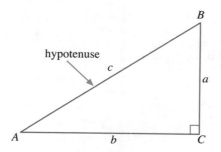

Note that we usually use the small letter of an angle in a triangle to denote the side opposite the angle. In this figure, a, b, and c denote the sides opposite $\angle A$, $\angle B$, and $\angle C$ respectively.

Have you heard of Pythagoras, the Greek philosopher?

Yes, there is a theorem named after him called Pythagorean Theorem.

MATH BITS

Pythagoras (569 BC – 475 BC) was a Greek philosopher who made considerable developments in mathematics, astronomy and the theory of music. It was believed he was the first to create the music scale used today.

The Pythagorean Theorem (or Pythagoras' Theorem) relates the lengths of the three sides of a right-angled triangle. Let us explore the theorem in Class Activity 1 using Sketchpad.

Objective: To explore the relationship between the sides of a right-angled triangle.

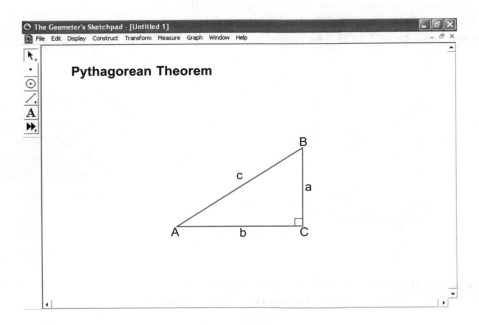

Tasks

(a) Draw a right-angled $\triangle ABC$ with $\angle C = 90°$.
(*Hint*: Use the command **Construct | Perpendicular line** to draw a line passing through C and perpendicular to AC.)

(b) Label the sides opposite $\angle A$, $\angle B$, and $\angle C$ as a, b, and c respectively.

(c) Measure the lengths of a, b, and c.

(d) Find the squares of a, b, and c.

(e) Select all the measurements in steps **(c)** and **(d)**. Then select the command **Graph | Tabulate** to create a table of values of a, b, c, a^2, b^2, and c^2.

(f) Drag the vertices of $\triangle ABC$ around to obtain another set of values of the sides and their squares. Double-click the table to add the current measurements as a new row to it.

(g) Repeat step **(f)** for two or more sets of measurements.

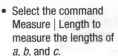

RECALL

- Select the command Measure | Length to measure the lengths of a, b, and c.
- Select the command Measure | Calculate to find the squares of the sides.

Question

What is the relationship between a^2, b^2, and c^2 in the right-angled $\triangle ABC$?

From Class Activity 1, we observe the following.

In a right-angled triangle, the square of the hypotenuse is equal to the sum of the squares of the other two sides.
(Abbreviation: Pythagorean Theorem)

REMARKS

In mathematics, a theorem is a statement that has been proven on the basis of previously established statements.

That is:

In $\triangle ABC$,

if $\quad\angle C = 90°$,

then $\quad AB^2 = BC^2 + AC^2$

or $\quad c^2 = a^2 + b^2 \qquad$ (Pythagorean Theorem)

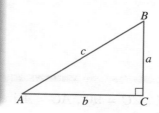

CLASS ACTIVITY 2

Objective: To explore one of the proofs of the Pythagorean Theorem.

Tasks

(a) A triangle with vertices $O(0, 0)$, $A(a, 0)$ and $B(0, b)$, and a square with vertices $O(0, 0)$, $P(a + b, 0)$, $Q(a + b, a + b)$, and $R(0, a + b)$, where a and b are real numbers, are drawn on the Cartesian plane in the diagram.

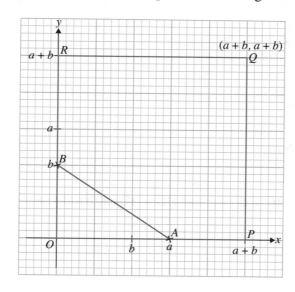

(b) On RQ, mark the point C with coordinates $(b, a + b)$ and on PQ, mark the point D with coordinates $(a + b, a)$. Join the points A, B, C, and D to obtain figure $ABCD$.

(c) Why is the figure $ABCD$ a square? Explain your answer.

(d) Giving your answers in terms of a and b, find
   (i) the area of the square $OPQR$,
   (ii) the area of each triangle.

(e) Suppose the length of AB is c units, find an expression in terms of a, b, and c for the area of $ABCD$.

(f) Relating your expression in (e) with $\triangle OAB$, what conclusion can you draw?

Example 1

In $\triangle ABC$, $\angle C = 90°$, $AC = 4$ in., and $BC = 3$ in. Find the length of AB.

Solution

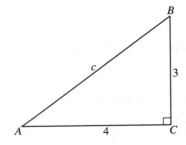

$\angle C = 90°$ (given)
$c^2 = a^2 + b$ (Pythagorean Theorem)
$\quad = 3^2 + 4^2$
$\quad = 25$
$\therefore \ c = \sqrt{25}$
$\quad = 5$

The length of AB is 5 in.

DISCUSS
When $c^2 = 25$, $c = 5$ or -5. Why is -5 excluded from the answer?

Try It! 1

In $\triangle ABC$, $\angle C = 90°$, $AC = 5$ in., and $BC = 12$ in. Find the length of AB.

Example **2**

In $\triangle PQR$, $\angle P = 90°$, $PQ = 24$ cm, and $QR = 25$ cm. Find the length of PR.

Solution

$\angle P = 90°$ (given)
$QR^2 = PQ^2 + PR^2$ (Pythagorean Theorem)
$25^2 = 24^2 + PR^2$
$PR^2 = 25^2 - 24^2$
$\quad = 49$
$\therefore\ PR = \sqrt{49}$
$\quad\quad = 7$ cm
The length of PR is 7 cm.

MATH WEB

There are more than 300 proofs of Pythagorean Theorem. You may access http://www-history.mcs.st-andrews.ac.uk/Biographies/Pythagoras.html and http://www.cut-the-knot.org/pythagoras/index.shtml for more information on Pythagoras and the proofs of the theorem.

Try It! **2**

$\triangle XYZ$ has a right angle at $\angle Z$ with $XY = 17$ cm and $XZ = 8$ cm. Find the length of YZ.

REMARKS

In the Sketchpad package, you may find interactive proofs in the directory C:\Program Files\Sketchpad\Samples\Teaching Mathematics\Shear Pythagoras.gsp.

Example **3**

In the figure, $\angle C = 90°$, $AD = 24$ cm, $BD = 15$ cm, and $DC = 10$ cm. Find the length of
(a) AC,
(b) AB.

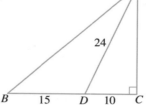

Solution

(a) In $\triangle ACD$,
$AD^2 = AC^2 + DC^2$ (Pythagorean Theorem)
$24^2 = AC^2 + 10^2$
$AC^2 = 24^2 - 10^2$
$\quad\quad = 476$
$\therefore\ AC = \sqrt{476}$
$\quad\quad\quad = 21.8$ cm (rounded to 3 sig. fig.)

(b) In $\triangle ABC$,
$AB^2 = BC^2 + AC^2$ (Pythagorean Theorem)
$\quad\quad = (15 + 10)^2 + 476$ $AC^2 = 476$ from (a)
$\quad\quad = 1,101$
$\therefore\ AB = \sqrt{1,101}$
$\quad\quad\quad = 33.2$ cm (rounded to 3 sig. fig.)

Try It! 3

In the figure, $\angle Q = 90°$, $PR = 12$ cm, $QR = 7$ cm, and $RS = 11$ cm. Find the length of
(a) PQ,
(b) PS.

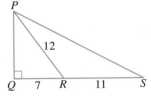

EXERCISE 10.1

In this exercie, give your answers rounded to 3 significant figures where necessary.

 BASIC PRACTICE

1. Find the unknown side of each of the following triangles, given that the measurements are in centimeters.

   (a)
   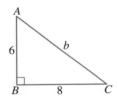

   (b)
   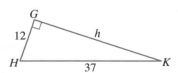

   (c)
   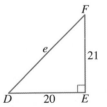

   (d)
   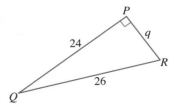

2. In $\triangle ABC$, $\angle B = 90°$, $AB = 9$ in., and $BC = 40$ in. What is the length of AC?

3. $\triangle PQR$ has a right angle at $\angle R$ with $PQ = 61$ cm and $QR = 11$ cm. What is the length of PR?

4. In $\triangle XYZ$, $\angle X = 90°$, $YZ = 7$ ft, and $XY = 3$ ft. Find the length of XZ.

 FURTHER PRACTICE

5. In the figure, $\angle BAD = \angle BDC = 90°$, $AB = 3$ cm, $AD = 1$ cm, and $CD = 2$ cm. Find the length of
   (a) BD,
   (b) BC.

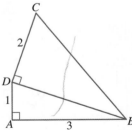

6. In the figure, $AC \perp BD$, $BC = 6$ m, $CD = 3$ m, and $AD = 5$ m. Find the length of
  (a) AC,
  (b) AB.

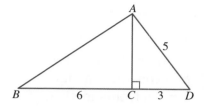

7. In the figure, $PQ \perp SQ$, $PR = 23$ m, $QR = 15$ m, and $RS = 17$ m. Find the length of
  (a) PQ,
  (b) PS.

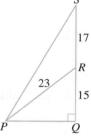

8. In the figure, $\angle TUV = \angle TVX = \angle VWX = 90°$, $TU = 8$ cm, $UV = 15$ cm, $VW = 16$ cm, and $WX = 30$ cm. Find the length of
  (a) TV,
  (b) VX,
  (c) TX.

 MATH@WORK

9. $ABCD$ is a rectangle in which $AB = 16$ cm and $BC = 9$ cm. Find the length of the diagonal AC.

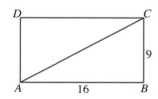

10. The length of a diagonal of a square is 12 cm. Find
  (a) the length of a side of the square,
  (b) the area of the square.

11. This question is one of the proofs of Pythagorean Theorem. Assume that the theorem is unknown. In the figure, $\triangle ABC$ is right-angled at $\angle C$. Triangles BAP, DBQ, EDR, and AES are congruent to $\triangle ABC$. They are placed in the square $ABDE$ on the hypotenuse AB as shown.
  (a) Show that $PQRS$ is a square.
  (b) State the length of PQ in terms of a and b.
  (c) What is the area of $\triangle BAP$ in terms of a and b?
  (d) Find the sum of the areas of $\triangle BAP$, $\triangle DBQ$, $\triangle EDR$, $\triangle AES$, and the square $PQRS$ in terms of a and b.
  (e) Express the area of $ABDE$ in terms of c.
  (f) Hence, show that $c^2 = a^2 + b^2$.

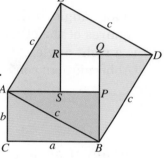

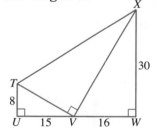 **BRAIN WORKS**

12. A Pythagorean Triple (or Pythagorean Triplet) is a set of three positive integers a, b, and c such that $a^2 + b^2 = c^2$. The following table shows two sets of Pythagorean Triples and three sets of incomplete Pythagorean Triples, where $a_n{}^2 + b_n{}^2 = c_n{}^2$ for $n = 1, 2, 3, \ldots$.

n	a_n	b_n	c_n
1	3	4	5
2	5	12	13
3	7	b_3	25
4	9	40	c_4
5	a_5	b_5	c_5

  (a) Using Pythagorean Theorem, find the values of b_3 and c_4.
  (b) By observing the pattern of values for a_n, b_n, and c_n, find the values of a_5, b_5 and c_5.
  (c) What is the relationship between b_n and c_n?
  (d) Express a_n, b_n, and c_n in terms of n.

10.2 *The Converse of Pythagorean Theorem*

A Definition

In ancient times, Egyptians tied knots equal distance apart for any two consecutive knots along a string. They used the string to construct a right angle by forming a triangle with sides 3, 4 and 5 units. In fact, this method applies the **converse of Pythagorean Theorem**.

We use Pythagorean Theorem and the concept of congruent triangles to prove the converse of Pythagorean Theorem. This is illustrated in question 7 of Exercise 10.2.

> In a triangle, if the square of the longest side is equal to the sum of the squares of the other two sides, then the angle opposite the longest side is a right angle.
> (Abbreviation: converse of Pythagorean Theorem)

> For any triangle with sides a, b, and c, if $c^2 = a^2 + b^2$, then the angle between a and b measures 90° and the triangle is a right-angled triangle.
> (converse of Pythagorean Theorem)

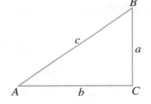

If we have a theorem that says "If P is true, then Q is true", then the converse of that is "If Q is true, then P is true".

B Determination of Right-Angled Triangles

If we know the lengths of the sides of a triangle, we can use the converse of Pythagorean Theorem to test whether the given triangle is right-angled.

Example **4**

Determine whether each of the following triangles is a right-angled triangle.
(a) $\triangle ABC$ with $a = 48$ cm, $b = 55$ cm, and $c = 73$ cm
(b) $\triangle PQR$ with $p = 30$ cm, $q = 20$ cm, and $r = 21$ cm

Solution

(a)
$$c^2 = 73^2$$
$$= 5{,}329$$
$$a^2 + b^2 = 48^2 + 55^2$$
$$= 5{,}329$$
$$\therefore \; c^2 = a^2 + b^2$$

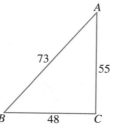

Hence, $\triangle ABC$ is right-angled at $\angle C$.
(converse of Pythagorean Theorem)

(b)
$$p^2 = 30^2$$
$$= 900$$
$$q^2 + r^2 = 20^2 + 21^2$$
$$= 841$$
$$\therefore \; p^2 \neq q^2 + r^2$$

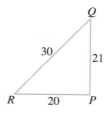

Hence, $\triangle PQR$ is not a right-angled triangle.

Note: There are other ways of showing the solution when determining if a triangle is a right triangle or not. We have $a^2 + b^2 = c^2$ the same as $c^2 - b^2 = a^2$.

When $c = 73$, $b = 55$, $c^2 - b^2 = (c - b)(c + b)$
$$= (73 - 55)(73 + 55)$$
$$= 18 \times 128$$
$$= 36 \times 64$$
$$= 6^2 \times 8^2$$
$$= (6 \times 8)^2$$
$$= 48^2 \quad \text{which is } a^2.$$

Hence, $\triangle ABC$ is right-angled at $\angle C$.
(converse of Pythagorean Theorem)

Try It! **4**

Determine whether each of the following triangles is a right-angled triangle.
(a) $\triangle GHK$ with $g = 89$ cm, $h = 38$ cm, and $k = 80$ cm
(b) $\triangle XYZ$ with $x = 17$ cm, $y = 144$ cm, and $z = 145$ cm

Example 5

In the figure, D is a point on the side AB of $\triangle ABC$. Given that $AD = 20$ cm, $DB = 25$ cm, $BC = 28$ cm, and $AC = 53$ cm, find the length of CD.

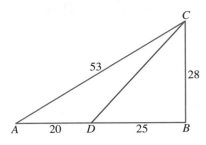

Solution

In $\triangle ABC$,
$$AC^2 = 53^2$$
$$= 2{,}809$$
$$AB^2 + BC^2 = (20 + 25)^2 + 28^2$$
$$= 2{,}809$$
$$\therefore \ AC^2 = AB^2 + BC^2$$

Hence, $\angle ABC = 90°$ (converse of Pythagorean Theorem)

In $\triangle BCD$,
$$CD^2 = BC^2 + BD^2 \quad \text{(Pythagorean Theorem)}$$
$$= 28^2 + 25^2$$
$$CD = \sqrt{1{,}409}$$
$$= 37.5 \text{ cm} \qquad \text{(rounded to 3 sig. fig.)}$$

> **REMARKS**
>
> We have to prove if $\angle B = 90°$ before applying Pythagorean Theorem to $\triangle BCD$ to find the length of CD.

Try It! 5

In the figure, R is a point on the side QS of $\triangle PQS$. Given that $PQ = 5$ cm, $QR = 3$ cm, $RS = 4$ cm, and $PS = \sqrt{74}$ cm, find the length of PR.

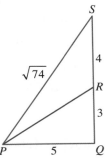

EXERCISE 10.2

In this exercise, give your answers rounded to 3 significant figures where necessary.

 BASICPRACTICE

1. Determine whether each of the following triangles is a right-angled triangle. If it is, name the right angle. The dimensions given are in meters.

    (a)

    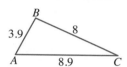

    (b)

    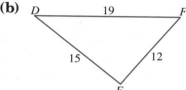

    (c)

    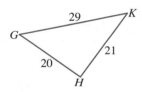

    (d)

    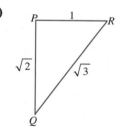

2. Determine whether each of the following triangles is a right-angled triangle. The dimensions given are in centimeters.
    (a) $\triangle ABC$ with $a = 10.1$, $b = 9.9$, and $c = 2$
    (b) $\triangle KMN$ with $k = 15$, $m = 48$, and $n = 50$
    (c) $\triangle TUV$ with $t = 63$, $u = 16$, and $v = 65$
    (d) $\triangle XYZ$ with $x = 13$, $y = 15$, and $z = 14$

 FURTHERPRACTICE

3. In the figure, $AB = 15$ cm, $BC = 20$ cm, $CD = 24$ cm, $DA = 8$ cm, and $AC = 25$ cm. What can you say about $\angle ABC$ and $\angle ADC$?

    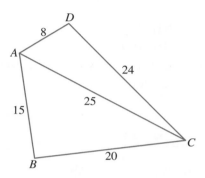

4. In the diagram, $QS \perp PR$, $PS = 9$ cm, $RS = 16$ cm and $QS = 12$ cm.
    (a) Find the lengths of PQ and RQ.
    (b) Is $\triangle PQR$ a right-angled triangle?

    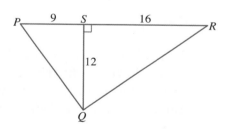

5. In the figure, XYZ is a straight line. Given that $XY = 6$ ft, $YZ = 4$ ft, $TZ = 7.5$ ft, and $TY = 8.5$ ft, what is the length of TX?

    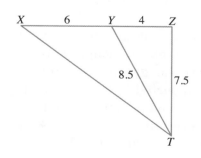

6. In the figure, $ABCD$ is a rectangle with $BC = 12$ cm, $CP = 5$ cm, $DP = 18$ cm, and $DQ = 7.5$ cm.

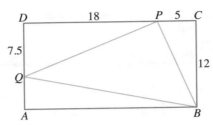

(a) Find the length of
  (i) BP,
  (ii) PQ,
  (iii) BQ.
(b) Determine whether $\triangle BPQ$ is a right-angled triangle.

7. The figure below shows $\triangle ABC$ and $\triangle XYZ$. Triangle ABC has sides of length a, b and c such that $c^2 = a^2 + b^2$. Triangle XYZ has a right angle at Z, and sides of length a, b, and z.

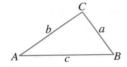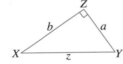

(a) What is the relationship between a, b and z in the right triangle XYZ?
(b) Is $c = z$? Explain your answer.
(c) Show that $\triangle ABC$ is congruent to $\triangle XYZ$.
(d) Find the measure of $\angle C$. What type of triangle is ABC?
(e) Hence, what conclusion can you draw for a triangle with sides a, b, and c where $c^2 = a^2 + b^2$?

8. In the diagram, AC is a pole 56 in. long. It rests on the ground AB and is supported by a wire BC. If $AB = 33$ in. and $BC = 64$ in., determine whether CA is perpendicular to AB.

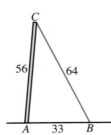

9. $\triangle PQR$ represents a piece of land in which $PQ = 53$ m, $QR = 28$ m, and $RP = 45$ m.
(a) Determine whether $\triangle PQR$ is a right-angled triangle.
(b) What is the area of $\triangle PQR$?
(c) Find the shortest distance from R to PQ.

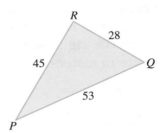

10. In the diagram, OA and OB are two roads where $OA = 420$ m, $OB = 400$ m, and $AB = 580$ m. Alex and Bella start walking from A and B respectively at the same time towards O. Alex's speed is 2 m/s and Bella's speed is 1 m/s. After 1 minute and 40 seconds, Alex reaches D and Bella reaches C.
(a) Show that $\angle AOB = 90°$.
(b) Find the lengths of OC and OD.
(c) What is the distance between C and D?

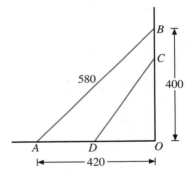

11. Rectangle $ABCD$ has sides 13 cm and 6 cm. Find a point P on CD such that $\angle APB = 90°$.

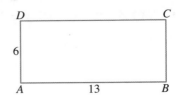

10.3 Applications Of Pythagorean Theorem

In construction and engineering, Pythagorean Theorem can be applied to find the unknown side of a right-angled triangle when the other two sides are given.

Example 6

In the diagram, a taut wire AB connects a point A on a vertical wall to a point B on the horizontal ground. A is 2 m above the ground and B is 0.6 m from the wall. What is the length of the wire?

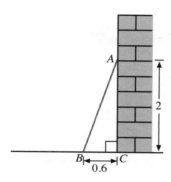

Solution

In $\triangle ABC$,

$AB^2 = AC^2 + BC^2$ (Pythagorean Theorem)

$ = 2^2 + 0.6^2$

$ = 4.36$

$AB = \sqrt{4.36}$

$ = 2.09$ m   (rounded to 3 sig. fig.)

The length of the wire is 2.09 m.

Try It! 6

The figure represents a rectangular door which is 1.1 m wide and 2 m high. Find the length of the diagonal AC of the door.

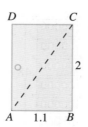

Example 7

The figure shows the cross-section of the roof of a barn. AB and AC are two sides of the roof, AD is a vertical supporting beam and BC is a horizontal beam. $AB = 3$ m, $AC = 2.1$ m, and $AD = 1.7$ m. What is the length of BC?

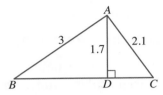

Solution

In $\triangle ABD$,

$$AB^2 = BD^2 + AD^2 \quad \text{(Pythagorean Theorem)}$$
$$3^2 = BD^2 + 1.7^2$$
$$BD^2 = 3^2 - 1.7^2$$
$$BD = \sqrt{6.11} \text{ m}$$

In $\triangle ACD$,

$$AC^2 = DC^2 + AD^2 \quad \text{(Pythagorean Theorem)}$$
$$2.1^2 = DC^2 + 1.7^2$$
$$DC^2 = 2.1^2 - 1.7^2$$
$$DC = \sqrt{1.52} \text{ m}$$
$$\therefore \ BC = BD + DC$$
$$= \sqrt{6.11} + \sqrt{1.52}$$
$$= 3.70 \text{ m} \quad \text{(rounded to 3 sig. fig.)}$$

The length of BC is 3.70 m.

In the diagram, TF is a vertical building of height 48 m. A and B are two cars at the same horizontal level as F. $AT = 88$ m and $BT = 60$ m. Find the distance between the two cars.

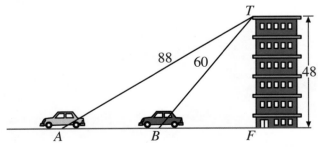

Example 8

The figure shows the cross-section of a trough in which $AB = CD = 9$ in., $BC = 12$ in., and the depth is 8 in. Find the width AD at the mouth of the trough.

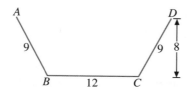

Solution

Draw BM and CN such that $BM \perp AD$ and $CN \perp AD$.

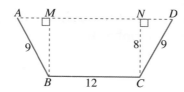

In $\triangle CDN$,

$$CD^2 = CN^2 + ND^2 \qquad \text{(Pythagorean Theorem)}$$
$$9^2 = 8^2 + ND^2$$
$$ND^2 = 81 - 64$$
$$ND = \sqrt{17} \text{ in.}$$

Similarly, $AM = \sqrt{17}$ in.

$\therefore \ AD = AM + MN + ND$
$\qquad = \sqrt{17} + 12 + \sqrt{17}$ $\quad MN = BC = 12$ in.
$\qquad = 20.2$ in. $\qquad$ (rounded to 3 sig. fig.)

The width of AD is 20.2 in.

Try It! 8

A dove-tail joint $EABCDF$ is cut from a piece of rectangular plank as shown. Given that $BC = 4.5$ in., $BE = CF = 2$ in., and $AB = DC = 2.3$ in., find the distance between A and D, rounded to 3 significant figures.

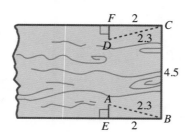

One of the consequences of the Pythagorean Theorem is line segments with lengths that are incommensurable can be constructed using a ruler and a pair of compasses. Pythagorean Theorem enables the construction of incommensurable lengths because the hypotenuse of a triangle is related to the sides by the square root operation.

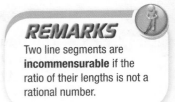

REMARKS

Two line segments are **incommensurable** if the ratio of their lengths is not a rational number.

CLASS ACTIVITY 3

Objective: To apply Pythagorean Theorem to construct lengths of irrational square-root values on the number line diagram.

Tasks

(a) On a sheet of graph paper and taking 2 cm to represent 1 unit, draw a unit square $OA_1A_2B_1$ as shown below. Extend the lines OB_1 and A_1A_2 to OX and A_1A respectively. Line OX is considered as a number line.

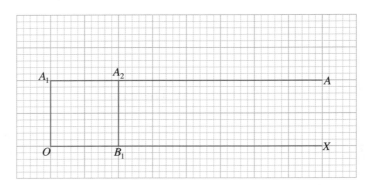

(b) Using a pair of compasses, draw an arc with center $O(0, 0)$ and radius OA_2 to cut OX at B_2. Using Pythagorean Theorem, find the length of the diagonal OA_2. How are OA_2 and OB_2 related? What is the value you have located at B_2 on OX? Copy and complete the following table.

Length of diagonal	Length of OB_n
$OA_2 = \sqrt{(A_2B_1)^2 + (OB_1)^2} = \sqrt{1^2 + 1^2} = \sqrt{2}$	$OB_2 =$
$OA_3 =$	$OB_3 =$
$OA_4 =$	$OB_4 =$
$OA_5 =$	$OB_5 =$

(c) Draw a perpendicular from B_2 to meet the line A_1A at A_3 so that you get the rectangle $OA_1A_3B_2$. Find the length of the diagonal OA_3.

(d) Using a pair of compasses, draw an arc with center $O(0, 0)$ and radius OA_3 to cut OX at B_3. What is the value you have located at B_3 on OX?

(e) Repeat the procedures **(c)** and **(d)** twice, and complete the corresponding values in the table.

(f) Suggest a formula for finding the length of OA_n and hence OB_n, where n is an integer greater than 1.

(g) What values have you constructed on the number line OX?

(h) What is OB_7? Use a similar method to locate OB_7 on the number line OX and state its approximate value.

Do you realize that you are actually locating square-root numbers on the number line in Class Activity 2? We obtain

$$OA_2 = OB_2 = \sqrt{2},\ OA_3 = OB_3 = \sqrt{3},\ OA_4 = OB_4 = \sqrt{4} = 2,\ ....$$

Pythagorean Theorem enables the construction of lengths which are the square roots of positive integers that are not a perfect square, such as $\sqrt{2}, \sqrt{3}, \sqrt{5}, \sqrt{7}, ...$. We are making approximations of such irrational numbers and locating them on a number line.

The figures below show another version of how to construct line segments whose lengths are in the ratio of the square root of any positive integer. Each triangle has a side (labeled "1") that is the chosen unit of measurement. In each right triangle, Pythagorean Theorem establishes the length of the hypotenuse in terms of this unit.

REMARKS

The spiral of Theodorus (also referred to as the square root spiral or the Pythagorean spiral) is a construction of right triangles into a spiral. Each triangle has a side length of one representing the a^2 of the Pythagorean theorem, with the other sides filling in the spaces for the b^2 and c^2 in the theorem.

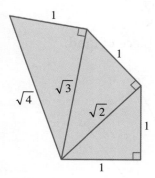

The spiral of Theodorus up to the triangle with hypotenuse $\sqrt{4}$

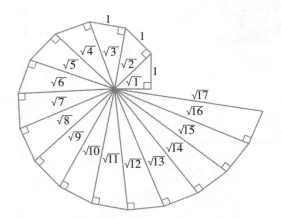

The spiral of Theodorus up to the triangle with hypotenuse $\sqrt{17}$

MATH WEB

You can find out more on the spiral of Theodorus from http://en.wikipedia.org/wiki/Spiral_of_Theodorus, http://en.wikipedia.org/wiki/Incommensurable_magnitudes#Ancient_Greece and http://eucc2011.wikis-paces.com/file/view/Tilted+Squares,+Irrational+Numbers+and+Pythagorean+Theorem.pdf.

EXERCISE 10.3

In this exercise, give your answers rounded to 3 significant figures where necessary.

BASIC PRACTICE

1. In the figure, *ABCD* represents the top of a billiard table where *AB* = 2.74 m and *BC* = 1.37 m. What is the distance between the corners *A* and *C*?

2. *KM* is a metal bar used to reinforce a wooden gate *HKLM*. Given that *KL* = 1.6 m and *LM* = 3 m, find the length of *KM*.

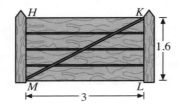

3. *PQRS* is a stamp in the shape of a rhombus, *PR* = 4 cm and *QS* = 2.6 cm. Find the length of a side of the stamp.

FURTHER PRACTICE

4. A square *DEFG* is cut from a circular tin plate as shown. If the diameter of the tin plate is 20 cm, what is the length of a side of the square?

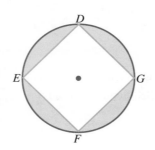

5. In the figure, △*XYZ* is an equilateral triangle of side 10 cm and *XM* ⊥*YZ*. Find
   (a) the length of *XM*,
   (b) the area of △*XYZ*.

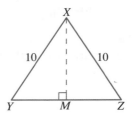

6. In the figure, *ABCD* is the cross-section of a shed with *AB* = 2 m, *BC* = 2.5 m, and *AD* = 1.5 m. Find the length of *CD*.

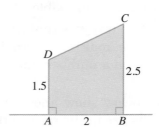

7. In the figure, *PQRS* represents a piece of land with ∠*PRQ* = ∠*PSR* = 90°, *PR* = 15 m, *PS* = 9 m, and *QR* = 8 m. Find
   (a) the length of *PQ*,
   (b) the length of *RS*,
   (c) the area of the piece of land.

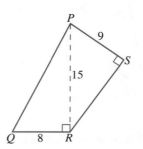

8. The figure represents a 5-m vertical pole AB supported by wires AP and AQ, where $AP = 8$ m and $AQ = 6$ m. P, B and Q are points on a straight line on the horizontal ground. What is the distance between P and Q?

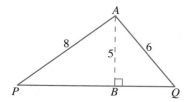

9. In the diagram, A and B represent two kites that are 50 m above the ground PQ. Given that $PA = 67$ m and $PB = 84$ m, find the distance between the two kites.

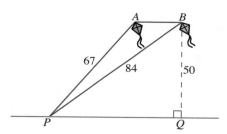

10. A ladder, PQ, leans against a vertical wall. As shown in the diagram, F is the base of the wall where $PF = 2.5$ m and $QF = 1.2$ m.
  (a) Find the length of the ladder.
  (b) The upper end P slides down 0.8 m to a point R. How far has the lower end Q slid away from its original position?

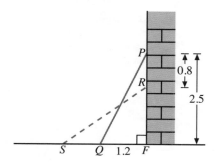

11. An engineer designs a slide for the children in a park. As shown in the diagram, the sliding part AB is 20 m long. It is required that the slope of the slide be greater than $\frac{1}{2}$ but less than 1. Find two possible sets of measurements for the lengths of AC and BC.

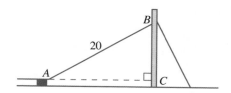

12. In the diagram, A and B are two points on a piece of cloth and $AB = 15$ cm. A stitch pattern is formed by using different positions for a variable point P above AB such that the threads along AP and BP form a right angle at P.

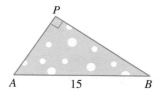

  (a) Find three possible sets of measurements for the lengths of AP and BP.
  (b) Copy the diagram and mark the points of P found in **(a)**.
  (c) If A, B, and the three points of P are joined by a smooth curve, name the curve.

Pythagorean Theorem

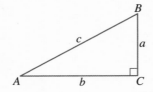

In $\triangle ABC$, if $\angle C = 90°$,

then $\qquad AB^2 = BC^2 + AC^2$

that is $\qquad c^2 = a^2 + b^2$.

Converse of Pythagorean Theorem

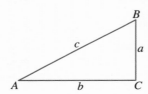

In any $\triangle ABC$, if $c^2 = a^2 + b^2$, then the angle between a and b, $\angle C = 90°$, and the triangle is a right-angled triangle.

In this exercise, give your answers rounded to 3 significant figures where necessary.

1. Find the value of x in each of the following figures, given that the measurements are in centimeters.

(a)

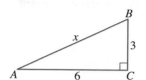

(b)

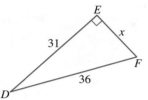

(c)

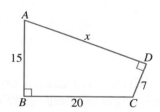

(d)

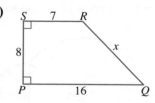

2. Find the values of x and y in each of the following figures, given that the measurements are in feet.
(a) BCD is a straight line.

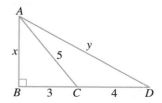

(b) BCD is a straight line.

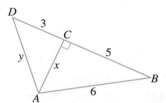

3. In the figure, $\angle CBD = \angle BAD = 90°$, $BC = 7$ cm, $CD = 9$ cm, and $AB = AD$. Find the length of
(a) BD,
(b) AB.

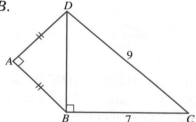

4. A softball diamond has sides of length 60 feet. A fielder throws the ball from second base. What is the distance that he has to throw to reach home base?

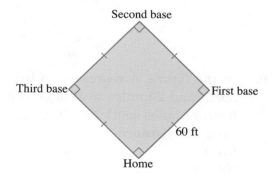

5. Determine whether each of the following triangles is a right-angled triangle. If it is, which angle is the right angle?
(a) $\triangle ABC$ with $a = 112$, $b = 15$, $c = 113$
(b) $\triangle PQR$ with $p = 83$, $q = 84$, $r = 13$

6. In the figure, $\angle YTZ = 90°$, $TX = 10$ cm, $XY = 6$ cm, $YZ = 17$ cm, and $TZ = 15$ cm.
(a) Find the length of TY.
(b) Show that $\angle TYX$ is a right angle.

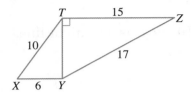

7. In the figure, AMN is a horizontal line, $AB = 10$ cm, $BC = 4$ cm, $CD = 6$ cm, $BM = 5$ cm, and $CE = 4.5$ cm. Find the length of
(a) AN,
(b) DN,
(c) AD.

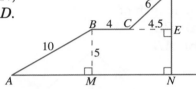

8. In the figure, $ABCD$ is a rectangle, $BC = x$ cm, $AB = (2x + 4)$ cm, and $AC = (2x + 6)$ cm. Find
(a) the value of x,
(b) the area of $ABCD$,
(c) the perpendicular distance from B to AC.

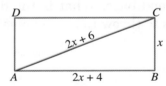

9. In the figure, A represents a town 9 miles north and 20 miles west of O; B is another town 21 miles south and 15 miles east of O. Find the distance
(a) OA,
(b) OB,
(c) AB.

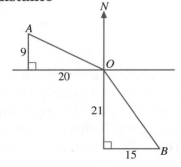

10. The lengths of the sides of a right-angled triangle are $(x - 1)$ cm, $3x$ cm and $(3x + 1)$ cm. Find
(a) the value of x,
(b) the perimeter of the triangle.

11. (a) In the figure, $ABPQ$, $CDPR$, and $EFQR$ are the squares on the sides of $\triangle PQR$. Their areas are 175 cm^2, 112 cm^2, and 63 cm^2 respectively. Find the area of $\triangle PQR$.

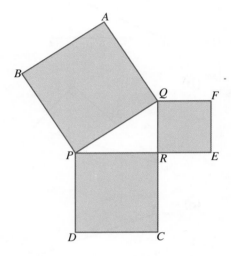

(b) If semicircles are drawn on the sides of the right-angled $\triangle ABC$, where $\angle ACB = 90°$, show the relationship between the areas of these semicircles.

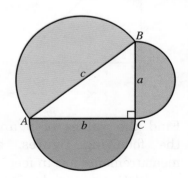

EXTEND YOUR LEARNING CURVE

Diagonal of a Prism

A rectangular prism is a 3-dimensional figure with a rectangular base and top of the same size which are parallel to each other, and each of the other sides is also a rectangle. A rectangular prism with edge lengths, l, w, and h is shown below.

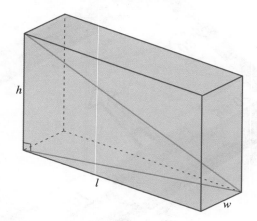

(a) Find the length of the diagonal which is drawn from one corner of the base to the opposite corner of the top, as shown in the figure, in terms of l, w, and h.

(b) What is the length of the diagonal joining the opposite corners of a prism whose base is 3 cm by 4 cm and height is 12 cm?

WRITE IN YOUR JOURNAL

1. What do you understand by the term 'hypotenuse' of a right-angled triangle? Does an equilateral triangle have a hypotenuse?

2. Can Pythagorean Theorem be applied to isosceles right-angled triangles? Why?

Playing

LET'S LEARN TO...

1 find the distance between two points in a coordinate system by applying the Pythagorean Theorem

2 find the slope of a straight line given the coordinates of two points on it

3 interpret and find the equation of a straight line graph in the slope-intercept form $y = mx + b$

4 solve geometric problems involving the use of coordinates

A global positioning system (GPS) receiver uses coordinates to locate the position of a place in the world. By detecting the coordinate of two places, it can find the shortest route from one place to another.

11.1 *Distance Between Two Points*

We can study geometry using a Cartesian coordinate plane. In a coordinate system, distances and lines can be represented by algebraic expressions and equations. This enables us to approach geometric problems using algebraic methods. Let us begin with the distance between two points on a coordinate plane.

 CLASS ACTIVITY 1

Objective: To find the distance between two points, that is the length of a line segment, on a coordinate plane, by applying the Pythagorean Theorem.

1.

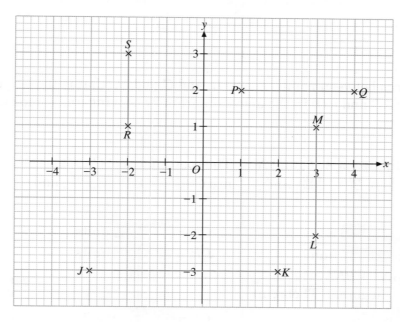

(a) The diagram above shows 4 line segments, *PQ*, *JK*, *RS*, and *LM*. Copy and complete the following table for the lengths of the line segments.

Line Segment	Coordinates of end points	Length (units)
PQ	*P*(1 , 2), *Q*(4 , 2)	$4 - 1 = 3$
JK	*J*(,), *K*(,)	
RS	*R*(,), *S*(,)	
LM	*L*(,), *M*(,)	

(b) If the end points of a line segment are $P(x_1, k)$ and $Q(x_2, k)$, where $x_2 > x_1$, what is the length of *PQ*?

(c) If the end points of a line segment are $P(h, y_1)$ and $S(h, y_2)$ where $y_2 > y_1$, what is the length of *RS*?

2.

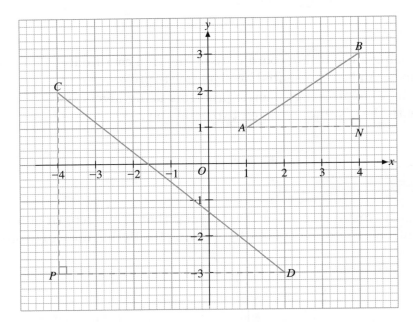

Find the distances between points, A and B, and C and D, (that is the lengths of line segments AB and CD) in the above diagram by copying and completing the following.

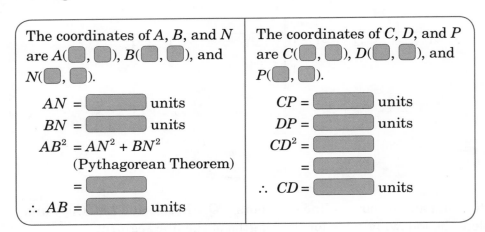

The coordinates of A, B, and N are $A(\boxed{}, \boxed{})$, $B(\boxed{}, \boxed{})$, and $N(\boxed{}, \boxed{})$.

$AN = \boxed{}$ units
$BN = \boxed{}$ units
$AB^2 = AN^2 + BN^2$
(Pythagorean Theorem)
$= \boxed{}$
$\therefore AB = \boxed{}$ units

The coordinates of C, D, and P are $C(\boxed{}, \boxed{})$, $D(\boxed{}, \boxed{})$, and $P(\boxed{}, \boxed{})$.

$CP = \boxed{}$ units
$DP = \boxed{}$ units
$CD^2 = \boxed{}$
$= \boxed{}$
$\therefore CD = \boxed{}$ units

Consider the line segment AB in the diagram where the points $A(x_1, y_1)$ and $B(x_2, y_2)$ are given.

We have $AB^2 = AN^2 + BN^2$ (Pythagorean Theorem)
$= (x_2 - x_1)^2 + (y_2 - y_1)^2$.

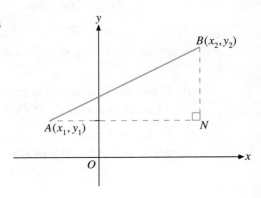

Hence, we have derived the following.

> The distance between two points, $A(x_1, y_1)$ and $B(x_2, y_2)$, is
> $$AB = \sqrt{(x_2 - x_1)^2 + (y_2 - y_1)^2}.$$

The length of the line segment AB is the distance between the two points A and B.

Example 1

$A(8, 6)$, $B(5, 5)$, and $C(-4, 2)$ are points on a coordinate plane.
(a) Find the lengths of AB, BC, and AC.
(b) Show that A, B, and C lie on a straight line.

Solution

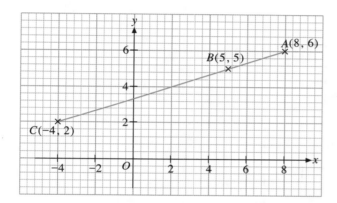

(a) $AB = \sqrt{(8 - 5)^2 + (6 - 5)^2}$

$\qquad = \sqrt{3^2 + 1^2}$

$\qquad = \sqrt{10}$ units

$\quad BC = \sqrt{[5 - (-4)]^2 + (5 - 2)^2}$

$\qquad = \sqrt{9^2 + 3^2}$

$\qquad = \sqrt{90}$ units

$\quad AC = \sqrt{[8 - (-4)]^2 + (6 - 2)^2}$

$\qquad = \sqrt{12^2 + 4^2}$

$\qquad = \sqrt{160}$ units

(b) $AB + BC - AC = \sqrt{10} + \sqrt{90} - \sqrt{160}$

$\qquad\qquad\qquad\quad = 0$

$\quad \therefore AB + BC = AC$

Therefore, A, B and C lie on a straight line.

DISCUSS

Would it make any difference if you write the distance formula as

$$\sqrt{(x_1 - x_2)^2 + (y_1 - y_2)^2}?$$

The coordinates of three points are $P(-7, -4)$, $Q(-4, -2)$, and $R(2, 2)$.
(a) Find the lengths of PQ, QR, and PR.
(b) Show that P, Q, and R lie on a straight line.

Example 2

The vertices of $\triangle ABC$ are $A(2, 3)$, $B(-2, 1)$, and $C(-1, -1)$.
(a) Find the lengths of AB, BC, and CA.
(b) Show that $\triangle ABC$ is a right-angled triangle.
(c) Find the perimeter of $\triangle ABC$, rounded to 3 significant figures.
(d) Find the area of $\triangle ABC$.

Solution

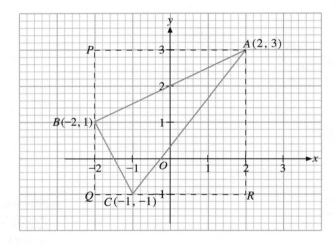

(a) $AB = \sqrt{[2 - (-2)]^2 + (3 - 1)^2}$

$= \sqrt{20}$ units

$BC = \sqrt{[-2 - (-1)]^2 + [1 - (-1)]^2}$

$= \sqrt{5}$ units

$CA = \sqrt{(-1 - 2)^2 + (-1 - 3)^2}$

$= 5$ units

(b) $AB^2 + BC^2 = (\sqrt{20})^2 + (\sqrt{5})^2$

$= 20 + 5$

$= 25$

$AB^2 + BC^2 = CA^2$

Hence, $\angle ABC = 90°$.   (converse of Pythagorean Theorem)

$\therefore$ $\triangle ABC$ is a right-angled triangle.

(c) Perimeter of $\triangle ABC = AB + BC + CA$

$$= \sqrt{20} + \sqrt{5} + 5$$

$$= 11.7 \text{ units} \quad \text{(rounded to 3 sig. fig.)}$$

(d) $\therefore$ area of $\triangle ABC = \dfrac{1}{2} \times AB \times BC \qquad \angle ABC = 90°$

$$= \dfrac{1}{2} \times \sqrt{20} \times \sqrt{5}$$

$$= 5 \text{ unit}^2$$

Alternative Method

Draw the square $APQR$ as shown in the figure.

Area of $\triangle ABP = \dfrac{1}{2} \times AP \times BP$

$$= \dfrac{1}{2} \times 4 \times 2$$

$$= 4 \text{ unit}^2$$

Area of $\triangle BCQ = \dfrac{1}{2} \times 2 \times 1$

$$= 1 \text{ unit}^2$$

Area of $\triangle ACR = \dfrac{1}{2} \times 3 \times 4$

$$= 6 \text{ unit}^2$$

Area of $\triangle ABC$ = Area of $APQR$ – Area of $\triangle ABP$
$\qquad\qquad$ – Area of $\triangle BCQ$ – Area of $\triangle ACR$

$$= 4^2 - 4 - 1 - 6$$

$$= 5 \text{ unit}^2$$

Note: The alternative method above can be applied to find the area of any triangle.

Try It! 2

The vertices of $\triangle PQR$ are $P(3, 2)$, $Q(-3, 0)$, and $R(4, -1)$.
(a) Find the lengths of PQ, QR, and RP.
(b) Show that $\triangle PQR$ is a right-angled triangle.
(c) Find the perimeter of $\triangle PQR$, rounded to 3 significant figures.
(d) Find the area of $\triangle PQR$.

EXERCISE 11.1

 BASIC PRACTICE

1. In each of following, find the distance between the pair of given points.
   (a) $A(3, 2)$, $B(7, 2)$
   (b) $C(4, 5)$, $D(4, -3)$
   (c) $O(0, 0)$, $E(-3, 4)$
   (d) $G(3, 1)$, $H(8, 13)$
   (e) $K(-2, 5)$, $L(-7, 6)$
   (f) $P(4, -3)$, $Q(-1, -7)$

2. A right-angled triangle ABC is as shown on the given coordinate plane.
   (a) What is the length of its hypotenuse?
   (b) Find the area of $\triangle ABC$.

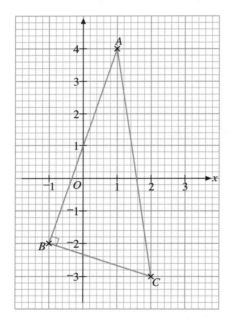

 FURTHER PRACTICE

3. In each of the following,
   (i) find the lengths of AB, BC, and AC,
   (ii) determine whether the points A, B, and C lie on a straight line.
   (a) $A(-4, 3)$, $B(-2, 2)$, $C(0, 1)$
   (b) $A(-3, -2)$, $B(1, -1)$, $C(3, 0)$

4. The vertices of $\triangle ABC$ are $A(-2, -1)$, $B(2, -1)$, and $C(1, 3)$.
   (a) Find the lengths of AB, BC, and CA.
   (b) Find the perimeter of $\triangle ABC$.
   (c) Find the area of $\triangle ABC$.

5. The vertices of $\triangle PQR$ are $P(-4, 4)$, $Q(5, 2)$, and $R(4, 6)$.
   (a) Find the lengths of PQ, QR, and RP.
   (b) Find the perimeter of $\triangle PQR$.
   (c) Show that $\triangle PQR$ is a right-angled triangle.
   (d) Find the area of $\triangle PQR$.

6. The distance between two points $P(-3, 2)$ and $Q(1, k)$ is 5 units. Find the possible values of k.

7. $A(4, 7)$ and $B(-3, 2)$ are points on a coordinate plane. Find the coordinates of a point C on the x-axis such that $AC = BC$.

 MATH@WORK

8. The coordinates of the points on opposite ends of the diameter of a circle are $(8, -5)$ and $(-4, 11)$.
   (a) What is the length of the radius of the circle?
   (b) Find, in terms of π, the circumference and area of the circle.

9. The vertices of a quadrilateral $ABCD$ are $A(5, 4)$, $B(-3, 2)$, $C(-4, -3)$, and $D(4, -1)$.
   (a) Draw $ABCD$ on a coordinate plane.
   (b) Show that $AB = DC$ and $AD = BC$ by finding the lengths of the sides.
   (c) What type of quadrilateral is $ABCD$?
   (d) Find the perimeter of $ABCD$.

 BRAIN WORKS

10. Given a point $G(1, 2)$, find the coordinates of two possible positions of a point $P(a, b)$ in the second quadrant such that the length of $PG = 5$ units.

11.2 *Slope of a Straight Line*

The slope of a straight line is a measure of its steepness, or how fast it rises vertically per unit length horizontally.

We have learned that the slope of a straight line is a measure of its steepness and we define slope $= \dfrac{\text{rise}}{\text{run}}$.

Suppose $A(x_1, y_1)$ and $B(x_2, y_2)$ are two points on the line as shown in the diagram.

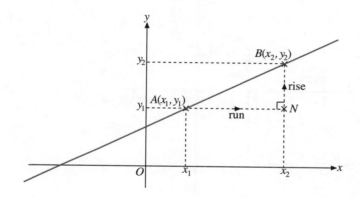

Then   rise $= BN = y_2 - y_1$

and   run $= AN = x_2 - x_1$.

Thus, we have

> The slope m of a line joining $A(x_1, y_1)$ and $B(x_2, y_2)$ is given by $m = \dfrac{y_2 - y_1}{x_2 - x_1}$, provided $x_1 \neq x_2$.

The difference in the y-coordinates is called the rise, and the difference in the x-coordinates is called the run. Thus slope is often given as

$$\text{slope} = \frac{\text{rise}}{\text{run}}.$$

Example 3

Find the slope of the line joining the points
(a) $A(-1, 3)$ and $B(3, 4)$,
(b) $C(3, 2)$ and $D(1, -2)$,
(c) $E(-2, -2)$ and $F(-3, 3)$.

Solution

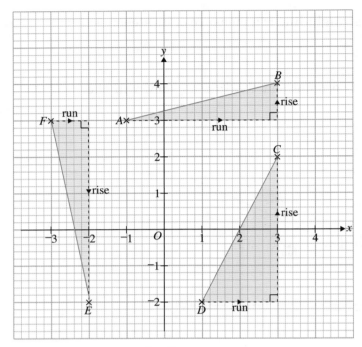

(a) Slope of $AB = \dfrac{y_2 - y_1}{x_2 - x_1}$

$= \dfrac{4 - 3}{3 - (-1)}$

$= \dfrac{1}{4}$

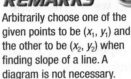

(x_1, y_1) (x_2, y_2)
$(-1, 3)$ $(3, 4)$

run $= 3 - (-1)$
    $= 4$ units
i.e. run $= x_2 - x_1$

(b) Slope of $CD = \dfrac{-2 - 2}{1 - 3}$

$= \dfrac{-4}{-2}$

$= 2$

(c) Slope of $EF = \dfrac{3 - (-2)}{-3 - (-2)}$

$= \dfrac{5}{-1}$

$= -5$

Note: As $\dfrac{y_2 - y_1}{x_2 - x_1} \neq \dfrac{y_2 - y_1}{x_1 - x_2}$, we must ensure that the order of the x-coordinates and the y-coordinates in the numerator and the denominators are consistent when computing the slope.

 **Try It!** ③ Find the slope of the line joining the points
   (a) $P(-1, 9)$ and $Q(4, -6)$
   (b) $R(2, -5)$ and $S(-7, -2)$
   (c) $T(2, 9)$ and $V(-4, 0)$

In Example 3, the lines AB and CD have a positive measure of the slope. The rise of these lines increases as you move from left to right. Line EF has a negative slope; the rise decreases as you move from left to right.

As shown in the diagram, the line CD is steeper than the line AB. The slope of CD is 2 and that of AB is $\frac{1}{4}$. Thus, the steeper a straight line is, the greater the value of its slope. If the slopes are positive, and for lines with negative slopes, steeper lines have slopes whose absolute values are larger.

 DISCUSS

If the slope of the line EF is -5 and the slope of the line GH is $-\frac{1}{5}$, which line is steeper?

CLASS ACTIVITY 2

Objective: To investigate the slope between any two distinct points on a straight line.

The diagram below shows the graph of a straight line ABC. Triangles ABO, BCD, and ACE are all right triangles with one side along the straight line.

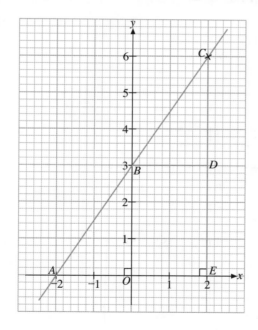

Questions

1. **(a)** Find the slope of the line using the coordinates of the points A and B.
   (b) Similarly, find the slope of the line using the coordinates of the points B and C, and then A and C.
   (c) What do you notice?

2. **(a)** Find the length of AO and of OB. Hence, find the value of ratio $\dfrac{AO}{OB}$.

   (b) Similarly, find the value of the ratio $\dfrac{BD}{DC}$ and $\dfrac{AE}{EC}$.

   (c) What do you notice?

   (d) Show that triangles BDC and AEC are similar to triangle AOB using a series of transformations.

3. **(a)** Since triangles are similar, we have $\dfrac{AO}{BD} = \dfrac{OB}{DC}$. From this equation, show that $\dfrac{OB}{AO} = \dfrac{DC}{BD}$.

   (b) Is $\dfrac{OB}{AO} = \dfrac{EC}{AE}$?

From the Class Activity 2, we observe that the slope is the same between any two distinct points on a sloping straight line. Therefore, a straight line has a uniform slope.

Example 4

In the diagram, the line joining $B(-2, 2)$ and $C(2, -4)$ intersects the y-axis at P. Find

(a) the slope of BC,

(b) the coordinates of P.

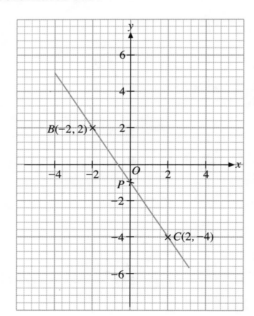

Solution

(a) Slope of $BC = \dfrac{2 - (-4)}{-2 - 2}$

$= \dfrac{6}{-4}$

$= -\dfrac{3}{2}$

(b) The x-coordinate of P is zero since point P is on the y-axis. Let the coordinates of P be $(0, k)$.

Slope of BP = slope of BC

$$\frac{k-2}{0-(-2)} = -\frac{3}{2}$$

$$\frac{k-2}{2} = -\frac{3}{2}$$

$$k-2 = -3$$

$$k = -1$$

$\therefore$ the coordinates of P are $(0, -1)$.

Try It! 4 The line joining the points $Q(-2, 3)$ and $R(6, -1)$ intersects the x-axis at T. Find
(a) the slope of QR,
(b) the coordinates of T.

When three or more points lie on the same straight line, they are said to be collinear. Collinear points can be identified by finding the slopes of any two line segments formed by the given points.

In Example 4, where points B, P, and C lie on the same straight line, besides a slope of BP = slope of BC, we also have slope of PC = slope of BC and slope of BC = slope of PC.

Example 5 Find the slope of the line
(a) $y = -\frac{3}{2}$,
(b) $x = 2$.

Solution

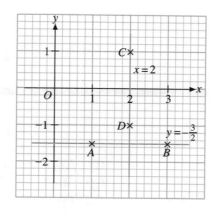

DISCUSS
Which of the following is a linear function?
(a) vertical line
(b) horizontal line
Why or why not?

(a) We choose two points, $A\left(1, -\frac{3}{2}\right)$ and $B\left(3, -\frac{3}{2}\right)$, on the line $y = -\frac{3}{2}$.

Slope of the line = slope of AB

$$= \frac{-\frac{3}{2} - \left(-\frac{3}{2}\right)}{3 - 1}$$

$$= \frac{0}{2}$$

$$= 0$$

∴ the slope of $y = -\frac{3}{2}$ is 0.

(b) We choose two points, $C(2, 1)$ and $D(2, -1)$, on the line $x = 2$.

Slope of the line = slope of CD

$$= \frac{-1 - 1}{2 - 2}$$

$$= \frac{-2}{0}$$

Since division by zero is undefined,
∴ the slope of the line $x = 2$ is undefined.

Try It! **5** Find the slope of the line
(a) $y = 1$, **(b)** $x = -3$.

We can generalize the results in Example 5 as follows:

> The slope of a horizontal line is zero.
> The slope of a vertical line is undefined.

EXERCISE 11.2

 BASIC PRACTICE

1. Find the slope of the straight line passing through each given pair of points.
   (a) $A(3, 4)$, $B(6, 7)$
   (b) $C(-5, 8)$, $D(-2, 5)$
   (c) $E(2, 3)$, $F(2, -5)$
   (d) $G(-7, -1)$, $H(3, -1)$
   (e) $I(2, -3)$, $J(-8, -11)$
   (f) $K(-1, 7)$, $L(4, -3)$
   (g) $M(-1, -2)$, $N(-9, 0)$
   (h) $P(ap^2, 3ap)$, $Q(aq^2, 3aq)$

2. The vertices of $\triangle ABC$ are $A(-5, -3)$, $B(4, 0)$, and $C(-1, 3)$. Find the slopes of the sides of the triangle.

3. Find the slopes of the line segments AB, CD, EF and GH as shown in the diagram.

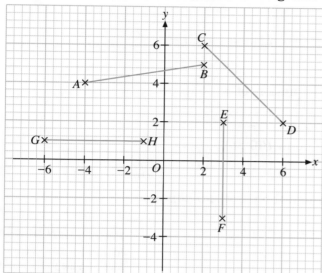

 FURTHER PRACTICE

4. The slope of the line passing through $A(2, 3)$ and $B(h, 7)$ is $\frac{2}{3}$. Find the value of h.

5. Three points A, B, and C have coordinates $(5, 8)$, $(-p, 9)$, and $(7p, 5)$ respectively. If the lines AB and AC have the same slope, find the value of p.

6. The points $A(-5, -3)$, $B(-2, k)$, and $C(4, 3)$ lie on a straight line. Find the value of k.

7. The line segment joining $P(-6, 7)$ and $Q(5, -2)$ intersects the y-axis at the point R. Find the coordinates of R.

8. The line segment joining the points $R(-1, t)$ and $S(4, 3t^2)$ has a slope of 2. Find the possible values of t.

 MATH@**WORK**

9. The vertices of a parallelogram $ABCD$ are $A(-2, -2)$, $B(2, -1)$, $C(3, 2)$, and $D(-1, 1)$.
  (a) Find the slopes of all four sides of the parallelogram.
  (b) What can you say about the slopes of the opposite sides of a parallelogram?

10. The vertices of a rectangle $PQRS$ are $P(-2, -3)$, $Q(4, 0)$, $R(2, 4)$, and $S(-4, 1)$.
  (a) Find the slopes of all four sides of the rectangle.
  (b) What can you say about the slopes of the adjacent sides of a rectangle?

11.

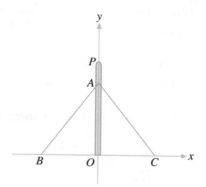

In the diagram, a vertical pole OP is supported by two pieces of wire, AB and AC, of equal lengths. The slope of AB is $\frac{4}{3}$ and the coordinates of B with reference to O are $(-75, 0)$. Find
  (a) the coordinates of the point C,
  (b) the coordinates of the point A,
  (c) the slope of AC,
  (d) the total length of the two pieces of wire, AB and AC.

 BRAIN WORKS

12. Given a point $P(4, -2)$, find two possible pairs of coordinates of a point Q such that the slope of PQ is $-\frac{3}{5}$.

11.3 *Equation of a Straight Line*

We have learned that the graphs of linear equations in two variables such as

$$y = 2x \quad \text{and} \quad 4x + 3y - 7 = 0$$

are straight lines. Let us see how we can find the equation of a linear graph when some information about the graph is known.

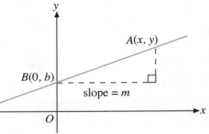

If a straight line has slope m and passes through the point $B(0, b)$, we can find its equation.

Let $A(x, y)$ be a point on the straight line passing through the point $A(0, b)$.

$$\text{Slope of } AB = m$$
$$\frac{y - b}{x - 0} = m$$
$$y - b = mx$$
$$\therefore \; y = mx + b$$

Every point (x, y) which lies on the line AB satisfies the equation $y = mx + b$. Thus, we have the following

> The equation of a straight line with slope m and y-intercept b is $y = mx + b$.

The equation $y = mx + b$ is called the **slope-intercept form** or the **gradient-intercept form** of the equation of a straight line.

For example, the line $y = \frac{1}{5}x - 2$ has slope $\frac{1}{5}$ and y-intercept -2.

The line $4x + 3y - 7 = 0$ can be rewritten in the slope-intercept form as

$$y = -\frac{4}{3}x + \frac{7}{3}.$$

Therefore, the line $4x + 3y - 7 = 0$ has slope $-\frac{4}{3}$ and y-intercept $\frac{7}{3}$.

Note: If the slope of a line is undefined, that is, the line is vertical, its equation is $x = a$, where a is its x-intercept.

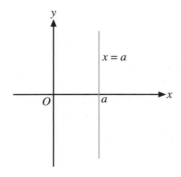

In general, we can find the equation of a straight line when we are given

> **(a)** the slope and any one point (x_1, y_1) on the line,
> or
> **(b)** any two points (x_1, y_1) and (x_2, y_2) on the line.

In case **(b)**, we first find the slope of the line using $\dfrac{y_2 - y_1}{x_2 - x_1}$.

The following examples will illustrate the forming of equation of a straight line in the slope-intercept form.

Example 6

Find the equation of the line

(a) L_1 with slope $= -\dfrac{4}{3}$ and passing through the origin,

(b) L_2 with slope $= -1$ and passing through the point $A\left(0, \dfrac{5}{6}\right)$.

(c) L_3 with slope $= 2$ and passing through the point $B(2, 3)$.

Solution

(a) When a line passes through the origin, its y-intercept $b = 0$.

Given slope $m = -\dfrac{4}{3}$, using the slope-intercept form $y = mx + b$, equation of the line L_1 is

$$y = -\frac{4}{3}x + 0,$$

i.e.

$$y = -\frac{4}{3}x.$$

(b) The point $A\left(0, \dfrac{5}{6}\right)$ lies on the y-axis, therefore the y-intercept $b = \dfrac{5}{6}$.

Given slope $m = -1$,

$\therefore$ equation of the line L_2 is

$$y = -x + \frac{5}{6}.$$

(c) Since slope = 2, the equation of L_3 is

$$y = 2x + b \quad\text{.............................. (1)}$$

where b is a constant.

Given $B(2, 3)$ is on L_3, putting $x = 2$ and $y = 3$ into (1), we obtain

$$3 = 2(2) + b$$
$$b = -1$$

$\therefore$ equation of the line L_3 is

$$y = 2x - 1.$$

Note: The equation of a line passing through the origin is of the form $y = mx$ or $x = 0$.

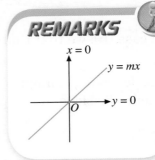
Try It! **6** Find the equation of the line

(a) AB with slope $\dfrac{2}{5}$ and passing through the origin,

(b) CD with slope -7 and passing through the point $(0, 8)$.

(c) EF with slope $-\dfrac{1}{2}$ and passing through the point $(4, 1)$.

Example 7 Find the equation of the straight line passing through the points
(a) $A(3, 2)$ and $B(-5, -4)$,
(b) $C(-3, 5)$ and $D(-3, -1)$.

• **Solution** **(a)** Slope of $AB = \dfrac{-4 - 2}{-5 - 3}$

$$= \dfrac{3}{4}$$

Equation of AB is of the form $y = \dfrac{3}{4}x + b$.

Since $A(3, 2)$ is on the line,

$$2 = \dfrac{3}{4}(3) + b$$

$$b = -\dfrac{1}{4}$$

$\therefore$ equation of the line AB is $y = \dfrac{3}{4}x - \dfrac{1}{4}$.

(b) Slope of $CD = \dfrac{-1 - 5}{-3 - (-3)}$

$\qquad\qquad\qquad = \dfrac{-6}{0}$ (undefined)

$\qquad \therefore$ CD is a vertical line and

$\qquad\qquad$ its x-intercept = x-coordinate of C and of D

$\qquad\qquad\qquad = -3.$

$\qquad \therefore$ equation of the line CD is $x = -3$.

Try It! **7**

Find the equation of the line passing through the points
(a) $P(-2, 3)$ and $Q(2, -1)$,
(b) $R(-4, 5)$ and $S(-1, 5)$.

Example **8**

The equation of a straight line L is $4x + 5y - 7 = 0$.
(a) Express the equation in the slope-intercept form.
(b) Hence, state the slope and the y-intercept of L.

Solution

(a) $4x + 5y - 7 = 0$

$\qquad\qquad 5y = -4x + 7$

$\qquad\qquad\; y = \dfrac{1}{5}(-4x + 7)$

$\qquad \therefore$ the slope-intercept form of the equation of L is

$\qquad\qquad\qquad y = -\dfrac{4}{5}x + \dfrac{7}{5}.$

(b) Comparing with $y = mx + b$, we have

$\qquad\qquad$ slope of $L = -\dfrac{4}{5}$,

$\qquad\qquad y$-intercept of $L = \dfrac{7}{5}$.

Try It! **8**

The equation of a straight line L is $2x - 3y + 4 = 0$.
(a) Express the equation in the slope-intercept form.
(b) Hence, state the slope and the y-intercept of L.

EXERCISE 11.3

BASIC PRACTICE

1. State the slope and y-intercept of each of the following lines.
   (a) $y = 5x - 8$
   (b) $y = 1 - 3x$
   (c) $y = \frac{4}{7}x$
   (d) $y = -9$

2. For each of the following, write down the equation of the line given its slope m and y-intercept b.
   (a) $m = 2, b = 3$
   (b) $m = -\frac{2}{7}, b = 7$
   (c) $m = -3, b = -5$
   (d) $m = \frac{4}{9}, b = 0$

3. For each of the following, find the equation of the line that has slope m and passes through the given point A.
   (a) $m = 3, A(1, 4)$
   (b) $m = -2, A(3, -5)$
   (c) $m = 0, A(-3, 4)$
   (d) $m = -\frac{4}{5}, A(-2, -7)$
   (e) $m = \frac{3}{4}, A(0, -8)$
   (f) $m = -1, A(-8, 0)$

4. Find the equation of the line that passes through the two given points A and B.
   (a) $A(-3, 5), B(0, 7)$
   (b) $A(3, -7), B(-3, 11)$
   (c) $A(4, 3), B(4, 9)$
   (d) $A(-5, -6), B(8, -6)$
   (e) $A(4, 2), B(-8, -13)$
   (f) $A(-3, -2), B(2, -3)$

5. For each of the following equations,
   (i) express it in the slope-intercept form,
   (ii) write down the slope and the y-intercept of the line.

   (a) $2x + y - 3 = 0$
   (b) $x - 4y - 8 = 0$
   (c) $3x + 7y + 6 = 0$
   (d) $\frac{x}{5} + \frac{y}{3} = 1$

FURTHER PRACTICE

6. Find the equations of the lines $L_1, L_2, L_3, L_4,$ and L_5 as shown in the diagram below.

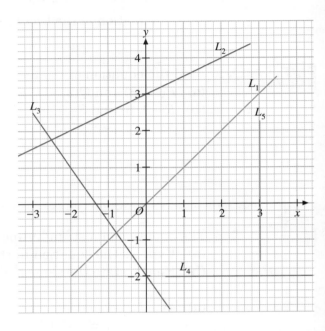

7. A line L cuts the x-axis at $A(4, 0)$ and the y-axis at $B(0, -3)$. Find
   (a) the slope of the line L,
   (b) the equation of the line L,
   (c) the area of $\triangle OAB$, where O is the origin,
   (d) the length of AB,
   (e) the perpendicular distance of O to L.

8. The slope of the line $6x + ky - 9 = 0$ is $-\frac{3}{4}$. Find
   (a) the value of k,
   (b) the y-intercept of the line.

9. A line L_1 passes through $A(2, -5)$. The slope of L_1 is the same as that of the line $L_2: 3x - 7y + 6 = 0$. Find the equation of L_1.

10. The slope of a line L_1 is $-\frac{4}{5}$. It cuts the y-axis at the same point as the line $L_2: 7x + 4y - 12 = 0$. Find the equation of L_1.

11. The vertices of $\triangle ABC$ are $A(-4, 1)$, $B(-4, -2)$, and $C(2, 5)$. Find

   (a) the equations of the lines AB, BC, and CA,

   (b) the coordinates of the point where AC cuts the y-axis,

   (c) the area of $\triangle ABC$,

   (d) the perpendicular distance from A to BC.

12. A hotel will cater for a party at the cost of \$30 per person plus a basic charge of \$200. Let \$$y$ be the total cost for x persons.

   (a) Copy and complete the following table.

Number of persons (x)	20	40	60	80	100
Total cost (\$$y$)					

   (b) Form a linear equation y in terms of x and y.

   (c) Suppose the graph of the linear equation in **(b)** is drawn on a coordinate plane.

      (i) What is the slope of the line? What does the slope represent?

      (ii) What is the y-intercept of the line and what does it represent?

13. On a coordinate plane where the same scale is used for both x and y-axes, a line L is drawn. The line passes through the point $A(-1, 3)$ and makes an angle of $45°$ with the x-axis. Find the equation of L.

14. The points $(2, 3)$ and $(4, 7)$ lie on a straight line. Explain why $\dfrac{y-3}{x-2} = \dfrac{7-3}{4-2}$ gives an equation for this line.

Distance Between Two Points

The distance between any two points $A(x_1, y_1)$ and $B(x_2, y_2)$

$$AB = \sqrt{(x_2 - x_1)^2 + (y_2 - y_1)^2}\,.$$

The distance between points A and B is considered as the length of the line segment AB.

Slope of a Straight Line

The slope of a line joining two points $A(x_1, y_1)$
and $B(x_2, y_2)$ is $m = \dfrac{\text{rise}}{\text{run}} = \dfrac{y_2 - y_1}{x_2 - x_1}$.

Slope m is undefined if $x_1 = x_2$.

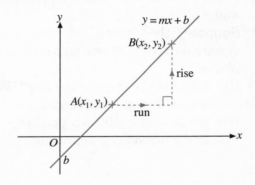

Equation of a Straight Line

The slope-intercept form or gradient-intercept form of the equation of a straight line is $y = mx + b$ where m is the slope and b is the y-intercept of the line.

1. **(a)** Find the values of p if the lines $3x - py - 5 = 0$ and $(p - 2)x = 5y + 1$ have the same slope.
   (b) Find the equation of the straight line passing through the point $(-6, 1)$ and having the same slope as the line $3x + 2y = 4$. If the line also passes through the point $(k, -5)$, find k.

2. P is the point $(6, 2)$ and Q is the point $(-3, 8)$.
   (a) Find the equation of PQ.
   (b) The line $y = 2$ is the line of symmetry of triangle PQR. Find the coordinates of R.
   (c) Find the area of $\triangle PQR$.
   (d) Find the length of line PQ, and hence find the perpendicular distance from R to PQ.

3. The vertices of ABC are $A(-1, 2)$, $B(1, 5)$ and $C(4, 3)$.
   (a) Find the lengths of the sides AB, BC and CA.
   (b) Show that $\angle ABC = 90°$.
   (c) What type of triangle is $\triangle ABC$?
   (d) Find the perpendicular distance from B to AC.
   (e) Find the coordinates of the point at which the line AC cuts the x-axis.

4. A line L passes through $A(-2, 3)$ and its slope is $\frac{1}{2}$.
   (a) Find the equation of the line L.
   (b) If the point $B(4, k)$ lies on L, find the value of k.
   (c) Find the lengths of OA and OB, where O is the origin.
   (d) Determine whether $\triangle OAB$ is a right triangle.

5. In the diagram, A is the point $(0, -10)$ and D is the point $(0, 6)$. CD is a horizontal line. The line AC meets the x-axis at B and its slope is $\frac{5}{2}$.

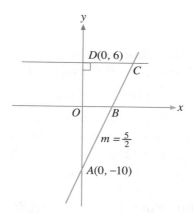

   (a) Find the equations of the lines CD and AC.
   (b) Find the coordinates of B and C.
   (c) Find the area of $\triangle ACD$.
   (d) What is the ratio of areas of $\triangle ABO$ and $\triangle ACD$?

6. The vertices of a quadrilateral $ABCD$ are $A(-3, 0)$, $B(4, 1)$, $C(5, 4)$ and $D(-2, 3)$. $G(1, 2)$ is a point inside $ABCD$.
   (a) Find the lengths of AG, BG, CG and DG.
   (b) Show that the points A, G and C lie on a straight line.
   (c) Show that the points B, G and D lie on a straight line.
   (d) From the results in **(a)**, **(b)** and **(c)**, what can you say about G?
   (e) What type of quadrilateral is $ABCD$?

7.

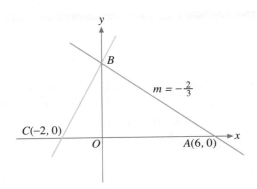

In the diagram, the coordinates of the points A and C are $(6, 0)$ and $(-2, 0)$ respectively. The slope of the line AB is $-\dfrac{2}{3}$.

(a) Find the equation of the line AB.

(b) State the coordinates of B.

(c) Find the equation of the line BC.

(d) Determine whether $\triangle ABC$ is a right triangle.

(e) Find the area of $\triangle ABC$.

8.

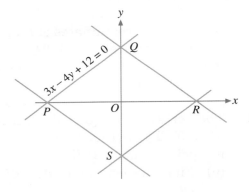

In the diagram, $PQRS$ is a rhombus and the equation of PQ is $3x - 4y + 12 = 0$.

(a) Write down the slope of PQ.

(b) Find the coordinates of P, Q, R, and S.

(c) Find the slope of QR.

(d) Find the equations of QR, RS, and PS in the slope-intercept form.

9. The vertices of a quadrilateral $ABCD$ are $A(-3, -2)$, $B(9, 2)$, $C(7, 8)$ and $D(-5, 4)$.

(a) Find the equation of the line passing through C that has the same slope as BD.

(b) Find the lengths of AB and AD, leaving your answers as square root numbers.

(c) Show that $ABCD$ is a rectangle.

(d) Find the areas of $ABCD$.

10. In the diagram, $OABC$ is a square and the vertex A is $(a, 0)$. Points P, Q, R and S are marked on the sides of the square such that $OP = AQ = BR = CS = 1$ unit.

(a) State the coordinates of the points B, C, P, Q, R and S.

(b) Find the lengths of PQ and QR.

(c) Show that $\angle PQR$ is a right angle.

(d) What type of quadrilateral is $PQRS$?

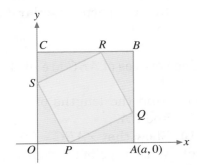

Families of Straight Lines

Consider the equations

$$T : y = kx + 2,$$

$$P : y = \frac{3}{4}x + k,$$

and $F : (2x - y - 3) + k(x + 3y - 5) = 0.$

(a) For each equation, substitute k with several values and draw the corresponding graphs on the same diagram using a sheet of graph paper. (You should have three different diagrams, each for T, P and F.)

(b) Turn to the classmate next to you and compare your diagrams with those of your classmate's. Hence, write down your findings about these three equations of straight lines.

WRITE IN YOUR JOURNAL

Some real-life contexts in which coordinate geometry is used in daily life are art, clothes, design and landscaping. Give an example of how you could use coordinate geometry at home.

MENSURATION OF PYRAMIDS, CYLINDERS, CONES AND SPHERES

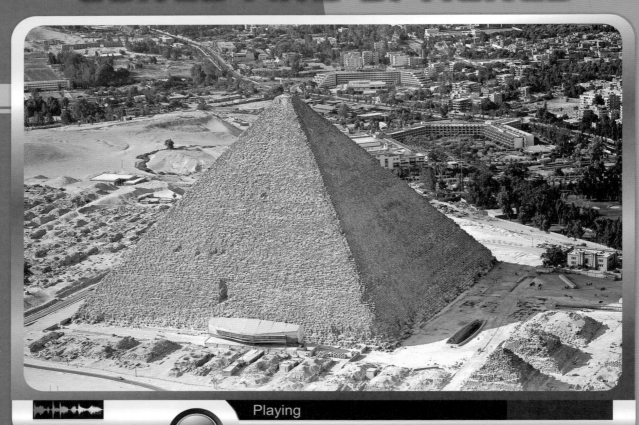

Playing

LET'S LEARN TO...

❶ sketch pyramids, cylinders, cones, and spheres

❷ use nets to visualize surface areas of solids such as pyramids, cylinders, and cones

❸ state the formulas for the volumes and surface areas of pyramids, cylinders, cones, and spheres

❹ find the surface areas and volumes of composite solids involving prisms, pyramids, cylinders, cones, and spheres

The Great Pyramid of Khufu at Giza, Egypt, was built around 2500 B.C. with more than 2 million stone blocks weighing 2 to 30 tons (1 ton = 1000 kg) each. This pyramid has a square base of side 230.38 m and a height of 146.5 m. Do you know how to find its volume?

12.1 *Pyramids*

A   Introducing Pyramids

Look at these 3-D objects. What do you notice about each of them? All of them have triangular faces that meet at a common point. We call these solids **pyramids** and those triangular faces **lateral faces**. The face that is opposite to the common point is called the **base** of the pyramid. Notice that the base of a pyramid is a polygon.

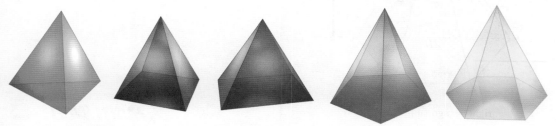

We can sketch and label pyramids as shown. We classify pyramids by their bases. For example, if the base of a pyramid is a triangle, we call it a triangular pyramid.

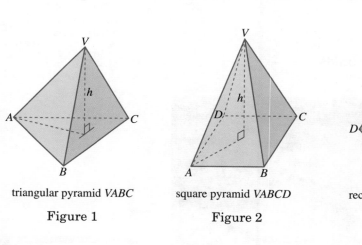

triangular pyramid *VABC*

Figure 1

square pyramid *VABCD*

Figure 2

rectangular pyramid *VABCD*

Figure 3

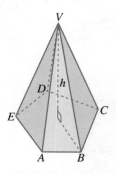

pentagonal pyramid *VABCDE*

Figure 4

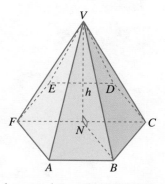

hexagonal pyramid *VABCDEF*

Figure 5

REMARKS

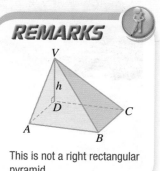

This is not a right rectangular pyramid.

The common edge between two adjacent lateral faces is called a **lateral edge** or **slant edge**. The common point at which the lateral faces meet is called the **vertex** or **apex**. The **perpendicular** from the vertex to the base of a pyramid is its **height**.

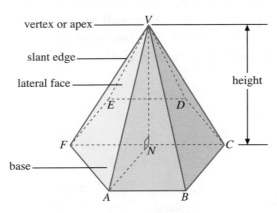

right hexagonal pyramid

REMARKS

The lateral faces of a right regular pyramid are congruent triangles. The height of each triangle is called the **slant height**.

Suppose the perpendicular meets the center of the base, then the pyramid is a **right pyramid**. If the base of a right pyramid is a regular polygon, then the pyramid is a **regular pyramid**.

These Egyptian pyramids are right square pyramids.

MATH WEB

You may access the website http://www.touregypt.net/featurestories/greatpyramid1.htm and http://www.ancientegypt.co.uk/pyramids/home..html for more information on the Great Pyramid of Khufu.

DISCUSS

Is a rectangular pyramid a regular pyramid?

B Nets and Surface Areas of Pyramids

We can construct models of pyramids by drawing their nets on a sheet of paper and folding up the sides. The nets of a triangular pyramid and a right square pyramid are as shown below. From the diagrams, we can see that the total surface area of a pyramid is equal to the area of its net.

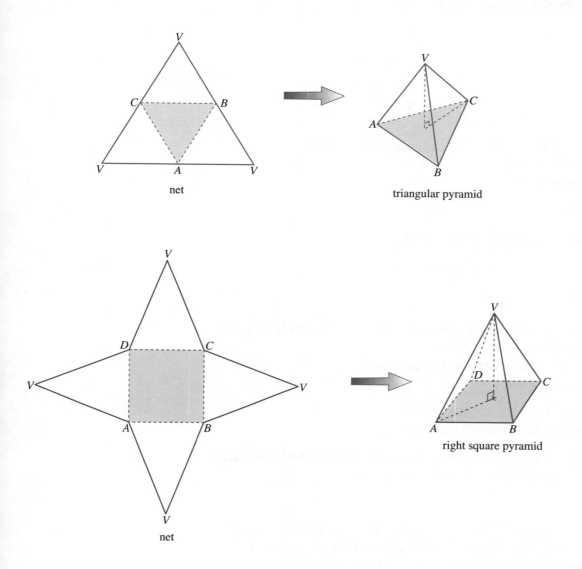

net   triangular pyramid

net   right square pyramid

Total surface area of a pyramid = Base area + Area of all lateral faces

Example **1**

Each lateral face of a triangular pyramid is an equilateral triangle of side 2 feet. What is the surface area of the pyramid?

Solution   Suppose VAB is a lateral face of the pyramid and $VM \perp AB$ as shown. Then $AM = MB = 1$ ft.

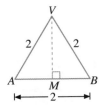

$$VA^2 = VM^2 + AM^2 \quad \text{(Pythagorean Theorem)}$$
$$2^2 = VM^2 + 1^2$$
$$VM^2 = 2^2 - 1^2$$
$$VM = \sqrt{3} \text{ ft}$$

$$\text{Area of } \triangle VAB = \frac{1}{2} \times AB \times VM$$
$$= \frac{1}{2} \times 2 \times \sqrt{3}$$
$$= \sqrt{3} \text{ ft}^2$$

Each of the 3 lateral faces and the base of this triangular pyramid are equal in area.

∴ total surface area of the pyramid

$$= 4 \times \sqrt{3}$$
$$= 4\sqrt{3}$$
$$= 6.93 \text{ ft}^2 \quad \text{(rounded to 3 sig. fig.)}$$

Note: Students may also refer to the net of the triangular pyramid on the previous page.

Try It! 1

In the figure, $VABCD$ is a right square pyramid with base $ABCD$ of side 2 feet. The length of each edge is 2.7 feet. What is the total surface area of the pyramid?

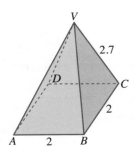

Example 2

$VPQRS$ is a right rectangular pyramid with height = 12 cm, PQ = 10 cm and QR = 8 cm. Find the total surface area of the pyramid.

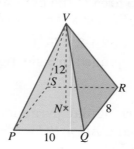

Solution

Construct perpendiculars VM and VT to QR and PQ respectively.

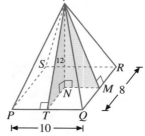

In $\triangle VNM$,

$$NM = TQ$$
$$= \frac{1}{2} \times PQ$$
$$= \frac{1}{2} \times 10$$
$$= 5 \text{ cm}$$

$$VM^2 = VN^2 + NM^2 \qquad \text{(Pythagorean Theorem)}$$
$$= 12^2 + 5^2$$
$$VM = \sqrt{12^2 + 5^2}$$
$$= 13 \text{ cm}$$

$$\text{Area of } \triangle VQR = \frac{1}{2} \times QR \times VM$$
$$= \frac{1}{2} \times 8 \times 13$$
$$= 52 \text{ cm}^2$$

In $\triangle VNT$,

$$NT = QM$$
$$= \frac{1}{2} \times QR$$
$$= \frac{1}{2} \times 8$$
$$= 4 \text{ cm}$$

$$VT^2 = VN^2 + NT^2$$
$$= 12^2 + 4^2$$
$$VT = \sqrt{12^2 + 4^2}$$
$$= \sqrt{160} \text{ cm}$$

$$\text{Area of } \triangle VPQ = \frac{1}{2} \times PQ \times VT$$
$$= \frac{1}{2} \times 10 \times \sqrt{160}$$
$$= 5\sqrt{160} \text{ cm}^2$$

Total surface area of the pyramid
= Area of $PQRS$ + 2 × Area of $\triangle VQR$ + 2 × Area of $\triangle VPQ$

= 10 × 8 + 2 × 52 + 2 × 5$\sqrt{160}$
= 310 cm^2 (rounded to 3 sig. fig.)

Try It!   2 $VABC$ is a triangular pyramid. The base $\triangle ABC$ is right-angled at C and $AC = BC = 3$ cm. VC is perpendicular to the base and $VC = 4$ cm. Find
(a) the sides of $\triangle VAB$,
(b) the total surface area of the pyramid.

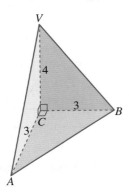

C Volumes of Pyramids

The volume of a pyramid is closely related to the volume of a prism of the same base and height. Let us explore the relationship in Class Activity 1.

CLASS ACTIVITY 1

Objective: To explore the relationship between the volume of a pyramid and the volume of a prism.

Tasks
(a) Use a piece of cardboard to draw the net below and then fold it to make an open square pyramid.

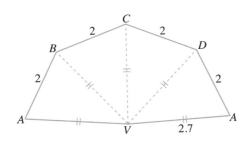

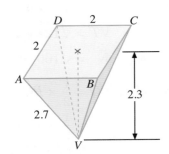

(b) Use a piece of cardboard to draw the net below and then fold it to make an open prism. Notice that the prism has the same square base of side 2 cm and height 2.3 cm as the pyramid in **(a)**.

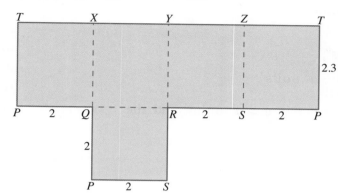 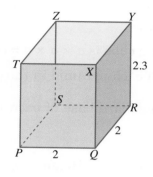

(c) Fill the inverted pyramid with cereal (beans or sand) to the brim. Then pour the cereal (beans or sand) into the prism. Continue to do this until the prism is full.

Questions

1. How many times must the pyramid be completely filled with cereal in order to fill the prism completely?

2. Describe the relationship between the volume of the pyramid and the volume of the prism.

   Volume of pyramid = ⬜ × Volume of prism with the **same base and height**

The result in Class Activity 1 can be applied to any pyramid and prism if they have the same base and height.

i.e. Volume of pyramid = $\frac{1}{3}$ × Volume of prism with the **same base and height**

We have learned that

$$\text{Volume of prism} = \text{Base area} \times \text{Height}.$$

This suggests that the following formula is true:

$$\text{Volume of pyramid} = \frac{1}{3} \times \text{Base area} \times \text{Height}$$

There are special pyramids whose volume can be computed exactly to add further support to the truth of this formula. Take a cube of edge length a units and draw lines from the center of the cube to the vertices. The cube has been divided into 6 congruent pyramids, each is a square pyramid of height $\frac{1}{2}a$ units and square base of side length a units.

The volume of the cube is $a \times a \times a = a^3$ units^3,

so, the volume of each pyramid in the cube $= \frac{1}{6}a^3$ units^3.

The area of the square base of each pyramid is $a \times a = a^2$ units^2 and the height is $\frac{1}{2}a$.

The product, Base area $\times$ Height is $a^2 \times \frac{1}{2}a = \frac{1}{2}a^3$.

Notice that the volume of each pyramid which is $\frac{1}{6}a^3$ can be expressed as $\frac{1}{3} \times \frac{1}{2}a^3$.

Thus, the formula for the volume of a pyramid as $\frac{1}{3} \times$ Base area $\times$ Height in this special case has been proven.

In the rest of this course, this formula will be used for other pyramids.

Example 3   A pentagonal pyramid has a base area of 21 cm^2 and a height of 8 cm. Find the volume of the pyramid.

Solution   Volume of the pyramid $= \frac{1}{3} \times$ Base area $\times$ Height

$$= \frac{1}{3} \times 21 \times 8$$
$$= 56 \text{ cm}^3$$

Try It! 3   A hexagonal pyramid has a base area of 42 cm^2 and a height of 9 cm. Find the volume of the pyramid.

Example 4

The figure shows a model of a building. It consists of a right square pyramid on top of a rectangular prism *ABCDEFGH*. *ABCD* is of side 10 cm, *CG* = 15 cm and the height of the model is 23 cm. Find

(a) the volume of the model,

(b) the total surface area of the model.

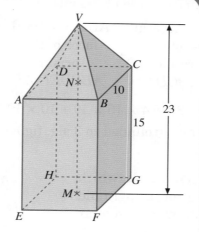

Solution

(a) Height of the pyramid = VN

$$= 23 - 15$$

$$= 8 \text{ cm}$$

Volume of the pyramid = $\frac{1}{3} \times$ Base area $\times$ Height

$$= \frac{1}{3} \times (10 \times 10) \times 8$$

$$= 266\frac{2}{3} \text{ cm}^3$$

Volume of the cuboid = Length $\times$ Breadth $\times$ Height

$$= 10 \times 10 \times 15$$

$$= 1{,}500 \text{ cm}^3$$

$\therefore$ Volume of the model = $266\frac{2}{3} + 1500$

$$= 1{,}766\frac{2}{3} \text{ cm}^3$$

(b) Draw $VP \perp BC$ as shown.

$$NP = \frac{1}{2} \times AB$$

$$= 5 \text{ cm}$$

$$VP^2 = VN^2 + NP^2 \quad \text{(Pythagorean Theorem)}$$

$$= 8^2 + 5^2$$

$$VP = \sqrt{89} \text{ cm}$$

Area of $\triangle VBC = \frac{1}{2} \times 10 \times \sqrt{89}$

$$= 5\sqrt{89} \text{ cm}^2$$

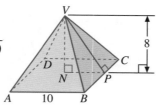

Total surface area of the model

$$= \begin{matrix} \text{Area of lateral} \\ \text{faces of the} \\ \text{pyramid} \\ VABCD \end{matrix} + \begin{matrix} \text{Area of lateral} \\ \text{faces of the} \\ \text{prism} \\ ABCDEFGH \end{matrix} + \begin{matrix} \text{base area} \\ EFGH \end{matrix}$$

$$= 4 \times 5\sqrt{89} + 4 \times 15 \times 10 + 10 \times 10$$

$$= 889 \text{ cm}^2 \quad \text{(rounded to 3 sig. fig.)}$$

Try It! ④ The figure shows a solid which is composed of a pyramid *VABCD* and a rectangular prism *ABCDEFGH*. *ABCD* is a square of side 8 cm. The height *VD* of the pyramid is 6 cm and *CG* = 12 cm. Find
(a) the volume of the solid,
(b) the total surface area of the solid.

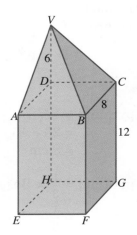

EXERCISE 12.1

In this exercise, give your answers rounded to 3 significant figures where necessary.

 BASIC PRACTICE

1. In each case, sketch and name the solid formed from the given net. Then find the total surface area of each solid. (The dimensions given are in centimeters.)
    (a)

    (b)

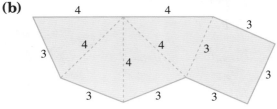

2. Find the volume of each of the following pyramids. (The dimensions given are in inches.)
    (a)

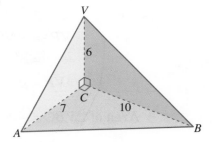

(b)

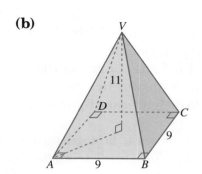

6. The figure shows a right square pyramid *VABCD* with *AB* = 10 cm and the height *VN* = 12 cm. Find
(a) the volume,
(b) the total surface area,
of the pyramid.

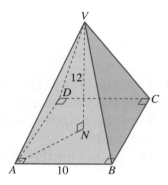

(c)

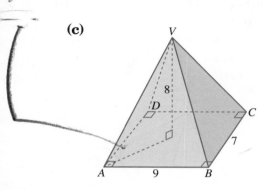

7. The figure shows a right rectangular pyramid *VPQRS* with *PQ* = 8 in., *QR* = 6 in., and *VR* = 13 in. Find
(a) the total surface area,
(b) the volume
of the pyramid.

(d)

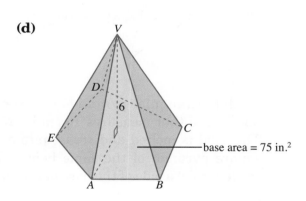

base area = 75 in.²

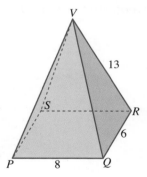

3. The base of a pyramid is an equilateral triangle of side 6 ft. The length of each slant edge is 5 ft. What is the total surface area of the pyramid?

4. The base area of an octagonal pyramid is 84 cm² and its height is 5 cm. What is the volume of the pyramid?

8. The volume of a pentagonal pyramid is 80 cm³. If the base area of the pyramid is 40 cm², what is its height?

5. The base of a pyramid is a rhombus whose diagonals are 14 m and 10 m. The height of the pyramid is 9 m. Find the volume of the pyramid.

9. The volume and height of a square pyramid are 1,275 ft³ and 17 ft respectively. What is the length of a side of its base?

10. The figure shows a regular hexagon *ABCDEF* of side 2 cm. It is the base of a right pyramid of height 5 cm.

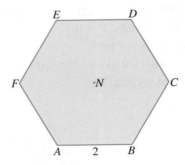

(a) Find the area of the hexagon.
(b) Find the volume of the pyramid.
(c) Find the length of a slant edge of the pyramid.
(d) Draw a net for the pyramid.

 MATH@WORK

11. In the figure, *V* is the center of the face *EFGH* of the wooden rectangular prism *ABCDEFGH*, with *AB* = 24 in., *BC* = 13 in., and *CG* = 30 in. The pyramid *VABCD* is cut out from the prism. What is the volume of the wood that is cut out?

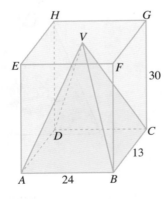

12. The Great Pyramid of Khufu is a right square pyramid in which the height is 480.6 ft and the length of a side of the base is 756 ft. Find the volume of the pyramid. Express your answer in scientific notation, rounded to 3 significant figures.

13. The figure shows a lantern formed using 8 congruent equilateral triangles, each of which has side 24 cm. Given that *ABCD* is a square, find
(a) the total surface area
(b) the volume,
of the lantern.

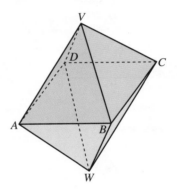

14. A solid rectangular pyramid made of metal has a base that measures 16 cm by 25 cm. The solid is melted and recast into a solid square pyramid of the same height. Find the length of a side of the base of the square pyramid.

 BRAIN WORKS

15. Suppose you are to construct a right square pyramid of volume 108 cm^3. Suggest two possible sets of measurements for its height and the length of a side of its base.

12.2 Cylinders

A Volume and Surface Area of a Cylinder

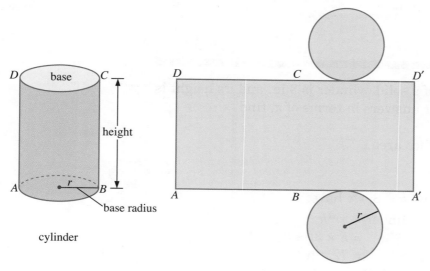

cylinder

net of cylinder

DISCUSS

By looking at the net, do you think the two circular bases can be at any other positions besides the ones indicated?

A closed **cylinder** is a solid with two parallel circular end faces and a uniform circular cross-section. Each end face is called a **base** of the cylinder. Its radius is called the **base radius**. The perpendicular distance between the two bases is called the **height** of the cylinder.

A cylinder can be considered as a prism whose base is an n-sided polygon where n is very large. Therefore:

> **Volume of cylinder = Base area × Height**

When the base radius is r units and the height is h units, base area of a cylinder = area of circular base = πr^2. Thus we have the formula:

> **Volume of cylinder = $\pi r^2 h$**

Study the net of the cylinder above. We can see that

AA' = circumference of the base circle

$\quad = 2\pi r$

∴ area of curved surface = Area of rectangle $AA'D'D$

$\qquad\qquad\qquad = 2\pi r \times h$

$\qquad\qquad\qquad = 2\pi rh$

Total surface area of a closed cylinder = Area of curved surface + 2 × Base area. Thus we have the following formula:

Total surface area of a closed cylinder = $2\pi rh + 2\pi r^2$

Example 5

The base radius of a solid cylinder is 3 in. and its height is 8 in. Leaving your answers in terms of π, find
(a) the volume,
(b) the total surface area,
of the cylinder.

Solution

(a) When $r = 3$ and $h = 8$, we have:

Volume of the cylinder = $\pi r^2 h$
$= \pi \times 3^2 \times 8$
$= 72\pi$ in.^{3}

(b) Total surface area of the cylinder
$= 2\pi rh + 2\pi r^2$
$= 2\pi \times 3 \times 8 + 2\pi \times 3^2$
$= 66\pi$ in.^{2}

Try It! 5

A solid cylinder has a base radius of 2 in. and a height of 7 in. Leaving your answers in terms of π, find
(a) the volume,
(b) the total surface area,
of the cylinder.

Example 6

The volume of a cylindrical can is 400 cm^3. If the height of the can is 13 cm, find the base radius of the can. Give your answer rounded to 3 significant figures.

Solution

Let the base radius of the can be r cm.

Then $\pi r^2 \times 13 = 400$

$r^2 = \dfrac{400}{13\pi}$

$r = \sqrt{\dfrac{400}{13\pi}}$

$= 3.13$ (rounded to 3 sig. fig.)

The base radius of the can is 3.13 cm.

The volume of a cylindrical disc is 150 cm³. If the thickness of the disc is 2 cm, find the base radius of the disc. Give your answer rounded to 3 significant figures.

Example **7**

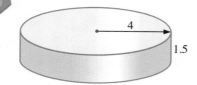
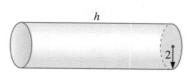

A metal cylindrical disc of base radius 4 cm and height 1.5 cm is melted and recast into a cylindrical bar of base radius 2 cm. Find

(a) the length of the bar,

(b) the ratio of the total surface area of the cylindrical disc to that of the bar.

Solution

(a) Let the length of the bar be h cm.

Volume of the bar = Volume of the original cylindrical disc

$$\therefore \ \pi \times 2^2 \times h = \pi \times 4^2 \times 1.5$$
$$4h = 24$$
$$h = 6$$

The length of the bar is 6 cm.

(b) Total surface area of original cylindrical disc
$$= 2\pi \times 4 \times 1.5 + 2 \times \pi \times 4^2$$
$$= 44\pi \ \text{cm}^2$$

Total surface area of the bar $= 2\pi \times 2 \times 6 + 2 \times \pi \times 2^2$
$$= 32\pi \ \text{cm}^2$$
$$\therefore \ \text{the required ratio} = 44\pi : 32\pi$$
$$= 11 : 8$$

Try It! **7**

A metal cylindrical bar of length 18 cm and base radius 2 cm is melted and recast into a solid cylinder of base radius 3 cm. Find

(a) the height of the new cylinder,

(b) the ratio of the total surface area of the bar to that of the new cylinder.

Example 8

The figure shows a cylindrical pipe. The external diameter of the pipe is 3 cm, its thickness is 0.3 cm and its length is 4 m.

(a) Find the internal radius of the pipe.

(b) Find the volume of material used in making the pipe.

(c) Find the total surface area of the pipe.

(d) If water flows through the pipe at 80 cm/s, find the volume of water delivered in 25 s.

Express your answers rounded to 3 significant figures where applicable.

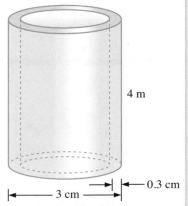

Solution

(a) External radius = 3 ÷ 2
$$= 1.5 \text{ cm}$$

Internal radius = 1.5 − 0.3
$$= 1.2 \text{ cm}$$

(b) External volume of the pipe
$$= \pi \times 1.5^2 \times 400 \qquad (4 \text{ m} = 400 \text{ cm})$$
$$= 900\pi \text{ cm}^3$$

Internal volume of the pipe $= \pi \times 1.2^2 \times 400$
$$= 576\pi \text{ cm}^3$$

∴ volume of material used
$$= 900\pi - 576\pi$$
$$= 324\pi$$
$$\approx 1{,}017.88$$
$$= 1{,}020 \text{ cm}^3 \quad \text{(rounded to 3 sig. fig.)}$$

(c) Total surface area of the pipe

$$= \begin{array}{c} \text{External} \\ \text{curved} \\ \text{surface area} \end{array} + \begin{array}{c} \text{Internal} \\ \text{curved} \\ \text{surface area} \end{array} + 2 \times \begin{array}{c} \text{Area of the} \\ \text{ring at each} \\ \text{end} \end{array}$$

$$= 2\pi \times 1.5 \times 400 + 2\pi \times 1.2 \times 400 + 2 \times (\pi \times 1.5^2 - \pi \times 1.2^2)$$
$$= 1{,}200\pi + 960\pi + 1.62\pi$$
$$= 2{,}161.62\pi$$
$$\approx 6{,}790.93$$
$$= 6{,}790 \text{ cm}^2 \quad \text{(rounded to 3 sig. fig.)}$$

(d) The amount of water flowing through the pipe in 1 second can be considered as the volume of water in a cylinder of base radius 1.2 cm and length 80 cm.

∴ volume of water delivered in 1 second
$= \pi \times 1.2^2 \times 80$
$= 115.2\pi$ cm^3

Volume of water delivered in 25 seconds
$= 115.2\pi \times 25$
$= 2,880\pi$
$= 9,050$ cm^3 (rounded to 3 sig. fig.)

Try It! 8

The external and internal diameters of a cylindrical water pipe are 4 cm and 3.2 cm respectively and the length of the pipe is 0.5 m.
(a) Find the volume of material used in making the pipe.
(b) Find the total surface area of the pipe.
(c) If water flows through the pipe at 10 cm/s, find the volume of water delivered in 30 seconds.

EXERCISE 12.2

In this exercise, give your answers rounded to 3 significant figures where necessary.

 BASIC PRACTICE

1. Find the volume and the total surface area of each cylinder. (The dimensions given are in inches.)

(a)

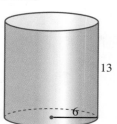

13

6

(b)

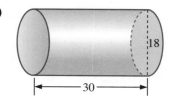

18

30

2. A cylindrical salami sausage is 11 in. long and has a radius of 1 in. Find its volume and total surface area.

3. A metal cylindrical disc is 3 cm thick and its diameter is 14 cm. Find its volume and total surface area.

4. The external base radius of a cylindrical drinking glass is 4 cm and its height is 9 cm. Find
   (a) its volume,
   (b) its external surface area.

5. Find the height of a cylinder if its
  (a) volume = 63π in.^{3}, base radius = 3 in.,
  (b) volume = 100 in.^{3}, base radius = 2 in.

6. Find the base radius of a cylinder if its
  (a) volume = 150π cm^3, height = 6 cm,
  (b) volume = 400 cm^3, height = 8 cm.

7. Find the circumference of a solid cylinder if its
  (a) curved surface area = 660 cm^2, height = 10 cm,
  (b) curved surface area = 1,200 cm^2, height = 15 cm.

8. A metal cylinder of base radius 6 in. and height 5 in. is melted and recast into a cylindrical metal bar of base radius 2 in. Find
  (a) the length of the bar formed,
  (b) the ratio of the total surface area of the original cylinder to that of the bar.

9. In the figure, AB = 10 cm, BC = 7 cm and AE = 12 cm. A hole of radius 2 cm is drilled completely through the rectangular prism. Find
  (a) the volume of the solid,
  (b) its total surface area.

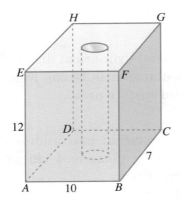

10. The figure shows a solid formed by two cylinders. The base radius of the cylinder on top is 3 in. and its height is 9 in. The base radius of the cylinder below is 9 in. and its height is 6 in. Find
  (a) the volume of the solid,
  (b) its total surface area.

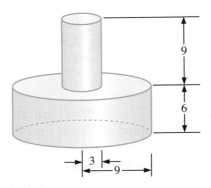

11. A rectangular tray of dimensions 35 cm by 10 cm by 4 cm is full of water. The water is poured into an empty cylindrical container of internal radius 6 cm. Find the depth of water in the container.

12. The figure shows a half solid cylinder with base diameter 20 mm and height 25 mm.
  (a) Find its volume.
  (b) Draw a net of the solid.
  (c) Find its total surface area.

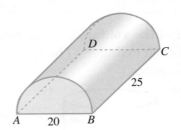

13. A measuring cylinder of internal diameter 5 cm is partially filled with water. When a stone is placed in the cylinder as shown, the water level rises by 3 cm.
Find
  (a) the volume of the stone,
  (b) the increase in the contact area between the water and the measuring cylinder.

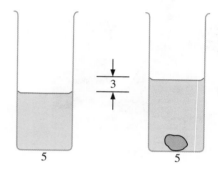

14. A cylindrical bucket of base radius 10 cm and height 18 cm is completely filled with water each time before the water is poured into a rectangular tank. The tank is 60 cm long, 45 cm wide and 36 cm high. Find
  (a) the volume of the bucket,
  (b) the volume of the tank,
  (c) the rise in the water level of the tank when seven full buckets of water are poured into the tank,
  (d) the number of full buckets of water required to fill the tank.

15. A cylindrical water hose of length 2 m has an internal diameter of 4 cm. The thickness of its wall is 0.5 cm.
  (a) Find the external radius of the hose.
  (b) Find the volume of material used in making the hose.
  (c) Find the total surface area of the hose.
  (d) Water flows through the hose at a rate of 45 cm/s. Find the volume of water delivered in 20 seconds.

BRAIN WORKS

16.

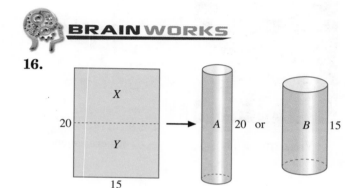

A sheet of rectangular paper measures 20 cm by 15 cm. It can be rolled up along either side to form two cylinders, A and B as shown.
  (a) Which cylinder has a greater volume?
  (b) Suppose the sheet is divided into two equal parts, X and Y, as shown and then rolled up to form two cylinders of height 15 cm each. Would the sum of the volumes of these two small cylinders be greater than the volume of cylinder B? Show how you arrived at your conclusion.

12.3 *Cones*

A Introducing Cones

We have come across many items that are in the shape of cones or conical in shape in our daily life. Some of them are shown below.

| Vietnamese hat | ice cream cones | tepee |

A **circular cone** (or simply a **cone**) is a solid figure that has a circular base and a vertex that is not on the plane of the base.

We can sketch and label cones and their parts as follows:

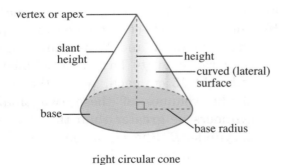

right circular cone

Figure 1

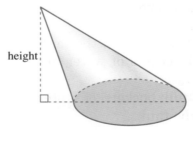

oblique circular cone

Figure 2

For a cone, the radius of its circular base is called the **base radius**. Its **slant height** is a line segment from its vertex to a point on the base circumference. Its **height** is the perpendicular distance from the vertex to its base. If its height passes through the center of its base, then the cone is a **right circular cone** (see Figure 1), otherwise it is an **oblique circular cone** (see Figure 2).

B   Net and Surface Area of a Cone

Suppose we have a conical paper drinking cup of slant height l cm and base radius r cm. If we cut along a slant height VA and lay the paper flat on a surface, we will get the net of the curved surface of the cone as shown below.

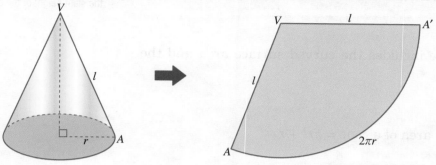

Net of the curved surface of a cone

Notice that the net is a part of a circle of center V and radius l cm. This part of a circle is called a **sector** of the circle. The arc AA', which is the circumference of the base of the cone, is thus $2\pi r$ cm long.

In Class Activity 2, we will explore how to find the curved surface area of the cone.

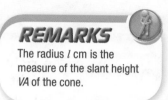

REMARKS
The radius l cm is the measure of the slant height VA of the cone.

 CLASS ACTIVITY 2

Objective: To find the curved surface area of a cone.

Task
Divide the curved surface of a cone into 24 equal parts and then arrange all the parts as shown below.

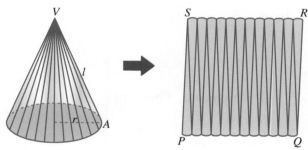

Questions

1. The length of $PQ \approx$ half the circumference of the base of the cone. $PQ \approx$ [ ].

2. $PS =$ [ ]

3. $PQRS$ is close to the shape of a rectangle, thus area of $PQRS \approx$ [ ].

4. Therefore, curved surface area of the cone = [ ].

From Class Activity 2, we have the following result:

> **Curved surface area of a cone = $\pi r l$**

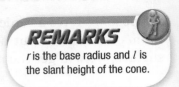

REMARKS

r is the base radius and l is the slant height of the cone.

The total surface area of a cone includes the curved surface area and the circular base area.

> **Total surface area of a cone = $\pi r l + \pi r^2$**

Example 9

A right circular solid cone has a base radius of 5 cm and a height of 12 cm. Find
(a) its curved surface area,
(b) its total surface area.
Leave your answers in terms of π.

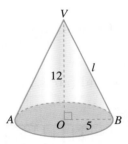

Solution

(a) In $\triangle BOV$,

$$BV^2 = OB^2 + OV^2 \quad \text{(Pythagorean Theorem)}$$
$$l^2 = 5^2 + 12^2$$
$$l = \sqrt{169}$$
$$= 13$$

Curved surface area of the cone $= \pi r l$
$$= \pi \times 5 \times 13$$
$$= 65\pi \text{ cm}^2$$

(b) Total surface area of the cone $= \pi r l + \pi r^2$
$$= 65\pi + \pi \times 5^2$$
$$= 90\pi \text{ cm}^2$$

A right circular solid cone has a slant height of 10 in. and a height of 8 in. Find
(a) its curved surface area,
(b) its total surface area.
Leave your answers in terms of π.

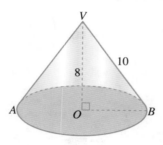

Example **10**

A semicircle of radius 8 in. is wrapped to form a cone such that OA coincides with OB. Find the base radius of the cone.

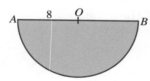

Let the base radius of the cone be r in.

Slant height of the cone = 8 in.

$$\text{Curved surface area of the cone} = \text{Area of the given semicircle}$$

$$\pi \times r \times 8 = \frac{1}{2} \times \pi \times 8^2$$

$$r = 4$$

The base radius of the cone is 4 in.

REMARKS

We can equate the circumference of the base of the cone to the length of arc AB. That is,

$$2\pi r = \pi \times 8$$
$$r = 4$$

A quarter of a circle of radius 12 cm is wrapped to form a cone such that OA coincides with OB. Find the base radius of the cone.

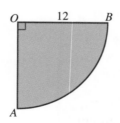

C Volume of a Cone

A circle can be regarded as a regular polygon with infinite number of sides. Therefore, a circular cone can be considered as a pyramid whose base is a regular polygon with an infinite number of sides.

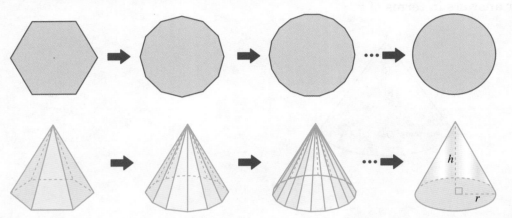

REMARKS
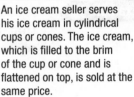
- A regular polygon becomes a circle when its number of sides is infinite.
- A right polygonal pyramid becomes a cone when the number of sides of its base is infinite.
- Use Sketchpad software to help you observe both cases.

$\therefore$ Volume of a cone $= \frac{1}{3} \times$ Base area $\times$ Height

$$= \frac{1}{3} \times \pi r^2 \times h$$

where r is the base radius and h is the height of the cone.

Thus, we have the following formula:

> Volume of a cone $= \frac{1}{3}\pi r^2 h$

DISCUSS

An ice cream seller serves his ice cream in cylindrical cups or cones. The ice cream, which is filled to the brim of the cup or cone and is flattened on top, is sold at the same price.

If the height of a cylindrical cup is half that of a cone, would you want to order your ice cream in the cone or the cylindrical cup to gain the best value for your money?

Example 11 Find the volume of a cone with a base radius of 3 cm and a height of 7 cm. Leave your answer in terms of π.

Solution Volume of the cone $= \frac{1}{3}\pi r^2 h$

$$= \frac{1}{3} \times \pi \times 3^2 \times 7$$

$$= 21\pi \text{ cm}^3$$

Try It! 11 Find the volume of a cone with
(a) a base radius of 6 cm and a height of 7 cm,
(b) a base radius of 3 cm and a height of 14 cm.

DISCUSS

What is the change in the volume of the cone when its radius and height are doubled?

Example *12*

A solid square pyramid made of metal has a base of side 5 cm and a height of 6 cm. It is melted and recast into a solid right circular cone of height 9 cm. Find
(a) the base radius of the cone,
(b) the curved surface area of the cone.

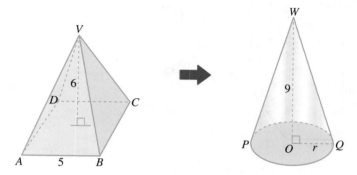

Solution

(a) Let the base radius of the cone be r cm.

Volume of the cone = Volume of the pyramid

$$\frac{1}{3}\pi r^2 \times 9 = \frac{1}{3} \times 5 \times 5 \times 6$$

$$3\pi r^2 = 50$$

$$r^2 = \frac{50}{3\pi}$$

$$r = \sqrt{\frac{50}{3\pi}}$$

$$= 2.30 \quad \text{(rounded to 3 sig. fig.)}$$

The base radius of the cone is 2.30 cm.

(b) In $\triangle WOQ$,

$$WQ^2 = WO^2 + OQ^2 \quad \text{(Pythagorean Theorem)}$$

$$WQ = \sqrt{9^2 + \frac{50}{3\pi}}$$

$$= 9.290$$

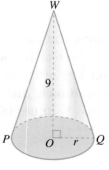

Curved surface area of the cone

$$= \pi \times \sqrt{\frac{50}{3\pi}} \times 9.290$$

$$= 67.2 \text{ cm}^2 \quad \text{(rounded to 3 sig. fig.)}$$

Note: We should use the value of π from a calculator for calculations in this chapter, unless stated otherwise.

In the diagram, the prism *ABCDEF* is a vessel full of water. *AB* = 6 cm, *BC* = 9 cm, *AD* = 10 cm and $\angle DEF = \angle ABC = \angle DAB = 90°$. The cone *VPQ* is a paper cup of height 15 cm. The amount of water in the vessel can fill up the cup completely. Find

(a) the base radius of the conical cup,

(b) its curved surface area.

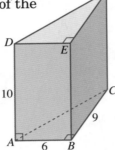
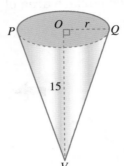

Example **13**

The figure shows a funnel which is an inverted cone with a cylindrical rim at the top. The cone has a base radius of 7 cm and a height of 12 cm. The height of the rim is 3 cm. Find the volume of the funnel.

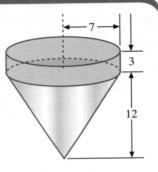

Solution

Volume of the cylindrical part = $\pi \times 7^2 \times 3$
$$= 147\pi \text{ cm}^3$$

Volume of the cone = $\frac{1}{3} \times \pi \times 7^2 \times 12$
$$= 196\pi \text{ cm}^3$$

Volu me of the funnel = $147\pi + 196\pi$
$$= 343\pi$$
$$= 1,080 \text{ cm}^3 \quad \text{(rounded to 3 sig. fig.)}$$

The figure shows the model of a rocket that consists of a cone of height 3 cm on top of a cylinder of height 6 cm and base diameter 4 cm. Find the volume of the model.

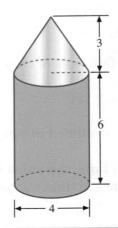

EXERCISE 12.3

In this exercise, give your answers rounded to 3 significant figures where necessary.

 BASIC PRACTICE

1. Find the curved surface area of each of the following cones. (The dimensions given are in centimeters.)

   (a)

   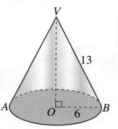

   (b)

   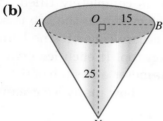

2. Find the total surface area of each of the following cones. (The dimensions given are in inches.)

   (a)

   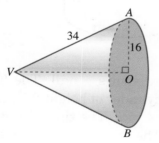

   (b)

   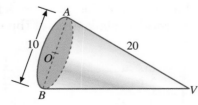

3. Find the volume of each of the following cones. (The dimensions given are in centimeters.)

   (a)

   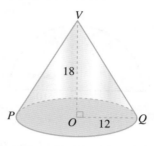

   (b)

   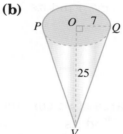

4. In the figure, O is the center of the base of the cone, $\triangle AOV$ is right-angled at O, $OA = 20$ cm and $OV = 21$ cm. Find its
   (a) curved surface area,
   (b) volume.

   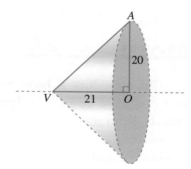

5. A semicircle of radius 10 in. is wrapped such that *VA* just touches *VB* to form a right circular cone. Find
 (a) the base radius of the cone,
 (b) its volume,
 (c) its curved surface area.

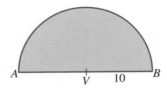

6. A cone has a base radius of 5 cm. The curved surface area is 65π cm^2. Find its
 (a) slant height,
 (b) height,
 (c) volume.

7. A cone has a base area of 9π cm^2 and a volume of 12π cm^3. Find its
 (a) height,
 (b) slant height,
 (c) total surface area.

8. 100 cm^3 of sand can completely fill up a conical vessel of height 7 cm. Find the base radius of the conical vessel.

 **MATH@WORK**

9. A traffic cone has a base radius of 6 in. and a height of 28 in. (not inclusive of base support). Find its
 (a) volume,
 (b) slant height,
 (c) curved surface area.

10. A piece of bamboo shoot in the shape of a cone has a base diameter of 12 cm and a height of 18 cm. Find its
 (a) volume,
 (b) mass if it weighs 0.75 g per cm^3.

11. A cylindrical tub of base radius 10.5 cm and height 12 cm is completely filled with ice cream. The ice cream in the tub is scooped up to fill ice cream cones to the brims and is flattened on top. If each ice cream cone has a base diameter at its top of 6 cm and a height of 12 cm, how many ice cream cones can be filled up?

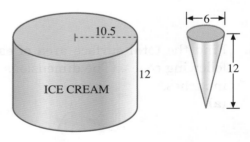

12. The figure shows a nail. The body of the nail is a cylinder of height 25 mm and base diameter 4 mm. The tip is a cone of height 5 mm. The head is a cylinder of base diameter 8 mm and is 2 mm thick. Find
 (a) the volume of the nail,
 (b) the total surface area of the nail.

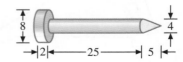

13. In the figure, V is the center of a circle with radius 10 cm. The length of the arc ACB is 12π cm. The sector $VACB$ is wrapped such that VA just touches VB to form a right circular cone. Find
   (a) the base radius,
   (b) the curved surface area,
   (c) the volume,
of the cone.

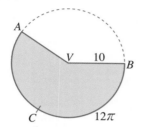

14. Make a right circular cone with height, h cm, and base radius, r cm, such that $h + r = 15$.
   (a) Find two possible sets of values of h and r, and the corresponding volume of each cone.
   (b) Determine the value of r such that the volume of the cone is the maximum.

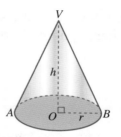

12.4 *Spheres*

A Introducing Spheres

The objects below are spheres. What special features do you notice in them?

Can you think of other examples of spheres that you have come across in your daily life?

A **sphere** is a solid where all the points on its surface are at a constant distance from a fixed point. The constant distance is the **radius** and the fixed point is the **center** of the sphere. A line segment joining two points on a sphere and passing through the center is called the **diameter**.

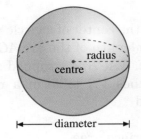

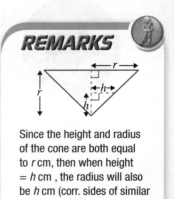
B Volume of A Sphere

Let us derive the volume of a sphere by studying the relationship between volumes of a hemisphere, a cylinder and a cone.

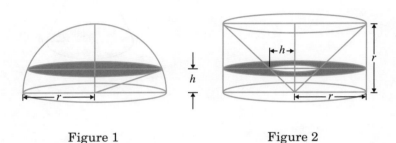

Figure 1   Figure 2

Figure 1 shows a hemisphere with radius r cm. Suppose we make a horizontal slice at a distance h cm above the flat base of the hemisphere. Using Pythagorean Theorem, the radius of the slice of hemisphere would be $\sqrt{r^2 - h^2}$ cm. The area of the cross-section of the hemisphere, which is a circle, will therefore be $\pi(r^2 - h^2)$ cm^2.

Figure 2 shows a cylinder of height r cm and radius r cm, with an inverted right circular cone inside. The base of the cone is at the top of the cylinder and its vertex at the bottom is at the center of the base of the cylinder. Thus, the height and radius of the cone are both equal to r cm.

Suppose we make a horizontal slice at a distance h cm (same as Figure 1) from the center of the base of the cylinder, the cross-section of the slice will consist of two concentric circles (shown in red in Figure 2). At the distance h cm from the vertex of the cone, the radius of the smaller concentric circle will also be h cm.

Hence the cross-sectional area of the slice in Figure 2
= area of bigger concentric circle – area of smaller concentric circle
= $\pi r^2 - \pi h^2$
= $\pi(r^2 - h^2)$ cm^2

The cross-sectional area of the slices in Figure 1 and Figure 2 are both the same, that is $\pi(r^2 - h^2)$ cm^2, and the height of the solids are the same, r cm, therefore the slices in the two figures have the same volume.

REMARKS
Cavalieri's Principle states two three-dimensional solids have the same volume if they share the same cross-sectional areas at equal heights.

Hence we have
Volume of hemisphere = volume of cylinder − volume of inverted cone

$$= \pi r^2 \times r - \frac{1}{3}\pi r^2 \times r$$

$$= \pi r^3 - \frac{1}{3}\pi r^3$$

$$= \frac{2}{3}\pi r^3$$

∴ Volume of a sphere = 2 × volume of hemisphere

$$= \frac{4}{3}\pi r^3$$

MATH WEB
You may access the following websites en.wikipedia.org/wiki/Cavalieri%27s_principle and www.cut-the-knot.org/Curriculum/Calculus/Cavalieri.shtml to find out more on Cavalieri's Principle.

Thus, we derive the formula:

$$\text{Volume of a sphere} = \frac{4}{3}\pi r^3$$

Note: The cross-sectional areas of the solids in both figures may change with different heights from the center of the base, but this does not affect the proof above.

C Surface Area of a Sphere

Suppose we have a sphere and a rectangular piece of paper as shown below.

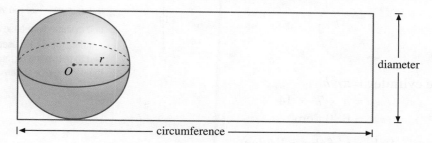

If the sphere has a radius of r cm, and the width and length of the rectangular piece of paper are equal to the diameter and circumference of the sphere respectively, then the paper will cover the entire sphere.
i.e. Surface area of the sphere
  = Area of the paper
  = Length × Width
  = Circumference of sphere × Diameter of sphere
  = $2\pi r \times 2r$
  = $4\pi r^2$

Thus, we have the formula:

$$\text{Surface area of a sphere} = 4\pi r^2$$

Archimedes was believed to be the first to prove the above amazing result. He stated that the surface area of a sphere was equal to the curved surface area of a cylinder with the same radius, in addition, the height was equal to the diameter of the sphere.

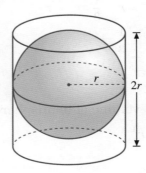

As curved surface area of the cylinder $= 2\pi rh$
$$= 2\pi r \times 2r$$
$$= 4\pi r^2,$$

we get the same formula for the surface area of the sphere.

Example 14

(a) Find the volume of a sphere with radius 7 cm.

(b) Hence find the ratio of the volume of a sphere with radius 7 cm to the volume of a cylinder with base radius 7 cm and height 14 cm.

Solution

(a) Volume of the sphere

$$= \frac{4}{3}\pi r^3$$
$$= \frac{4}{3}\pi \times 7^3$$
$$= \frac{1{,}372\pi}{3} \text{ cm}^3$$

Volume of the cylinder $= \pi r^2 h$
$$= \pi \times 7^2 \times 14$$
$$= 686\pi \text{ cm}^3$$

Volume of the sphere : Volume of the cylinder
$$= \frac{1{,}372\pi}{3} : 686\pi$$
$$= 2 : 3$$

REMARKS

Archimedes found that the volume of a sphere with radius r was $\frac{2}{3}$ of the volume of a cylinder with base radius r and height $2r$. He used this fact to derive the formula for the volume of a sphere.

Try It! 14

Find the ratio of the volume of a sphere with radius 6 cm to the volume of a cone with base radius 6 cm and height 12 cm.

Example 15

A watermelon is in the shape of a sphere of radius 12 cm. Its skin is 1 cm thick. Find the volume of the skin of the watermelon.

Solution

The figure shows the cross-section of the watermelon when it is sliced through its center.

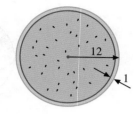

Radius of the fleshly part = 12 − 1

$\qquad\qquad\qquad\qquad\qquad$ = 11 cm

Volume of the skin

= Volume of the watermelon − Volume of its fleshly part

$= \frac{4}{3}\pi \times 12^3 - \frac{4}{3}\pi \times 11^3$

$= \frac{4}{3}\pi \times (12^3 - 11^3)$

= 1,660 cm^3 (rounded to 3 sig. fig.)

Try It! 15

A hollow crystal ball has an external radius of 5 cm and the thickness of crystal is 1 cm. Find the volume of the crystal in the ball.

Example 16

A tennis ball has a diameter of 6.8 cm. Find its surface area.

Solution

Radius $= \frac{1}{2} \times 6.8$

$\qquad\quad$ = 3.4 cm

Surface area of the tennis ball

$= 4\pi \times 3.4^2$

= 145 cm^2 (rounded to 3 sig. fig.)

Try It! 16

A table tennis ball has a diameter of 4 cm. Find its surface area.

Example 17

The surface area of a sphere is equal to the total surface area of a cone with base radius 5 cm and slant height 9 cm. Find the radius of the sphere.

Solution

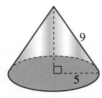

Let the radius of the sphere be r cm.

Total surface area of the cone = $\pi \times 5 \times 9 + \pi \times 5^2$
$$= 70\pi \text{ cm}^2$$

Surface area of the sphere = $4\pi r^2 \text{ cm}^2$

$$4\pi r^2 = 70\pi$$
$$r^2 = \frac{70}{4}$$
$$r = \sqrt{\frac{70}{4}}$$
$$= 4.18 \quad \text{(rounded to 3 sig. fig.)}$$

The radius of the sphere is 4.18 cm.

RECALL

Total surface area of a cone
$= \pi r l + \pi r^2$.

Try It! 17

The surface area of a sphere is equal to the total surface area of a cube of side 10 cm. Find the radius of the sphere.

Example 18

The figure shows a test tube that consists of a cylindrical body and a hemispherical end. The tube is 8 cm long and has a diameter of 2 cm. Find
(a) the volume,
(b) the external curved surface area
of the test tube.

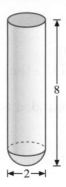

Solution

(a) Radius of the hemispherical part = $\frac{1}{2} \times 2$
$$= 1 \text{ cm}$$

Volume of the hemispherical part = $\frac{1}{2} \times \frac{4}{3}\pi \times 1^3$
$$= \frac{2}{3}\pi \text{ cm}^3$$

$$\text{Height of the cylindrical part} = 8 - 1$$
$$= 7 \text{ cm}$$
$$\text{Volume of the cylindrical part} = \pi \times 1^2 \times 7$$
$$= 7\pi \text{ cm}^3$$
$$\text{Volume of the test tube} = \frac{2}{3}\pi + 7\pi$$
$$= \frac{23\pi}{3}$$
$$= 24.1 \text{ cm}^3$$
(rounded to 3 sig. fig.)

(b) External curved surface area of the test tube
= Surface area of the hemispherical part
+ Curved surface area of the cylindrical part
$$= \frac{1}{2} \times 4\pi \times 1^2 + 2\pi \times 1 \times 7$$
$$= 16\pi$$
$$= 50.3 \text{ cm}^2 \quad \text{(rounded to 3 sig. fig.)}$$

Try It! **18**
The shape of a glass stopper is composed of a hemisphere of radius 3 cm and a right circular cone as shown. The height of the glass stopper is 7 cm. Find
(a) the volume,
(b) the total surface area,
of the glass stopper.

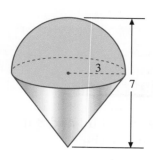

EXERCISE 12.4

In this exercise, give your answers rounded to 3 significant figures where necessary.

 BASIC PRACTICE

1. Find the surface area and volume of a sphere with the given radius in each case.
   (a) 6 cm
   (b) 1.5 ft
   (c) 9 mm

2. Find the surface area and volume of a sphere with the given diameter in each case.
   (a) 13 cm
   (b) 0.4 ft
   (c) 7 in.

3. The diameter of a basketball is 9.45 in. Find
(a) its surface area,
(b) its volume.

4. A spherical soap bubble has a radius of 2.1 cm. Find
(a) its surface area,
(b) the volume of air inside the bubble.

5. The radius of a solid hemisphere is 11 cm. Find its
(a) total surface area,
(b) volume.

 FURTHER PRACTICE

6. The radii of two spheres are 6 in. and 8 in. respectively. Find the ratio of their
(a) radii,
(b) surface areas,
(c) volumes.

7. The surface area of a snowball is 225π cm². Find the radius of the snowball.

8. A spherical stone has a volume of 36π cm³. Find its
(a) radius,
(b) surface area.

9. A 2-cm thick hollow glass sphere has an external diameter of 9 cm. Find
(a) its surface area,
(b) the volume of glass in the sphere.

10. A solid right circular metal cone has a base radius of 8 cm and a height of 13.5 cm. It is melted and recast into a sphere. Find
(a) the radius of the sphere,
(b) its surface area.

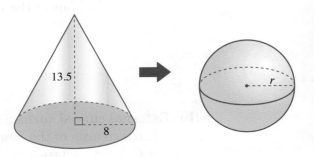

 MATH@WORK

11. The figure shows a cylindrical container of base radius 6 in. that is filled with water to a depth of 5 in.
(a) Find the volume of water.
(b) A metal sphere of radius 2 in. is totally submerged in the water. Find the rise in the water level.

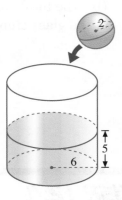

12. Three solid metal spheres of radii 3 cm, 4 cm and 5 cm respectively are melted and recast into a large solid sphere. Find
(a) the radius of the new sphere,
(b) the change in the total surface area as a result of the melting and recasting.

13. A toy is made up of a right circular cone attached to a hemisphere as shown in the figure. The overall height of the toy is 17 cm. The surface area of the hemisphere is 50π cm². Find

(a) the radius of the hemisphere,

(b) the volume of the toy,

(c) the total surface area of the toy.

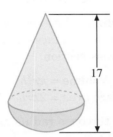

14. The figure shows a hemispherical clay pot of internal radius 7 in. and thickness 1 in. Find

(a) the capacity of the pot,

(b) the volume of clay used to make the pot,

(c) the total surface area of the pot.

15. A rivet consists of a hemispherical head of radius 5 mm, a cylindrical pin of length 25 mm and diameter 4 mm as shown in the figure. Find

(a) the volume,

(b) the total surface area,

of the rivet.

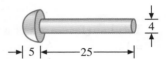

BRAINWORKS

16. A manufacturer is designing a rectangular box to pack 8 table-tennis balls of diameter 4 cm each.

(a) What should the dimensions of the box be so that its surface area is the minimum?

(b) Find the volume of space in the box from **(a)** which is not occupied by the balls.

Pyramid

Total surface area of a pyramid
= Base area + Area of all lateral faces

Volume of a pyramid
= $\frac{1}{3}$ × Base area × Height

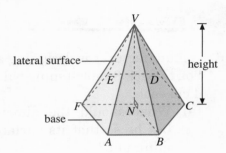

Cylinder

A solid cylinder has two parallel and equal circular end faces and a uniform circular cross-section.

$$\text{Volume} = \pi r^2 h$$
$$\text{Total surface area} = 2\pi rh + 2\pi r^2$$

where r is the base radius and h is the height of the cylinder.

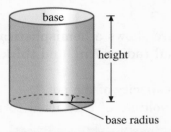

Cone

Curved surface area of a cone = πrl
Total surface area of a cone = $\pi rl + \pi r^2$

Volume of a cone = $\frac{1}{3}\pi r^2 h$

where r = base radius,
            l = slant height,
and h = height.

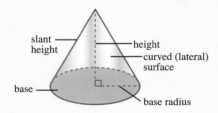

Sphere

Surface area of a sphere = $4\pi r^2$

Volume of a sphere = $\frac{4}{3}\pi r^3$,

where r is the radius of the sphere.

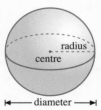

In this exercise, give your answers rounded to 3 significant figures where necessary.

1. In the figure, *ABCDEFGH* is a solid rectangular prism with *AB* = *BC* = 4 in. and *CG* = 5 in. A pyramid *HACD* is cut out from the cuboid. Find
   (a) the volume of the prism,
   (b) the volume of the pyramid *HACD*,
   (c) the total surface area of the pyramid *HACD*.

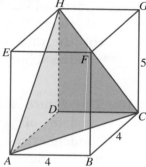

2. Figure 1 shows a part of a net for the rectangular pyramid *VABCD* (Figure 2) in which *VN* is perpendicular to the base *ABCD*. It is given that *AB* = 18 cm, *BC* = 12 cm and *VA* = *VD* = 7.5 cm.

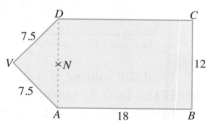

Figure 1

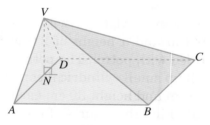

Figure 2

   (a) Find the volume of the pyramid.
   (b) Find the length of the slant edge *VB* of the pyramid.
   (c) Draw a complete net of the pyramid.
   (d) Find the total surface area of the pyramid.

3. The figure shows a piece of crystal which has identical right square pyramids at both ends of a prism. If *AB* = *BC* = 16 cm, *AE* = 24 cm and *VW* = 54 cm, find
   (a) the volume,
   (b) the total surface area
   of the piece of crystal.

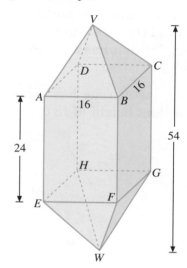

4. The figure shows a semicircular cone with *OB* = 12 cm and *VB* = 37 cm. Find its
   (a) volume,
   (b) total surface area.

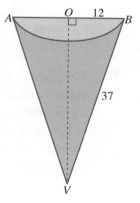

5. A right circular conical container is filled with 500 cm³ of water to a depth of 15 cm. Find
   (a) the radius of the circular water surface,
   (b) the area of the curved surface of the container in contact with the water.

6. In $\triangle ABC$, $\angle C = 90°$, $AC = 9$ cm and $BC = 5$ cm.

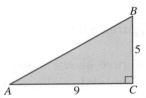

(a) Find the length of AB.
(b) A cone is formed by rotating $\triangle ABC$ through 360° about the side BC or AC. Determine which would result in a cone of greater volume.
(c) Find the total surface area of the cone in (b) that has a greater volume.

7. A solid metal cone has a height of 15 cm and a slant height of 18 cm.

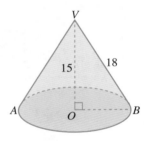

(a) Find its total surface area.
(b) Find its volume.
(c) If the cone is melted and recast into a solid sphere, find the radius of the sphere.

8. The figure shows a solid that consists of a right conical top, a cylindrical body and a hemispherical bottom. The radius of each of the three parts is 5 cm. The height of the cone is 12 cm high and the total height of the remaining two parts is 20 cm.

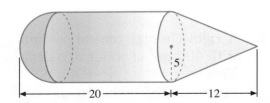

Find its
(a) volume,
(b) total surface area.

9. The rim of the base and the vertex of a right circular cone are on the surface of a sphere as shown in the figure.

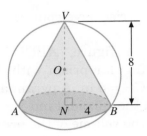

Given that the cone has a height of 8 in. and a base radius of 4 in., find
(a) the radius of the sphere,
(b) the ratio of the volume of the cone to the volume of the sphere.

10. The figure shows a water tank which consists of a cylindrical body and a hemispherical end. The cylindrical body has a length of 1.4 m and a diameter of 0.6 m. When the tank is placed horizontally, the water just fills to a depth of 0.3 m as shown.

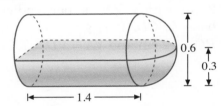

(a) Find the volume of water in the tank.
(b) If the tank is placed upright with the hemispherical part as the base, find the depth of water in the tank.

11. A cylindrical tank with a base radius of 0.8 m and a height of 2.0 m is completely filled with petrol. The petrol in it is used to fill up small cylindrical cans of base radius 10 cm and height 30 cm each.
(a) Find the volume of the tank
  (i) in m^3,   (ii) in cm^3.
(b) Find the volume of a can
  (i) in cm^3,   (ii) in m^3.
(c) What is the greatest possible number of cans that can be filled with the petrol from the tank?

12. The figure shows the uniform cross-section of a tray. *ABF* and *CDE* are quarters of a circle. *AF* = *DE* = 10 cm, *EF* = 30 cm and the length of the tray is 40 cm.

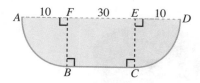

(a) Find the external surface area of the tray.
(b) Find the volume of the tray.
(c) A cylindrical bin of height 40 cm has a volume equal to that of the tray. Find its base radius.

13. The figure shows the uniform cross-section of a girder which is 5 feet long. *ABCD* is a trapezium and *EFG* is a semicircle. *AB* = *DC* = 20 in., *BC* = 26 in., *AM* = *DN* = 12 in., *GE* = 20 in. and *MG* = *NE*.

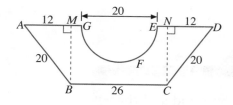

(a) Find the length of *BM*.
(b) Find the total surface area of the girder.
(c) Find its volume.
(d) What is its weight in pounds if it is made of material that weighs 0.28 pounds per cubic inch?

14. A circular pipe is 1.2 m long. Its internal and external diameters are 3 cm and 4 cm respectively.

(a) Find the volume of material used in making the pipe.
(b) Find the total surface area of the pipe.
(c) If water flows through the pipe at a rate of 25 cm/s into an empty rectangular tank, find the volume of water delivered in 1 minute.
(d) If the rectangular tank is 48 cm long and 30 cm wide, find the depth of water in the tank after 1 minute.

15. The figure shows a solid of uniform cross-section consisting of a rectangle *ABCD* and a quadrant *DEC* of a circle, center *D*. The length of side *AB* = 7 cm, *AD* = 4 cm, and *BG* = 20 cm.

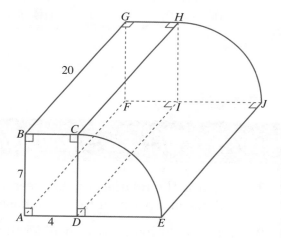

(a) Draw a net of the prism.
(b) Find the total surface area and the volume of the solid.
(c) If 10 of such solid metal prisms are melted and recast to form a solid cylinder with a height of 40 cm, find the radius of the cylinder.
(d) If 10 of such prisms are to be coated with lacquer and each bottle of lacquer is sufficient to cover 0.6 m², how many bottles of lacquer are needed to coat these prisms?

EXTEND YOUR LEARNING CURVE

Cannonball Pyramid

Oranges are arranged in the shape of square pyramids as shown below.

$n = 1$

$n = 2$

$n = 3$

(a) With the same pattern of oranges, find the number of oranges in the pattern for

(i) $n = 4$,   **(ii)** $n = 5$,   **(iii)** $n = 10$.

(b) Assume that each orange is a sphere of radius 3 cm. Find the height of the pyramid for

(i) $n = 2$,   **(ii)** $n = 3$,   **(iii)** $n = 10$.

WRITE IN YOUR JOURNAL

1. What is the relationship between the volume of a pyramid and the volume of a prism of the same base and height as the pyramid?

2. How would you try to remember the formulas for finding the surface areas and volumes of a pyramid, cone and sphere?

13 DATA ANALYSIS

Playing

LET'S LEARN TO...

1. organize data
2. construct and interpret tables, bar graphs, histograms, line graphs and scatter plots
3. describe the purposes, advantages and disadvantages of different forms of statistical representations
4. draw simple inferences from statistical diagrams
5. use line graphs to predict trends of data over time
6. use scatter plots to describe the correlation between two variables

Bar graphs and line graphs are just two examples of representations of data. Discuss with your classmates one such representation that you have come across in newspapers and from the Internet.

13.1 *Organizing Data in Frequency Tables*

Previously we learned that data can be collected using surveys. The data collected in a survey are called **raw data** because they have not been organized. The following is an example of the raw data obtained in a random survey of 40 families on the total number of mobile phones owned by each family.

2	3	4	3	2	3	0	5	4	1
3	2	1	2	4	2	1	3	5	3
1	3	3	2	2	5	4	3	2	2
3	2	5	4	1	1	5	4	2	1

We can hardly see any patterns in this set of raw data. Therefore, we organize the data using a table.

Steps in organizing data:

STEP ❶ Set up a table with three columns. Each item in the first column is called a **class** of the table.

Number of mobile phones	Tally	Frequency
0		
1		
2		
3		
4		
5		
Total		

STEP ❷ Read the data one by one and mark a **stroke** (or tally) in the Tally column in the same row as its class. To make the counting easier, mark every 5th stroke with cross stroke like '*////*'.

Number of mobile phones	Tally	Frequency
0	/	
1	//// //	
2	//// //// /	
3	//// ////	
4	//// /	
5	////	
Total		

144

STEP ❸ The number of times each class occurs is called the **frequency** of the class. We write down the frequency of each class by counting its corresponding tally marks. Then we add the frequencies and write the sum as shown. This is to check whether the tallying is correct.

Number of mobile phones	Tally	Frequency
0	/	1
1	### //	7
2	### ### /	11
3	### ###	10
4	### /	6
5	###	5
	Total	40

REMARKS

Check the total number of families in the frequency column to ensure that all families have been accounted for.

The table thus formed is called a **frequency table**. It provides clear and specific information about the data set. For example, at a glance we know which class has the highest frequency and what the difference between the frequencies of any two classes is.

Example ❶

The following list shows the ratings given by owners of a certain model of car in a survey.

B	B	A	C	D	B	A	C
A	C	B	B	A	D	C	B
B	A	C	D	B	B	A	B
B	B	A	B	C	C	A	A

Grade
A: Very good
B: Good
C: Average
D: Poor

Construct a frequency table to represent the data.

Solution

We can obtain the frequency table by using the method of tallying as shown below.

Rating	Tally	Frequency
A	### ////	9
B	### ### ///	13
C	### //	7
D	///	3
	Total	32

The following list shows the grades for Physical Education of 36 students.

B	B	A	C	B	C	A	B	A
C	A	D	B	C	F	D	C	B
D	A	F	A	D	B	C	B	A
A	C	B	C	A	C	B	C	B

Represent the data using a frequency table.

Example ②

The following list shows the time taken (in hours) by each of 30 students to finish their homework on a certain day.

1.5	1.3	0.7	1.0	1.8	3.1	0.8	1.6	1.2	3.2
3.3	1.7	2.0	0.8	2.9	1.1	2.1	1.0	2.4	1.8
0.7	1.4	0.9	1.5	2.1	1.8	1.3	0.9	2.8	2.2

(a) Construct a frequency table for the data.
(b) Find the percentage of students who took more than 3 hours to finish their homework.

Solution

(a) If we use classes like 0.7, 0.8, 0.9, ... to construct a frequency table, there will be too many classes and quite a number of them may have zero frequencies. Therefore, we group the data into convenient non-overlapping class intervals as shown below.

Time (x hours)	Tally	Frequency
$0 < x \leqslant 1$	#### ///	8
$1 < x \leqslant 2$	#### #### ///	13
$2 < x \leqslant 3$	#### /	6
$3 < x \leqslant 4$	////	3
Total		30

REMARKS

In the class interval $0 < x \leqslant 1$, the number of hours to be considered must be greater than zero and less than or equal to 1 hour.

(b) From the frequency table, we can see that there were 3 students who took more than 3 hours to finish their homework.

$$\therefore \text{ the required percentage} = \frac{3}{30} \times 100\%$$
$$= 10\%$$

Note:
- The data represented by the above frequency table are called **grouped data**.
- The class intervals must be non-overlapping so that no single item can fall into two classes.
- The class intervals should cover the smallest item and the largest item in the data set.
- In a class interval $a < x \leqslant b$, the difference $b - a$ is called the **class width** of the class. For example, in the class $2 < x \leqslant 3$, the class width $= 3 - 2 = 1$ hour.
- When the class widths of all the classes are equal, the frequency table is said to have **uniform intervals** (refer to the table in **(a)**).

Try It! 2

The following list shows the prices (in dollars) of 24 books.

23	45	19	18	33	36	25	37
47	30	29	40	34	25	38	12
32	13	41	20	26	34	28	22

(a) Represent the data in a frequency table with class intervals $10 < x \leqslant 20$, $20 < x \leqslant 30$ and so on.

(b) Find the percentage of books that cost more than $30.

The choice of class intervals of the form $a < x \leqslant b$ or $a \leqslant x < b$ is merely a matter of preference.

The set of data in Example 2 and in Try It! 2 each has only one variable, that is, the time taken to complete the homework and the prices of books respectively. This type of data is known as **univariate data** and it does not deal with relationships, but rather it is used to describe something. To be more specific, the data in those two questions are univariate numerical data. **Numerical data** involves quantities that are countable or measurable. Examples of numerical data include height, weights, ages, time taken, distances traveled, wages, and points scored in a test.

In contrast, **categorical data** is data which is divided into categories. Examples include gender (male and female), grade level (like 7th grade, 8th grade, etc.), age group (such as 15 years and under, 16–25 years, etc.) and test grades (A, B, C, D). The numerals in the names or titles of categories are not countable; they place subjects in categories defined by **numerals**.

Bivariate data is data involving two different variables. Unlike univariate data, bivariate data deals with an association between these two variables. The purpose of bivariate data is to analyze and explain this relationship. Since bivariate data includes two variables, and it is used to examine the association between these variables, how do you think we would want to organize and examine this data? We will learn to organize and interpret bivariate categorical data using two-way frequency tables in the next example, and then investigate patterns of association in bivariate data in the next section.

A **two-way frequency table** is a useful tool for summarizing data on two categorical variables and for examining possible associations between the variables. The entries in the cells of a two-way table can be absolute frequency counts or relative frequencies. Generally relative frequencies are written as a decimal or percentage. You can even use the relative frequency as probability to determine how often a value may occur in the future.

Example 3

The following lists show the ages of a group of 40 people who, when exposed to the virus of a highly contagious disease, either contracted or did not contract the disease.

Ages of those who contracted the disease

12	18	34	9	5	65	3	72	80
9	4	7	67	8	83	45	70	10

Ages of those who did not contract the disease

42	19	12	54	70	13	26	38	62	40	15
6	21	19	58	35	19	43	50	13	10	33

(a) Represent the data in a frequency table with the age categories 12 and under, 13 to 59 , and 60 and above.

(b) Find the percentage of people who, when exposed to the virus, contracted the disease.

(c) Find the percentage of people in each age category who contracted the disease.

(d) What conclusions can you draw from the data?

Solution

(a) Since the data involves two variables – age and whether or not they contracted the disease, we use a two-way frequency table to organize the bivariate data as shown below.

Disease Contraction and Age

Age	12 and under	13 to 59	60 and above	Total
Contracted Disease	9	3	6	18
Did Not Contract Disease	3	17	2	22
Total	12	20	8	40

Note: 1. It is useful to identify the independent and dependent variables where possible, since it is the usual practice to display the independent variable in the columns and the dependent variable in the rows of the table.

       2. In the above case, it may be reasonable to expect that incidence of disease contraction upon viral exposure depends on the person's age. So, the age category is the independent variable and the disease contraction is the dependent variable.

(b) From the table, 18 of the 40 people contracted the disease when exposed to the virus.

The required percentage is $\dfrac{18}{40} \times 100\% = 45\%$.

(c) Percentage of people who contracted the disease in the age category

12 years and under is $\dfrac{9}{12} \times 100\% = 75\%$.

13 to 59 years is $\dfrac{3}{20} \times 100\% = 15\%$.

60 years and above is $\dfrac{6}{8} \times 100\% = 75\%$.

(d) We can conclude that although 45% of the people contracted the disease when exposed to the virus, the disease was more contagious for the young and the elderly. 75% of those in each of the age categories, 12 years and under, and 60 years and above, contracted the disease.

Try It! 3   Miss Sanders asked 25 sixth grade and 25 eighth grade students about their favorite kinds of movies, Action (A), Comedy (C) or Romance (R). The following lists show the findings.

Favorite Kind of Movie for 6th Grade Students

A	A	R	C	R	A	C	C	R	A
C	C	A	C	C	R	A	A	R	A
C	C	C	A	A					

Favorite Kind of Movie for 8th Grade Students

R	R	A	R	C	A	C	R	R	A
C	R	C	A	A	R	A	R	R	A
R	R	A	R	C					

(a) Organize the above data in a two-way frequency table.
(b) Find the percentage of students who like each kind of movie.
(c) Find the percentage of sixth graders who like each kind of movie.
(d) Find the percentage of eighth graders who like each kind of movie.
(e) Compare the movie preference of the sixth and eighth graders.

In Example 3, the total number of people in each age category is unequal and thus we use percentages to get a more accurate picture of the data. These percentage values can be put into a two-way table to form a **two-way relative frequency table** as shown.

Two-way Relative Frequency Table

Age	12 and under	13 to 59	60 and above	Total
Contracted Disease	75	15	75	45
Did Not Contract Disease				
Total	100	100	100	100

Two-way Frequency Table

Age	12 and under	13 to 59	60 and above	Total
Contracted Disease	9	3	6	18
Did Not Contract Disease	3	17	2	22
Total	12	20	8	40

For example, to obtain the percentage of those aged 12 years and under who contracted the disease, we divide 9 by 12, and multiply by 100%. Refer to how you have obtained the percentages in the first row of the two-way relative frequency table from Example 3 part (c). Similarly fill in the table by expressing the number in each cell as a percentage of its **column's total**.

Two-way Relative Frequency for Columns Table

Age	12 and under	13 to 59	60 and above	Total
Contracted Disease	75	15	75	45
Did Not Contract Disease	25	85	25	55
Total	100	100	100	100

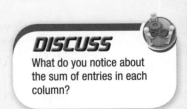

DISCUSS

What do you notice about the sum of entries in each column?

The two-way table above shows **relative frequencies for columns**. We can also calculate percentages from the table rows, rather than columns, to get a table that shows relative frequencies for rows. To do that we would, for example, have divided the number of people who are age 12 years and under and who contracted the disease (=9) by the total number of people who contracted the disease (=18) and multiply by 100% , and so on. The table below shows this:

Two-way Relative Frequency for Rows Table

Age	12 and under	13 to 59	60 and above	Total
Contracted Disease	50	16.7	33.3	100
Did Not Contract Disease	13.6	77.3	9.1	100
Total	30	50	20	100

DISCUSS
What do you notice about the sum of entries in each row?

By doing so, you have obtained the percentage of the people that contracted the disease who are of age 12 and under (50%), the percentage of the people that contracted the disease who are of age 13 to 59 (16.7%), and so on. The **relative frequencies for rows** table highlights facts different from those in the relative frequencies for columns table.

In other words, different association between the two variables can be obtained by calculating percentages in different ways. Two-way tables can also show **relative frequencies for the whole table**, besides for rows or for columns, where the percentages are calculated from the table total (in this case 40 people).

REMARKS
Entries in the "Total" row and "Total" column are called **marginal frequencies**. The relative frequencies in the body of the table are called **conditional frequencies**.

In general, when the independent variable (in this case the age category) is placed in the columns of the table, percentages are often calculated in terms of the column total.

EXERCISE 13.1

 BASIC PRACTICE

1. The following list shows the ages, measured to the nearest year, of students in a seventh grade class.

13	14	13	12	15	14	13	13
12	13	13	14	14	15	12	13
13	12	14	14	13	14	13	12
14	15	13	13	12	13	14	13

Construct a frequency table for the data.

2. Alan, Ben and Cliff are candidates for the post of councillor of a class. The following list shows the votes received by the three candidates from the 40 students in the class.

Ben	Ben	Alan	Ben	Cliff	Cliff	Alan	Ben	Cliff	Alan
Alan	Cliff	Cliff	Ben	Ben	Alan	Cliff	Ben	Alan	Cliff
Cliff	Ben	Ben	Alan	Cliff	Ben	Alan	Cliff	Ben	Ben
Alan	Ben	Cliff	Cliff	Ben	Ben	Alan	Cliff	Cliff	Ben

(a) Construct a frequency table for the data.

(b) Who will be the class councillor based on majority votes?

3. Display each of the following set of data in a two-way table.

    (a) A group of 230 men and women were asked whether they approved or disapproved of a proposed new shopping mall in their suburb. Ninety-eight of the 135 women interviewed approved and 74 men disapproved.

        (i) How many people disapproved this proposal?

        (ii) How many men approved this proposal?

    (b) A survey on breakfast eating habit was conducted among some seventh, eighth and ninth graders. Of the seventh graders, 53 eat their breakfast regularly but 9 do not eat their breakfast regularly. Thirty of the 52 ninth graders do not eat their breakfast regularly. Among the eighth graders, the number who do not eat their breakfast regularly is half of the number who eat regularly. A total of 79 students from the three grades do not eat their breakfast regularly.

        (i) Find the total number of students in this survey.

        (ii) How many eighth graders eat their breakfast regularly?

        (iii) What is the total number of students who eat their breakfast regularly?

4. Three hundred boys and girls were asked whether they prefer to study alone, to study in pairs, or to study in a group. The results are shown below.

Study Preference and Gender

Study Preference	Boys	Girls	Total
Study alone	24	56	80
Study in pairs	16	80	96
Study in a group	60	64	124
Total	100	200	300

    (a) Present these data in percentage form in a two-way table.

    (b) Using your results, compare the study preference of the boys and of the girls.

FURTHER PRACTICE

5. The following list is a record of the grades of 40 students in a mathematics examination.

B	C	A	D	F	A	B	C	C	B
D	C	C	A	B	D	F	C	D	C
B	B	D	F	A	D	B	D	F	F
C	F	C	B	D	C	C	A	D	C

    (a) Construct a frequency table for the data.

    (b) What was the grade obtained by the most number of students?

    (c) Find the percentage of students who obtain grade A or grade B.

6. The following list shows the distances (in km) which 30 adults have to travel from home to their work place.

7.2	2.8	4.2	6.0	6.5	3.3
4.1	3.7	8.1	3.6	4.7	6.4
9.3	5.8	6.9	5.7	1.6	2.3
5.3	9.0	7.1	0.8	4.8	4.0
8.4	1.5	5.5	7.9	9.2	6.5

    (a) Construct a frequency table of uniform intervals for the data, using the intervals $0 < x \leq 2$, $2 < x \leq 4$, and so on.

    (b) Find the percentage of adults whose work place is more than 6 km from their home.

7. Martin and Liz surveyed 20 seventh graders and 20 eighth graders about their favorite type of music out of the following genres: Country (C), Hip Hop (H), Jazz (J) or Rock (R). The following lists show the data from their surveys.

Favorite Type of Music of 7th Graders

R	H	R	J	R	C	R	R	C	R
R	H	R	H	C	H	R	J	H	C

Favorite Type of Music of 8th Graders

H	H	J	R	R	C	R	C	J	R
R	J	H	H	J	H	R	H	H	J

(a) Construct a two-way frequency table for the data.

(b) What is the percentage of 8th graders who like Hip Hop music?

(c) Present the data in percentage form in a two-way table.

(d) Using your results, compare the music preference of the 7th and 8th graders.

8. The two-way frequency table below shows the numbers of eighth grade male and female students who are involved in after-school clubs.

After-school Clubs Attended by 8th Grade Students

	Male	Female	Total
Drama Club	8	14	
Math Club	8	4	
Chess Club	8	12	
Literary Club	4	6	
Total			

(a) Find the missing values and complete the table.

(b) Construct a two-way table showing relative frequencies for columns.

(c) What conclusions can you draw from the data?

MATH@WORK

9. The following two-way frequency table (Table 1) shows the preferred weekend leisure activities for a group of 50 people in a town.

Table 1
Preferences for Weekend Leisure Activities

	Men	Women	Children	Total
Shopping	2	13	0	15
Sports	12	5	7	24
Watching TV	6	2	3	11
Total	20	20	10	50

(a) The following table shows **relative frequencies for the whole table** for the above data. The number in each cell of Table 1 is expressed as a ratio of the total number of people (50). The ratios of each category of people who prefered watching TV have been completed.

Table 2
Relative Frequency for the Whole

	Men	Women	Children	Total
Shopping				0.3
Sports				0.48
Watching TV	0.12	0.04	0.06	0.22
Total				1.0

Copy and complete the table. Express your answers as decimals.

(b) The table below shows relative frequencies for rows, that is the relative frequencies are expressed in terms of the total number at the end of each row in Table 1.

Table 3
Relative Frequency for Rows

	Men	Women	Children	Total
Shopping				
Sports				
Watching TV	0.55	0.18	0.27	1.0
Total				1.0

Copy and complete the table.

(c) What conclusions can you draw from Table 2?

(d) What conclusions can you draw from Table 3?

(e) You are the town planner working on the 3-year development plan for the town. Based on the above data of the current preference and leisure needs of the people, what facilities would you propose to add to this town? Elaborate on the nature of the proposed facilities.

10. A quality control officer inspected 30 cases of vases produced by a factory. The list below shows the number of defective vases found in each case of 10 vases.

1	3	1	4	1	2	0	0	4	0
4	2	0	1	3	0	1	3	1	2
0	1	3	0	2	1	0	1	2	1

(a) Construct a frequency table for the data.

(b) Find the percentage of cases that contain at most one defective vase.

11. In a survey, the number of hours that a person surfs the Internet per day is recorded. The following list shows the survey results of 27 people who surfed the Internet.

1.5	3.2	2.1	3.0	0.8	4.2	11.6	2.7	6.6
4.1	1.6	6.3	2.5	2.0	5.8	2.4	8.8	5.4
0.4	9.2	2.9	5.7	7.8	1.0	3.9	10.3	2.9

(a) Construct a frequency table of uniform intervals, using the intervals $0 < x \leqslant 3$, $3 < x \leqslant 6$ and so on.

(b) Find the percentage of people in the survey who spend more than 3 hours but fewer than or equal to 9 hours per day surfing the Internet.

BRAIN WORKS

12. In a factory, the lifetime of each of 30 batteries was tested. The results (in hours) are shown below.

9.2	3.2	7.7	8.0	5.2	8.8
6.9	7.6	3.8	4.1	7.6	8.4
9.9	3.6	8.4	9.0	5.1	7.5
4.9	9.5	8.1	4.5	7.2	9.5
6.4	6.9	7.4	5.7	7.9	6.3

(a) Construct a frequency table of uniform intervals, with 4 or 5 intervals for the data.

(b) Compare your table with those of your classmates.

13.2 *Bar Graphs and Histograms*

A Bar Graphs

The organized data in a frequency table can be represented by suitable graphs so that patterns and trends can be readily recognized. One of the many techniques used to present data in a visual form is drawing a bar graph. A **bar graph** is useful for comparing facts. The bars provide a visual display for comparing quantities in different classes or categories. Bar graphs help us to see relationships quickly.

Bar graphs can have horizontal or vertical bars. The height or length of the bar will represent the number of observations or **frequency** in that class, and is proportional to the frequency of the class it represents. The greater the frequency of the class, the greater the length or height of the bar. The width of each bar in a bar graph should be consistent. Let us look at some examples.

Example 4

In a survey, the favorite colors of a group of students are summarized in the following table.

Favorite color	Blue	Green	Red	White	Yellow
Number of students	10	15	12	5	8

(a) What is the total number of students in this survey?
(b) Represent the data with a bar graph.
(c) Which color do the students like most?

Solution

(a) Total number of students = 10 + 15 + 12 + 5 + 8
    = 50

(b) There are five classes in this survey and the range of values in the vertical scale is 0 to 15. We choose a scale of 1 cm for the width of each bar and a vertical scale of 2 cm to 5 units to represent the number of students. The bar graph is shown below.

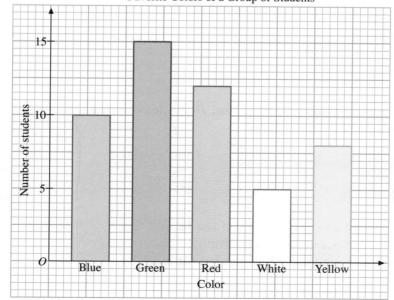
Favorite Colors of a Group of Students

REMARKS

In a bar graph, the bars should have equal width and the gaps between the bars should be uniform.

REMARKS

Steps for constructing a bar graph:
1. Find the range in values.
2. Determine a scale.
3. Label the axes.
4. Draw the bars.
5. Give the graph a title.

(c) The tallest bar indicates the greatest frequency.
∴ the color which the students like most is green.

Note: • A statistical diagram should have a title and be labeled.
• A bar graph with horizontal bars may be drawn as shown below. The horizontal bar graph uses the vertical axis for labeling the classes. One advantage of horizontal bar graphs over the vertical ones is that there is more room to fit long text labels of each class.

Favorite Colors of a Group of Students

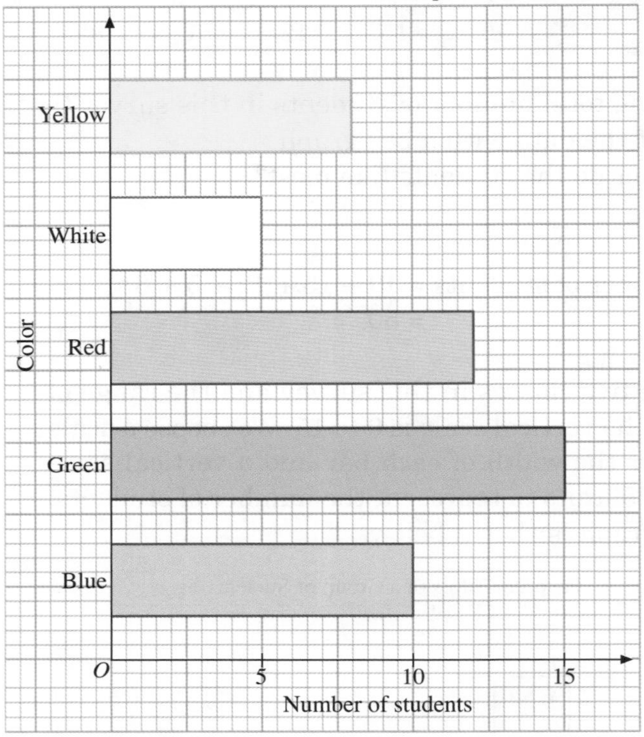

Try It! 4 The stock (in kg) of grades *A*, *B*, *C* and *D* tea leaves in a store is shown in the following table.

Grade of tea leaves	A	B	C	D
Mass (kg)	5	10	13	8

(a) Find the total mass of the stock of tea leaves.
(b) Represent the data using a bar graph.
(c) Which grade of tea leaves has the lowest stock?

Example **5**

The bar graph shows the expenditure and revenue of *ABC* Company for each quarter in its first year of operation.

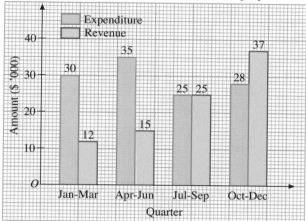

Expenditure and Revenue of *ABC* Company

(a) Compare its revenue over the four quarters.

(b) Describe the company's performance in the third quarter of the year.

(c) In which quarter did the company make a profit?

(d) Was the company profitable in its first year of operations?

• **Solution**

(a) There was a steady increase in revenue from one quarter to the next as shown by an increase in the height of the bar that represents the company's revenue.

(b) During the third quarter,
   expenditure = revenue = $25,000.
   Thus, the company broke even in the third quarter.

(c) In the fourth quarter, the revenue bar was higher than the expenditure bar.
   ∴ the company made a profit in the fourth quarter.

(d) Total expenditure in the four quarters
   = $(30 + 35 + 25 + 28) × 1,000
   = $118,000
   Total revenue in the four quarters
   = $(12 + 15 + 25 + 37) × 1,000
   = $89,000
   Total expenditure – total revenue
   = $118,000 – $89,000
   = $29,000

   The company lost $29,000 during the year.
   Hence, the company was not profitable in its first year of operations.

REMARKS

The double (or group) bar graph allows a direct comparison of different sets of data within each class. As in Example 5, expenditure and revenue can be compared within each quarter and across quarters.

REMARKS

1st quarter: Jan - Mar
2nd quarter: Apr - Jun
3rd quarter: July - Sep
4th quarter: Oct - Dec

Try It! **5** The bar graph shows the sales of coffee and tea at a café in 4 hours on a certain morning.

Sales of Coffee and Tea at a Café

(a) Compare the sales of coffee over the 4 hours.
(b) During which period were the sales of tea more than those of coffee?
(c) How many cups of coffee were sold during the four hours?

Another type of bar graph is the **stacked bar graphs** (also called **segmented bar graphs**) which is useful for displaying two-way tables to make relationships easier to detect. A stacked bar graph, like other bar graphs, has a bar for each class of a categorical variable. However, each bar is divided into "segments", where each data item of the class is represented as a segment in the bar.

The diagram on the right shows a stacked bar graph which displayed the number of 8th grade girls and boys in each of their favorite sport – basketball, softball and tennis. There are 3 bars for the three classes (Basketball, Softball and Tennis) of the categorical variable, Sports, and each bar is divided into 2 segments to represent the two data categories (girls and boys).

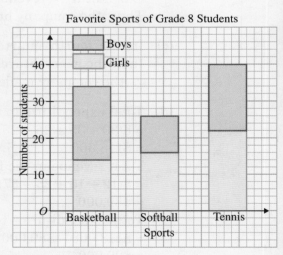

Favorite Sports of Grade 8 Students

A stacked bar graph can show how each value contributes to a total. Each bar represents a total or a whole. In the given bar graph, 40 eighth graders like tennis, of which 22 are girls. The length of each segment indicates a proportion or a percentage of observations in a second variable.

B Histograms

Bar graphs are useful when the data are in categories, such as "Basketball" or "Softball". But when data are continuous such as a person's height, weight, or age, we use a **histogram** to represent such grouped data with class intervals. A histogram consists of rectangles whose **areas** are proportional to the **frequencies** in the classes. The bases of the rectangles being equal to the class intervals are on the horizontal axis. In this section, we shall only consider grouped data with uniform class intervals.

RECALL

In a frequency table, each group of data is called a **class**. When the class widths of all the classes are equal, the frequency table is of uniform intervals.

In a histogram, the base of each rectangle is the same when all the class widths are equal.

That's right! The heights of the rectangles are therefore proportional to the frequencies.

Example 6

The following table shows the heights of 50 students.

Height (x cm)	Frequency
$150 < x \leqslant 155$	7
$155 < x \leqslant 160$	12
$160 < x \leqslant 165$	18
$165 < x \leqslant 170$	10
$170 < x \leqslant 175$	3

(a) Represent the data using a histogram.

(b) Describe the shape of the histogram.

Solution

(a) The histogram is as shown.

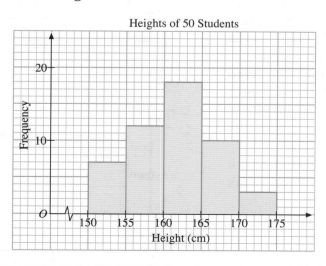

Heights of 50 Students

(b) The histogram shows that the heights of most students lie between 155 cm and 170 cm. There are more students in the lowest class than in the highest class.

Note: • Unlike a bar graph, a histogram has no gaps between adjacent rectangles.
• In a bar graph, the width of each rectangle has no special meaning. But in a histogram, the width of each rectangle represents the class width.

Try It! 6

The following table shows the times taken by 50 students to complete a mathematics assignment.

Time (t min)	Frequency
$30 < t \leq 40$	4
$40 < t \leq 50$	9
$50 < t \leq 60$	17
$60 < t \leq 70$	12
$70 < t \leq 80$	8

(a) Represent the data using a histogram.
(b) Describe the shape of the histogram.

EXERCISE 13.2

BASIC PRACTICE

1. The students in Mrs. Costa's school were surveyed about snacks and asked to pick one snack food they liked most from a list. The bar graph on the right summarizes the data collected from this survey.
   (a) Which snack food was most preferred by the students in Mrs. Costa's school?
   (b) How many students preferred fruit?
   (c) Which snack food were preferred equally by the students?
   (d) Name the top three preferred snack food among the students in Mrs. Costa's school.

Preferred Snack Choices of Students at Mrs. Costa's School

2. The bar graph shows the numbers of rainy days in Sunshine City over a period of four months.
   (a) Which month had the least number of rainy days?
   (b) What is the ratio of the number of rainy days in June to that in August?
   (c) Find the average number of rainy days in the four months.

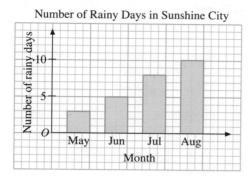

Number of Rainy Days in Sunshine City

3. The following table shows the examination results in mathematics of 7th grade students in a particular school.

Grade	A	B	C	D	F
Number of students	30	46	60	40	24

   (a) Represent the data with a
      (i) bar graph,   (ii) pictogram.
   (b) Which graph in (a) is easier to draw?

4. The histogram shows the distances between the homes and the school of some students.
   (a) What is the class width of each class?
   (b) Find the percentage of students who live more than 6 km from their school.
   (c) Describe the shape of the histogram.

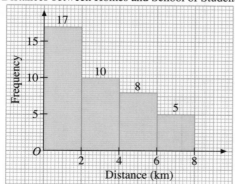

Distances between Homes and School of Students

5. The histogram shows the daily wages of some workers in a survey.
   (a) Find the number of workers whose daily wages are not more than $80.
   (b) Describe the distribution of the daily wages of these workers.

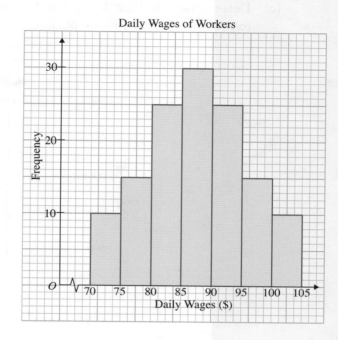

Daily Wages of Workers

6. The bar graph shows Andrew's income and expenditure for each month from January to March.
   (a) Compare Andrew's monthly income over the three months.
   (b) In which month was his income less than his expenditure and by how much?
   (c) Determine whether his total income in the three months was greater than his total expenditure for the same period.

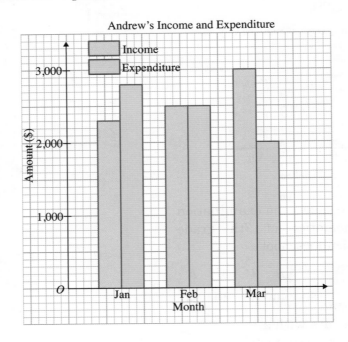

7. The bar graph shows the number of production and sales staff in four companies.
   (a) What is the ratio of the number of production staff to that of sales staff in company *A*?
   (b) Which company has the most number of sales staff?
   (c) How many more staff does company *C* have as compared to company *B*?

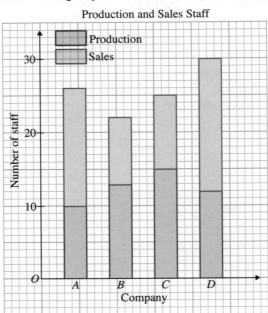

8. The following frequency table shows the distribution of floor areas of 50 residential apartments.

Area (A m²)	Frequency
30 < A ≤ 50	9
50 < A ≤ 70	15
70 < A ≤ 90	10
90 < A ≤ 110	7
110 < A ≤ 130	5
130 < A ≤ 150	4

(a) Draw a histogram to represent the data.
(b) Find the percentage of apartments with areas that are greater than 110 m².
(c) Describe the distribution of the areas of the apartments.

9. The times taken by a technician to complete 120 repair jobs are recorded in the following frequency table.

Time (t minutes)	Frequency
25 < t ≤ 30	5
30 < t ≤ 35	6
40 < t ≤ 45	24
45 < t ≤ 50	35
50 < t ≤ 55	26
55 < t ≤ 60	14

(a) Given that the distribution has uniform class width, state the missing information in the table.
(b) Draw a histogram to represent the data.
(c) Find the percentage of the jobs that took the technician more than 45 minutes to repair.
(d) Which is the most common time duration of the repair jobs?

10. Mrs. Costa had sampled an equal number of boys and girls at her school when she surveyed their preferred snack choice (refer to Question 1). The table below shows the results of the survey.

Preferred Snack Choices of Students at Mrs. Costa's School

	Boys	Girls
Candy	76	84
Chips	178	95
Chocolate bars	140	118
Cookies	72	92
Fruit	64	146
Ice cream	90	105
Popcorn	80	80
Pretzels	100	80

(a) Draw one suitable bar graph to show a comparison of snack food preferences by gender in Mrs. Costa's school.
(b) Which snack foods were preferred by more girls than boys?
(c) Which snack food was preferred by considerably more boys than girls?
(d) Which snack food was preferred equally by both boys and girls?

11. The following frequency table shows the transportation expenses of 60 office executives in a particular week.

Transportation expenses ($x)	Frequency
30 < x ≤ 40	7
40 < x ≤ 50	15
50 < x ≤ 60	21
60 < x ≤ 70	11
70 < x ≤ 80	6

(a) Draw a histogram to represent the data.
(b) Find the percentage of the executives who spent between $40 and $60 on transportation in that week.
(c) If the transportation expenses were increased by $5 a week and a new histogram was drawn, describe how the new histogram would compare with the earlier one.

12. The following list shows the shot put throwing distances (in meters) of 32 boys.

5.3	6.2	6.8	3.2	5.5	6.1	7.7	5.9
4.2	5.8	6.4	7.6	6.5	3.9	4.8	7.0
6.6	5.0	5.1	6.9	5.3	7.9	6.4	4.1
7.2	3.5	6.0	4.8	6.7	5.9	4.7	6.8

(a) Group the data using a frequency table with uniform class intervals starting from $3 < x \leqslant 4$.

(b) Draw a histogram to present the grouped data in **(a)**.

(c) Those students whose throws were less than or equal to 5.0 m were required to attend a training program. How many students were required to attend the training program?

BRAINWORKS

13.

Annual Sales of Cars

(bar graph titled "Annual Sales of Cars" with y-axis "Number of cars sold (thousands)" ranging from 20 to 24, x-axis "Brand" with AA = 21, BB = 22, CC = 23, DD = 24)

The bar graph shows the annual sales of four models of cars. It was used in a promotional advertisement by the *DD* Brand Company. Is it a fair comparison chart? Explain your answer.

14. The following table shows the lengths of service of the staff in a school.

Length of service (x years)	Frequency
$0 < x \leqslant 1$	6
$1 < x \leqslant 2$	13
$2 < x \leqslant 3$	9
$3 < x \leqslant 4$	4
$4 < x \leqslant 5$	3
$5 < x \leqslant 10$	5

(a) Find the class width of
  (i) the 5th class interval,
  (ii) the 6th class interval.

(b) A student drew the following histogram to represent the data.

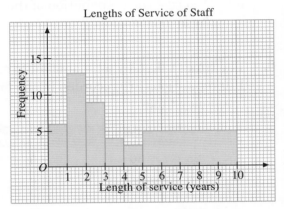

Lengths of Service of Staff

Do you think the histogram is drawn correctly? Explain your answer.

13.3 Line Graphs and Scatter Plots

A Line Graphs

A **line graph** is useful in displaying data or information that changes continuously over time. It compares two variables – shown on a vertical and a horizontal axis. The horizontal axis often measures units of time. As a result, the line graph is often viewed as a time series graph. In a line graph, data values are plotted on a grid and the adjacent data points are joined by line segments.

Line graphs, especially useful in the fields of statistics and science, are more popular than all other graphs combined because their visual characteristics reveal data trends clearly. Line graphs allow us to observe trends of data such as an increase or a decrease in data over time. Thus, we may use a line graph to make predictions about certain results of data not recorded yet.

Example 7

The following table shows the population of the United States at intervals of ten years between 1970 and 2010.

Year	1970	1980	1990	2000	2010
Population (millions)	203	227	249	281	309

Source: National Center for Health Statistics, U.S. Bureau of the Census

(a) Draw a line graph to represent the data.
(b) Describe the trend of the population between 1970 and 2010.
(c) Based on the graph, estimate the U.S. population in the year 2020.

Solution

(a) The line graph of the data is shown below.

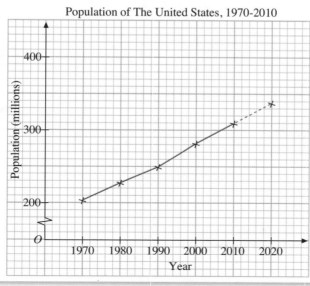

Population of The United States, 1970-2010

(b) The graph shows that the U.S. population increased steadily from 1970 to 2010. The changes from 1970 to 1990 was smaller than the later changes, and the largest growth, from 1990 to 2000, was followed by somewhat slower growth.

(c) We can project the population in the year 2020 by extending the line graph. Thus, the estimated population in 2020 is 340 millions.

REMARKS
The estimation method used in question **(c)** is called **extrapolation** where a value is estimated by following a pattern and going beyond the values already known. However, be careful when extrapolating. Extrapolation gets less accurate the further we extrapolate.

Try It! 7

The following table shows the crude birth rate per 1,000 population of the United States at intervals of ten years between 1970 and 2010.

Year	1970	1980	1990	2000	2010
Crude Birth Rate	18.4	15.9	16.7	14.4	13.0

Source: National Center for Health Statistics, U.S. Bureau of the Census

(a) Draw a line graph to represent the data.
(b) Describe the trend of the crude birth rate between 1970 and 2010.
(c) Based on the graph, estimate the U.S. crude birth rate in the year 2020.

REMARKS
Crude Birth rate:
This is the average annual number of childbirths during a year per 1,000 persons in the population. The birth rate is usually the dominant factor in determining the rate of population growth. It depends on both the level of fertility and the age structure of the population.

Example 8

The line graph below shows the closing values of the SSSX Index for the Global Stock Market on five transaction days.

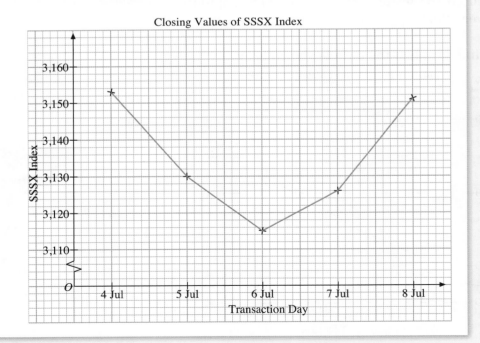

Closing Values of SSSX Index

REMARKS
You can click on Chart Wizard icon in Microsoft Excel software to draw line graphs.

(a) Describe the trend of the SSSX Index between 4 July and 6 July.

(b) Find the lowest closing value of SSSX Index during these five days.

(c) On which date did the index have the largest rise between 5 July and 8 July? What was the largest rise?

Solution

(a) Since the index on 5 July was lower than that on 4 July, the index fell on 5 July. Similarly, the index fell on 6 July.

(b) The graph has the lowest point on 6 July. Thus, the lowest closing value = 3,115.

(c) Increase in the index on 7 July = 3,126 − 3,115
$$= 11$$
Increase in the index on 8 July = 3,151 − 3,126
$$= 25$$

∴ the index had the largest rise of 25 points on 8 July.

Note: The break on the vertical axis indicates that the scale does not start from zero and there is no scale below the '3110' mark. This scale will give us a better view for the variation of data.

Try It! 8

The line graph below shows the Consumer Price Index (CPI) of Country X from 2005 to 2011, where the index in 2009 is set to 100.

Consumer Price Index of Country X, 2005-2011
(2009 = 100)

(a) Describe the trend of the Consumer Price Index of Country X between 2005 and 2011.

(b) Find the lowest CPI in this period.

(c) Which year had the greatest rise in the index and what was the value of the greatest rise?

Note : A consumer price index (CPI) measures changes in the price level of consumer goods and services purchased by households. The annual percentage change in a CPI is used as a measure of inflation.

When drawing a line graph, it is important to use appropriate scales on the axes. Otherwise, the shape and slope of the line can give readers the wrong impression about the data. For instance, let us consider the decline in number of vandalism cases of a town being represented by two line graphs using different scales. Compare the line graphs in Diagram 1 and Diagram 2 below.

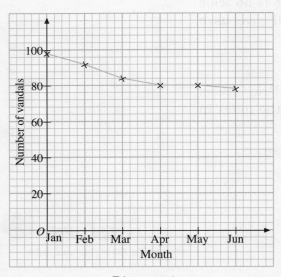

Diagram 1

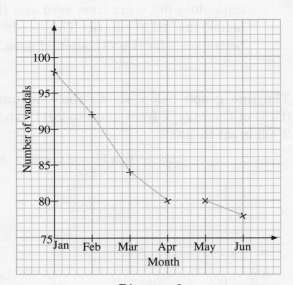

Diagram 2

Using a scale of 75 to 100 in Diagram 2 focuses on a small range of values which makes the vandalism rate appear to have decreased much faster than it appears in Diagram 1. It does not accurately depict the trend in vandalism between January and June since it exaggerates that trend and does not relate it to the bigger picture. However, choosing a scale of 0 to 100 (Diagram 1) better displays how small or slow the decline in the number of vandals really was. Thus, starting the vertical scale at 75 in this set of data gives a graph that is misleading.

B Scatter Plots

We can learn much more about sets of data by displaying bivariate data in a graphical form that maintains the pairing of two variables. **Scatter plots** are particularly useful as a good visual means of seeing relationships between the two variables of bivariate numerical data. Scatter plots are similar to line graphs in that data points are plotted on horizontal and vertical axes. The difference is that with a scatter plot, the plotted data points are not connected together with line segments; the resulting pattern of the data points on the scatter plot reveals the relationship between the variables. Statisticians and quality control technicians often use scatter plots to determine if there is a relationship, or what we called a **correlation**, between two variables.

We draw a **line of best fit** in a scatter plot to analyze the correlation. The closer the data points are when plotted in making a straight line, the higher (or stronger) the correlation between the two variables. If the slope of the line is positive (rising from left to right), then the variables are said to have a **positive correlation**. If the slope of the line is negative (falling from left to right), the variables have a **negative correlation**.

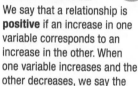

REMARKS

We say that a relationship is **positive** if an increase in one variable corresponds to an increase in the other. When one variable increases and the other decreases, we say the relationship is **negative**.

In general terms, a scatter plot gives us an idea of what kind of correlations (or patterns) our bivariate data has. We may have:

❶ Positive (negative) linear correlation
❷ Positive (negative) non-linear correlation
❸ No correlation

Example 9

Amy surveyed her basketball teammates to find out if there is a correlation between the average number of hours they practiced each day and the average number of points they scored per game. The table below shows the data she has collected.

Average number of hours of daily practice	Average number of points scored per game	
0.5	4	
1	6	
1	8	
1.5	9	
2	12	
2	10	
1.5	10	
2.5	14	
0.5	12	

(a) Construct a scatter plot to display the data.
(b) Describe the pattern of points on the scatter plot.

(c) Draw a line of best fit that passes through two or more points that represent the data.

(d) What type of slope is the line of best fit? Describe the correlation between the average number of hours a player practices each day and the average number of points the player scores per game.

Solution

(a) The scatter plot is shown below.

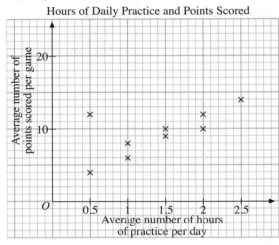

Hours of Daily Practice and Points Scored

(b) All the data points are clustered in the shape of a straight line, except for one point (0.5, 12).

Note: The data point (0.5, 12) is considered an **outlier**. It stands out because it deviates from the other points. Outliers are often disregarded when drawing a line of best fit because they do not "fit" within the normal trend of the data. However, they may provide important information to analysts when investigating relationships between the two sets of data.

(c) One possible line of best fit is shown in the scatter plot below.

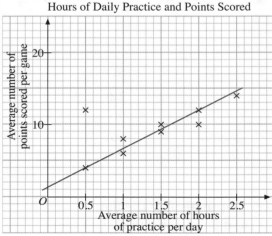

Hours of Daily Practice and Points Scored

(d) The line which runs through the data points has a positive slope. Thus, there is a positive correlation between the average number of hours a player practices in a day and the average number of points the player scores per game.

Note: If a correlation is positive, an increase in the value of the variable on the horizontal axis is more likely associated with an increase in the value of the variable on the vertical axis. The closer the points are to the line, the higher the correlation.

Try It! 9

Ernie surveyed his friends about the number of hours they watched TV per night and the number of A's they scored in an examination. The data he collected is shown in the table below.

Number of Hours Spent Watching TV per Night	Number of A's Scored
5	0
3	2
2	3
3	3
1	5
4	1
6	1
2	6
1	6
2	4

(a) Construct a scatter plot for the data.
(b) Describe the distribution of points on the scatter plot.
(c) Draw a line of best fit that passes through two or more points that represent the data.
(d) Hence, describe the relationship between the number of hours spent watching TV per night and the number of A's scored.

Objective: To examine the pattern of data points on a scatter plot and the relationship between two variables.

Carefully examine each of the following scatter plots and then answer the questions.

Scatter Plot A

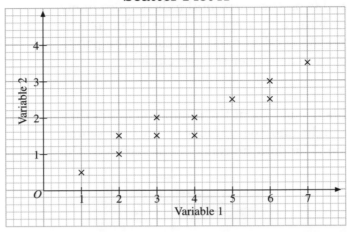

Scatter Plot B

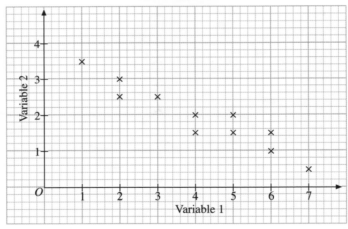

Scatter Plot C

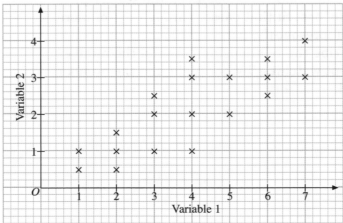

Scatter Plot D

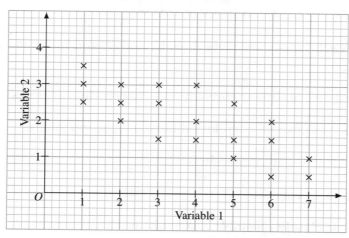

Scatter Plot E

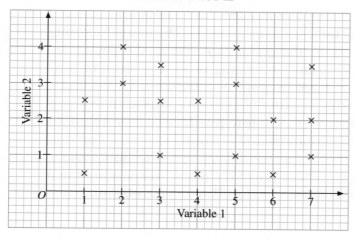

Scatter Plot F

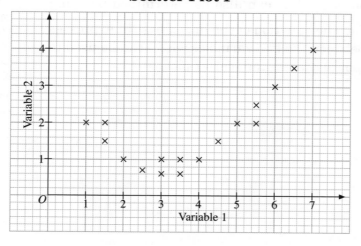

Questions

(a) Describe how the points are clustered in each scatter plot.

(b) Draw a line of best fit each for scatter plots A, B, C, and D, and hence estimate the slope of each line.

(c) Which scatter plot shows a non-linear correlation between the variables?

(d) Which scatter plots show a positive correlation between the variables?

(e) Which scatter plots show a negative correlation?

(f) Which scatter plot shows no correlation?

(g) Which scatter plots most closely resemble a straight line?

From Class Activity 1, we notice that the way the data points are clustered reveals the degree of correlation between two variables. The more the points resemble a straight line, the higher the correlation. When the points are clustered in a way that closely resembles a rising or falling straight line, there is a **high positive** or a **high negative** correlation in the data. When the points "tend" to be rising or falling but are not clustered in a way that clearly shows a straight line, there is a **low positive** or **low negative** correlation. When the data points are randomly scattered in such a way that they do not approximate a line (as they do not appear to rise or fall), there is **zero correlation** between the variables. When the points are clustered in a way that closely resemble a curve, there is a **non-linear correlation**.

> ### REMARKS
> A strong correlation does not necessarily mean that changes in one variable will cause changes in the other variable. A third factor could be involved.

When both variables are quantitative, the line of best fit which connects two or more points on the graph expresses a slope, which can be determined by $\dfrac{\text{rise}}{\text{run}}$ or $\dfrac{y_2 - y_1}{x_2 - x_1}$. The equation of the line can also be determined by using two points on the line of best fit. The equation of the line of best fit expresses a mathematical relationship between the two variables which can be used to predict information that was not plotted in the scatter plot.

> ### REMARKS
> In general, we can find the equation of a straight line using two points (x_1, y_1) and (x_2, y_2) on the line. In this case, we first find the slope m of the line using $\dfrac{y_2 - y_1}{x_2 - x_1}$. The equation of a straight line can be expressed in the slope-intercept form as $y = mx + c$.

EXERCISE 13.3

BASIC PRACTICE

1. The line graph shows the changes in the body temperature (°C) of a patient from 9 A.M. to 12 A.M. on a certain day.

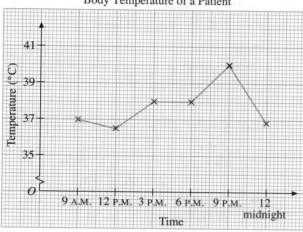

Body Temperature of a Patient

(a) What was the highest body temperature of the patient? When did the patient have it?

(b) Find the number of readings with temperatures above 37 °C.

2. The line graph below shows the total number (in millions) of mobile phone subscribers in one town from 2004 to 2012.

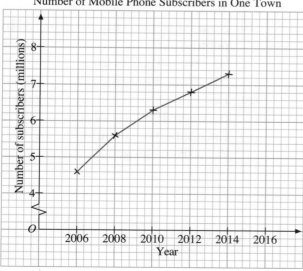

Number of Mobile Phone Subscribers in One Town

(a) Describe the trend of mobile phone subscriptions between 2006 and 2014.

(b) Based on the graph, estimate the number of mobile phone subscribers in the town in the year 2016.

3. The following table shows the closing prices of a stock in a week.

Day	Mon	Tue	Wed	Thu	Fri
Closing price ($)	23.00	21.50	22.00	20.50	19.50

(a) Draw a line graph to represent the data.

(b) Describe the trend in the price of the stock.

4. For each of the scatter plots below, describe whether or not a relationship exists between the variables, and if it does, comment on whether it is positive or negative, whether it has a linear form, and whether it is low, moderate, or high.

(a)

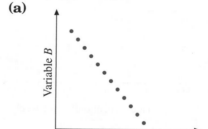

(b)

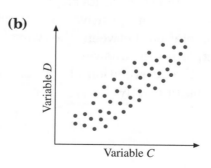

(c)

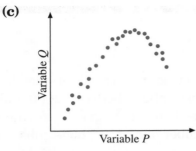

(d)

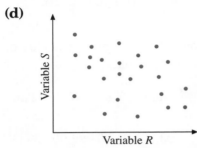

5. The scatter plot below shows the relationship between the number of hours a group of middle school students spent on online activities per week and their grade point average.

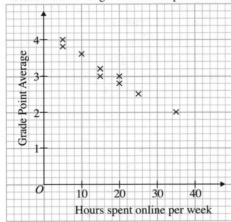

Grade Point Average and Hours Spent Online

(a) Draw a line of best fit on the scatter plot and estimate its slope.

(b) Is there a positive or negative correlation between the variables? Explain your answer.

(c) Is the correlation high or low? Explain briefly.

(d) What can you conclude about the correlation between the number of hours the students spent on online activities and their academic performance?

FURTHER PRACTICE

6. A boy recorded his height from his 8th birthday to his 14th birthday.

Age (year)	8	9	10	11	12	13	14
Height (cm)	136	143	150	156	162	167	169

(a) Draw a line graph to represent the data.

(b) Describe the boy's growth in height over this period of time.

(c) What do you think is the likely height of the boy when he is
  (i) 15 years old?
  (ii) 24 years old?

7. The following table shows the population of a country between 1997 and 2012.

Year	1997	2000	2003	2006	2009	2012
Population (million)	3.95	4.02	4.13	4.17	4.19	4.24

(a) Draw a line graph to represent the data.

(b) Find the percentage growth in the population
  (i) from 1997 to 2000,
  (ii) from 2009 to 2012.

(c) Describe the trend of the population between 1997 and 2012.

(d) Estimate the population in the year 2015 from the graph.

8. As part of a biology experiment, Denise gave 10 plants each different amounts of sunlight per day and measured their growth. The data is shown in the following table.

Amount of Sunlight Exposure Per Day (hours)	Total Growth (cm)
1	1.5
1	2
2	2
2	3
3	5
3	4.5
4	6
4	6
5	7.5
5	7

(a) Display the data on a scatter plot.
(b) Comment on the distribution of the data points.
(c) Draw a line of best fit and hence describe the relationship between the amount of sunlight exposure and plant growth.

9. The age and pulse rate of a group of young people were recorded in the table below.

Age	Pulse Rate	Age	Pulse Rate
15	79	19	76
17	74	17	77
18	75	15	72
16	85	17	70
19	82	18	71

(a) Draw a scatter plot for the data given in the table.
(b) Describe the pattern of the data points.
(c) Determine from your graph whether there is a correlation between the two variables.

MATH@WORK

10. The following table shows the unemployment rate of the United States between 2004 and 2011.

Year	Unemployment Rate (%)
2004	5.5
2005	5.1
2006	4.8
2007	4.6
2008	5.8
2009	9.3
2010	9.7
2011	8.9

Source: CIA World Factbook & Bureau of Labor Statistics

Note: The unemployment rate refers to the percent of the labor force that is without jobs.

(a) Draw a line graph to represent the data.
(b) Describe the trend of the unemployment between 2004 and 2011.
(c) Based on the graph, estimate the U.S. unemployment rate in the year 2012.
   Note: Compare information from the sources to see how accurate is your estimation from the line graph.
(d) Do you think you are able to use the line graph to accurately estimate the unemployment rate in 2013 or after? Explain briefly.

11. The line graph below shows the blood alcohol concentration (BAC) of Jack over time after a shot of liquor.

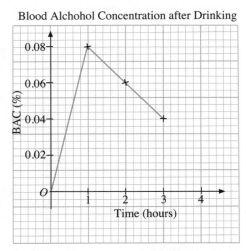

Blood Alchohol Concentration after Drinking

(a) How many hours after drinking did the BAC reach the highest level? What was its value?

(b) What would be the expected BAC 4 hours after the shot of liquor?

(c) A person should not drive a car until the BAC drops below 0.05%. After having the drink, how long should Jack wait before driving?

12. The table below shows the amount of fat (in grams) and number of calories in some food items at a fast food restaurant.

Item	Total Fat (g)	Total calories
Regular Hamburger	9	270
Regular Cheeseburger	13	330
Hamburger Deluxe	21	430
Cheeseburger Deluxe	30	530
Fish Fillet Sandwich	26	470
Crispy Chicken Sandwich	25	500
Grilled Chicken Sandwich	15	430
Breakfast Sandwich	22	440
Yogurt with Granola	4	280
Chocolate Sundae	12	340

(a) Draw a scatter plot relating total fat to total calories and a line of best fit for the data given in the table.

(b) Describe the relationship, if any, between the total fat and the total calories in fast food.

(c) Choose two points on your line of best fit and find
  (i) the slope of the line, rounding your answer to 3 decimal places,
  (ii) the equation of the line of best fit.

(d) Predict the total calories in a fast food item which contains 20 grams of fat.

BRAIN WORKS

13. The following table shows the profits of a company between 2009 and 2012.

Year	2009	2010	2011	2012
Profits($'000)	100	101.5	102	103

(a) Copy the following coordinate planes on a sheet of graph paper. Draw two line graphs, one in each figure, with the given data.

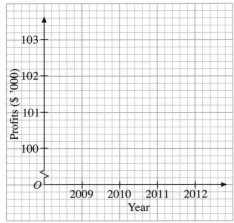

Figure 1

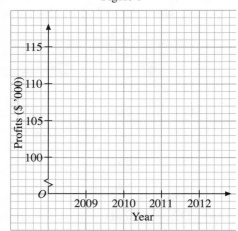

Figure 2

(b) Compare the line graphs drawn in **(a)**.

(c) If you were a manager in the company, which line graph would you use to show the profits? Explain your answer.

14. Investigate how you can create a scatter plot using an Excel spreadsheet. Use it to create scatter plots that show a high positive correlation, a high negative correlation, a low positive correlation and a low negative correlation.

IN A NUTSHELL

Steps in Organizing Data

- divide the raw data in several non-overlapping classes
- construct a frequency table
- complete the table by tallying

Frequency Tables

1. One-way tables are suitable for summarizing univariate data
2. Two-way tables are suitable for bivariate categorical data
   - able to display frequencies and relative frequencies
   - describe possible association between two variables.

Presentation of Data

- Bar graphs: easy to draw and compare classes

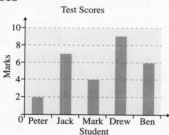

- Histograms: show the distribution of grouped data in class intervals

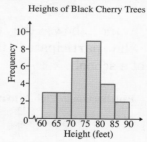

- Line graphs: suitable for time-related data, able to show the trend of data

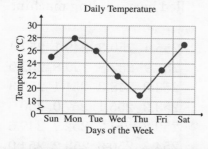

- Scatter plots: show correlation between two numerical variables

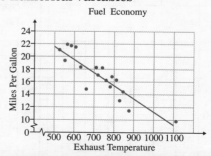

Uses of Statistical Diagrams

- provide visual impression of data
- analyze, infer and predict data

1. Students in a class were asked about their favorite games. The results are shown in the bar graph.

Favorite Games of Students

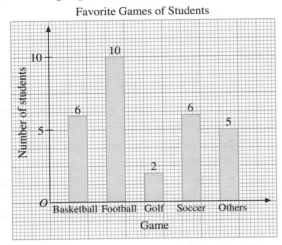

(a) How many students are there in the class?

(b) Which games are equally popular among the students?

2. The bar graph shows the numbers of students who participated in the club activities of a school.

Participation in Club Activities

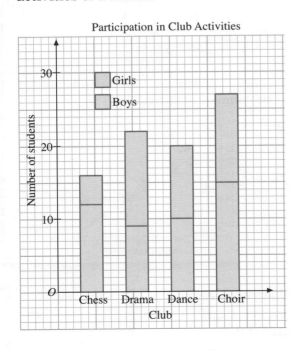

(a) Find the ratio of the number of boys to that of girls in the chess club.

(b) Which club was the most popular among all the students?

(c) Which club had equal numbers of boys and girls?

(d) Find the total number of girls in the four clubs.

3. The following table shows the heights of a girl at different ages.

Age (year)	11	12	13	14	15	16	17
Height (cm)	154	156	162	166	168	169	169

(a) Draw a line graph to represent the data.

(b) Describe the growth in height of the girl.

(c) Estimate the girl's height when she is 18 years old based on the data.

(d) A doctor proposed that the normal mass, in kg, of a girl with height, h cm, where $h > 160$, is given by the formula $m = 60 + 0.9(h - 160)$.

   (i) Find m when $h = 168$.

   (ii) Find h when $m = 63$.

4. The following list shows the volume, V (in cm³), of 36 cups of coffee which are filled by a vending machine.

255.4 250.3 249.1 252.4 251.7 254.7
251.9 252.8 250.8 252.0 256.2 251.6
253.9 248.3 251.1 253.3 255.4 253.4
253.9 255.1 257.0 250.6 254.8 257.9
250.8 251.7 252.7 249.6 251.4 250.9
254.3 250.6 253.2 254.0 253.1 255.1

(a) Construct a frequency table for the data with uniform class intervals starting from $248 < V \leqslant 250$.

(b) Draw a histogram corresponding to the frequency table in **(a)**.

(c) The cups of coffee with volumes less than or equal to 250 cm³ are considered underweight. Find the percentage of underweight cups.

5. The average annual currency exchange rate for the Singapore Dollars (SGD) and US Dollar (USD) between the years 2005 and 2012 is shown in the following table.

Year	SGD per USD
2005	1.66
2006	1.59
2007	1.51
2008	1.41
2009	1.45
2010	1.36
2011	1.26
2012	1.23

(a) Draw a line graph to represent the data.

(b) Describe the trend of the SGD per USD exchange rate between 2005 and 2012.

(c) Based on the graph, estimate the exchange rate in the year 2013.

6. The table below shows the average daily summer temperatures, in degrees Fahrenheit, for Happy Beach City, recorded over 7 days.

Day	Temperature (°F)
1	85
2	90
3	89
4	90
5	92
6	91
7	95

(a) Draw an appropriate graph to represent the data.

(b) How many days was the temperature above 90 °F?

(c) Which day had the greatest rise in temperature? What was the greatest rise?

7. The number of beach visitors and the corresponding average daily temperature on the day of their visit over a period of 12 days in summer were recorded in the table below.

Temperature (°F)	88	90	92	93	88	90
Number of beach visitors	100	150	220	300	80	200

Temperature (°F)	95	94	91	89	93	95
Number of beach visitors	330	300	170	115	250	295

(a) Draw a scatter plot and a line of best fit for the data.

(b) Describe the correlation, if any, between the number of people going to the beach and the average daily temperature.

8. (a) The table below shows the number of hours spent in the shopping mall and the number of dollars spent.

Hours in Mall	4	2	1	3	5	1	6	3	2	3
Dollars Spent	100	120	200	240	220	50	80	280	400	500

(i) Construct a scatter plot for the given data.

(ii) Determine from your graph whether there is a correlation between the number of hours spent in the mall and the number of dollars spent.

(b) The two-way frequency table below shows the number of people in different age categories and their main intention of going to a shopping mall most of the time.

Main Intention of Going to the Mall and Age

	29 and below	30 to 50	51 and above	Total
Shopping	18		28	
Meeting up friends	57	9		88
Total		75		

Copy and complete the table.

(c) Copy and complete the following table showing the relative frequencies of the data in **(b)**. Express your answers as percentages.

Relative Frequency for Columns

	29 and below	30 to 50	51 and above	Total
Shopping				
Meeting up friends				
Total	100%	100%	100%	100%

(d) What conclusions can you draw regarding the main intention of people in the different age categories of going to the shopping mall?

EXTEND YOUR LEARNING CURVE

Conduct a survey among your fellow 8th graders on whether or not they have curfew on school nights and whether or not they have assigned chores at home. The project should involve the following:

- design a simple questionnaire or interview
- design a way to collect the data
- organize the data
- present the data using graphs and summarize the data
- write briefly on your findings
- examine for possible association between the two variables
- is there evidence that those who have a curfew also tend to have assigned chores?

WRITE IN YOUR JOURNAL

1. What are the specific purposes and plus points of different forms of statistical representation?

2. Some statistical graphs can be misleading. Write down what you should observe when interpreting a statistical graph.

Playing

LET'S LEARN TO...

1 solve quadratic equations by factorization, completing the square method, quadratic formula and graphical method

2 solve fractional equations that can be reduced to quadratic equations

3 apply quadratic equations to solve real world problems

Quadratic equations are necessary to understand the mechanics of motion. If the distance, s metres, traveled by a car in time t seconds is given by $s = 3t^2 + 4t$, do you know how long it takes the car to travel 100 m?

14.1 Solving Quadratic Equations by Factorization

An equation that can be expressed in the general form

$$ax^2 + bx + c = 0,$$

where a, b and c are constants and $a \neq 0$, is called a **quadratic equation in one variable** x. A **root** or a solution of the equation is a value of x that satisfies the equation.

Quadratic equations can be solved using any one of the methods that we will be learning in this chapter. Let us first review how quadratic equations can be solved using the **factoring method** which we have learned in Book 8A, Chapter 4. This method makes use of the following property of real numbers.

> For any two real numbers P and Q,
> if $P \times Q = 0$, then either $P = 0$ or $Q = 0$ or $P = Q = 0$.

Example 1

Solve the equation $5x^2 - 58x - 24 = 0$.

Solution

We first factorize the expression $5x^2 - 58x - 24$.
Writing $5x^2 - 58x - 24$ as $(x + p)(5x + q) = 5x^2 + (5p + q)x + pq$,
we have $5p + q = -58$ and $pq = -24$.

Since both the product pq and the sum $5p + q$ are negative, -24 can be factored as $(-12) \times 2$, $(-2) \times 12$, $(-8) \times 3$, etc.

Consider the product pq as $(-12) \times 2$,
$5p + q = 5(-12) + 2 = -58$.   This is correct.
Thus, $p = -12$ and $q = 2$.
$\therefore 5x^2 - 58x - 24 = (x - 12)(5x + 2)$.

$5x^2 - 58x - 24 = 0$
$(x - 12)(5x + 2) = 0$ Factorize $5x^2 - 58x - 24$.
$x - 12 = 0$ or $5x + 2 = 0$ Either one of the factors is 0.
$x = 12$ or $x = -\dfrac{2}{5}$

$\therefore x = 12$ and $x = -\dfrac{2}{5}$ are the roots of the equation.

Note: We can substitute the values of x in the expression to check if the answers are correct.

Try It! 1

Solve the equation $5x^2 - 8x - 21 = 0$.

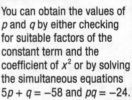

RECALL

You can obtain the values of p and q by either checking for suitable factors of the constant term and the coefficient of x^2 or by solving the simultaneous equations $5p + q = -58$ and $pq = -24$.

Check:
When $x = 12$,
$5x^2 - 58x - 24$
$= 5(12)^2 - 58(12) - 24$
$= 0$.

When $x = -\dfrac{2}{5}$,
$5x^2 - 58x - 24$
$= 5\left(-\dfrac{2}{5}\right)^2 - 58\left(-\dfrac{2}{5}\right) - 24$
$= 0$.
$\therefore$ the roots $x = 12$ and $x = -\dfrac{2}{5}$ are correct.

Example 2

Solve the equation $(4x + 1)(x - 3) = 9x - 28$.

Solution

$$(4x + 1)(x - 3) = 9x - 28$$
$$4x^2 - 11x - 3 = 9x - 28 \qquad \text{Expand the LHS.}$$
$$4x^2 - 20x + 25 = 0 \qquad \text{Rewrite in the form } ax^2 + bx + c = 0.$$
$$(2x - 5)^2 = 0 \qquad \text{Factorize the LHS.}$$
$$\therefore \ 2x - 5 = 0$$
$$x = \frac{5}{2}$$

Note: Since the factor $2x - 5$ occurs twice, the root $x = \dfrac{5}{2}$ is repeated. That is, the equation has two equal roots.

Try It! 2

Solve the equation $(9x - 1)(x - 2) = -7x - 2$.

REMARKS

Equal roots are also known as double roots or repeated roots.

Example 3

Solve the equation $4x(3x + 5) = 7(3x + 5)$.

Solution

$$4x(3x + 5) = 7(3x + 5)$$
$$4x(3x + 5) - 7(3x + 5) = 0 \qquad \text{Move the terms to one side.}$$
$$(3x + 5)(4x - 7) = 0 \qquad \text{Factor out the common factor } (3x + 5).$$
$$3x + 5 = 0 \quad \text{or} \quad 4x - 7 = 0$$
$$x = -\frac{5}{3} \quad \text{or} \quad x = \frac{7}{4}$$

Note: 1. This equation can be solved by expanding both sides and rewriting the equation in the form $ax^2 + bx + c = 0$.

2. We cannot "cancel" the factor $3x + 5$ from both sides of the original equation. Otherwise, we will lose the root $x = -\dfrac{5}{3}$.

Try It! 3

Solve the equation $2x(5x + 3) = 9(5x + 3)$.

EXERCISE 14.1

 BASICPRACTICE

1. Solve the following equations.
   (a) $x^2 - 14x + 24 = 0$
   (b) $x^2 + 13x - 30 = 0$
   (c) $2x^2 - 13x - 7 = 0$
   (d) $3x^2 - 10x + 8 = 0$
   (e) $5x^2 + 7x - 6 = 0$
   (f) $8x^2 + 10x + 3 = 0$
   (g) $15x^2 - 2x - 1 = 0$
   (h) $14x^2 - 29x = 15$
   (i) $9x^2 + 7x = 0$
   (j) $16x^2 + 40x + 25 = 0$

 FURTHERPRACTICE

2. Solve the following equations.
   (a) $4x^2 = 7(4x - 7)$
   (b) $x(x + 11) = 2(x + 5)$
   (c) $3x(2x + 5) = 4(2x + 5)$
   (d) $36 - 25x^2 = 0$
   (e) $(7x + 2)(2x - 3) = 5x - 6$
   (f) $(x + 1)^2 = 9(x + 1)$
   (g) $(2x - 1)^2 - 4(2x - 1) - 5 = 0$
   (h) $2(3x + 4)^2 - 5(3x + 4) + 3 = 0$
   (i) $(2y - 11)^2 = (3y + 4)^2$
   (j) $(2y + 9)^2 = 4(y - 2)^2$

 MATH@WORK

3. The sum of the areas of two squares is 269 cm². The side of one square is 3 cm longer than that of the other square. Find the length of a side of the smaller square.

x $x + 3$

4. The three sides of a right-angled triangle are $(x + 2)$ cm, $(2x + 3)$ cm and $(3x - 1)$ cm. Find the value of x.

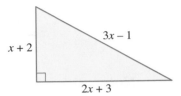

 BRAINWORKS

5. Peter solved the equation $(5x - 2)^2 = (2x + 1)^2$ as follows. Is his solution correct? Explain your answer.

$(5x - 2)^2 = (2x + 1)^2$
Taking square roots of both sides,
$5x - 2 = 2x + 1$
$3x = 3$
$\therefore\ x = 1.$

14.2 *Completing the Square Method*

When factorization fails to solve a quadratic equation, a more general method known as the **completing the square** method can be used to obtain its roots. This method is based on the fact that any quadratic equation may be written in the form $(x + p)^2 = q$, where p and q are real numbers.

Example 4

Solve the following equations.
(a) $(x + 3)^2 = 16$
(b) $(x - 2)^2 = 5$

Solution

(a) $(x + 3)^2 = 16$

$$x + 3 = \pm\sqrt{16}$$ 　　　　Take square root of both sides.

$$x + 3 = 4 \quad \text{or} \quad x + 3 = -4$$
$$\therefore \ x = 1 \quad \text{or} \qquad x = -7$$

Note: Since 16 is a perfect square, you can also bring it to the left-hand side and then factorize the expression $(x + 3)^2 - 16$ using the "difference of two squares" method.

(b) $(x - 2)^2 = 5$

$$x - 2 = \pm\sqrt{5}$$

$$x = \sqrt{5} + 2 \quad \text{or} \quad x = -\sqrt{5} + 2$$
$$\therefore \ x = 4.24 \qquad \text{or} \quad x = -0.236 \ \ \text{(rounded to 3 sig. fig.)}$$

RECALL

$a^2 - b^2 = (a + b)(a - b)$

Try It! 4

Solve the following equations.
(a) $(x - 1)^2 = 36$
(b) $(x + 4)^2 = 23$

Let us now learn an algebraic method that involves adding a term to the expression $x^2 + bx$ to make it a perfect square in order to solve the given quadratic equation. In other words, we need to find a constant c which, when added to $x^2 + bx$, will make $x^2 + bx + c$ a perfect square of the form $(x + p)^2$ for some real values of p.

Objective: To make $x^2 + bx$ a perfect square of the form $(x + p)^2$ for some real values of p.

Questions

1. Each of the following figures is made up of a square and two identical rectangles.
    (i) State the total area of **I**, **II** and **III**.
    (ii) To make the figure a square, draw the shape that should be added to the figure on the right. State the area of the shape that should be added to the original figure to make it a complete square,
    (iii) What is the area of the square thus formed?

(a)

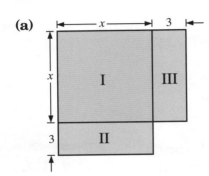 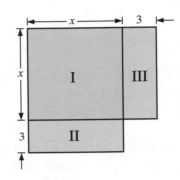

(i) Total area of **I**, **II** and **III** =

=

(ii) Complete the square by adding $\left(\right)^2$.

(iii) Area of the square =

$= \left(\right)^2$

(b)

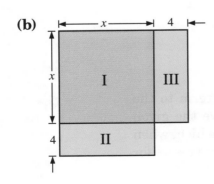 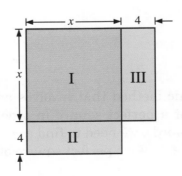

(i) Total area of **I**, **II** and **III** =

=

(ii) Complete the square by adding $\left(\right)^2$.

(iii) Area of the square =

$= ()^2$

(c)

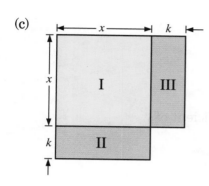 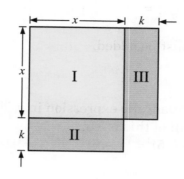

(i) Total area of **I**, **II** and **III** =

$=$

(ii) Complete the square by adding $\left(\right)^2$.

(iii) Area of the square =

$= ()^2$

2. Suppose the area of the given figure is $x^2 + bx$. To complete the square, you have added $(p)^2$ to it. What is the relationship between p and b?

In general, to make $x^2 + bx$ a perfect square, we add $\left(\dfrac{b}{2}\right)^2$ to it.

Thus,

$$x^2 + bx + \left(\frac{b}{2}\right)^2 = \left(x + \frac{b}{2}\right)^2$$

Notice that the quantity to be added is the **square of half the coefficient of x**, provided the **coefficient of x^2 is 1**.

Example **5**

Find the constant term that must be added to each of the following expressions to obtain a perfect square.

(a) $x^2 + 3x$,　　　　　　　　(b) $y^2 - 10y$

Solution

(a) $x^2 + 3x$

The coefficient of x is 3. Half of this is $\dfrac{3}{2}$.

$$x^2 + 3x + \left(\dfrac{3}{2}\right)^2 = \left(x + \dfrac{3}{2}\right)^2 \qquad a^2 + 2ab + b^2 = (a+b)^2$$

$\therefore$ $\left(\dfrac{3}{2}\right)^2$ must be added.

(b) $y^2 - 10y$

This is a quadratic expression in y. The coefficient of y is -10. Half of this is -5.

$$y^2 - 10y + (-5)^2 = (y - 5)^2 \qquad a^2 - 2ab + b^2 = (a-b)^2$$

Try It! 5

What constant term must be added to each of the following expressions to obtain a perfect square?

(a) $z^2 - z$,　　　　　　　　(b) $w^2 + \dfrac{4}{5}w$.

Solving a quadratic equation by making the expression $x^2 + bx$ a perfect square is called the **completing the square method**.

Example 6

Solve the equation $x^2 - x - 3 = 0$ using the completing the square method.

Solution

$$x^2 - x - 3 = 0$$
$$x^2 - x = 3 \qquad \text{\small{$b = -1$. Move the constant term to the RHS.}}$$
$$x^2 - x + \left(-\dfrac{1}{2}\right)^2 = 3 + \left(-\dfrac{1}{2}\right)^2 \qquad \text{\small{Add $\left(-\dfrac{1}{2}\right)^2$ to both sides.}}$$
$$\left(x - \dfrac{1}{2}\right)^2 = \dfrac{13}{4} \qquad \text{\small{Write the LHS as a perfect square.}}$$
$$x - \dfrac{1}{2} = \pm\sqrt{\dfrac{13}{4}} \qquad \text{\small{Take the square root of both sides.}}$$
$$\therefore\ x - \dfrac{1}{2} = -\dfrac{\sqrt{13}}{2} \quad \text{or} \quad x - \dfrac{1}{2} = \dfrac{\sqrt{13}}{2}$$
$$x = \dfrac{1}{2} - \dfrac{\sqrt{13}}{2} \quad \text{or} \quad x = \dfrac{1}{2} + \dfrac{\sqrt{13}}{2}$$
$$\therefore\ x = -1.30 \quad \text{or} \quad x = 2.30 \quad \text{(rounded to 3 sig. fig.)}$$

REMARKS

For any positive number k, if $y^2 = k$

then $y = -\sqrt{k}$ or $y = \sqrt{k}$.

Try It! 6

Solve the equation $x^2 - 3x - 5 = 0$ using the completing the square method.

Example 7

Solve the equation $3x^2 + 18x + 2 = 0$ by completing the square.

Solution

$3x^2 + 18x + 2 = 0$

$x^2 + 6x + \dfrac{2}{3} = 0$ Make the coefficient of x^2 to be 1.

$x^2 + 6x = -\dfrac{2}{3}$ $b = 6$.

$x^2 + 6x + \left(\dfrac{6}{2}\right)^2 = -\dfrac{2}{3} + \left(\dfrac{6}{2}\right)^2$ Add $\left(\dfrac{6}{2}\right)^2$ to both sides.

$x^2 + 6x + 3^2 = \dfrac{25}{3}$

$(x + 3)^2 = \dfrac{25}{3}$ Write LHS as a perfect square.

$x + 3 = \pm\sqrt{\dfrac{25}{3}}$

$x = -3 - \sqrt{\dfrac{25}{3}}$ or $x = -3 + \sqrt{\dfrac{25}{3}}$

$\therefore \ x = -5.89$ or $x = -0.113$

(rounded to 3 sig. fig.)

> **MATH BITS**
> A number in the form
> $a + b\sqrt{n}$, is called a **number in surd form**, where a and b are integers or fractions, $b \neq 0$, n is a positive integer and $\sqrt{n}$ is not an integer.

Try It! 7

Solve the equation $2x^2 - 9x + 6 = 0$ by completing the square.

EXERCISE 14.2

BASIC PRACTICE

1. Find the constant term that must be added to each of the following expressions to make it a perfect square.
   (a) $x^2 + 2x$
   (b) $x^2 - 4x$
   (c) $x^2 - 8x$
   (d) $x^2 + 7x$
   (e) $x^2 + x$
   (f) $x^2 - 11x$

2. Solve the following equations, giving your answers rounded to 3 significant figures.
   (a) $(x + 3)^2 = 49$ (b) $\left(x - \dfrac{5}{2}\right)^2 = \dfrac{9}{4}$
   (c) $(x + 4)^2 = 7$ (d) $(x - 3)^2 = 10$

3. Solve the following equations using the completing the square method, giving your answers rounded to 3 significant figures.
   (a) $x^2 + 10x - 3 = 0$ (b) $x^2 - 14x - 5 = 0$
   (c) $2x^2 + 7x + 2 = 0$ (d) $3x^2 - 36x + 20 = 0$

4. Solve the following equations using the completing the square method, giving your answers rounded to 2 decimal places.
   (a) $x^2 + 7x - 5 = 0$
   (b) $x^2 - x - 1 = 0$
   (c) $5x^2 + 30x - 18 = 0$
   (d) $3x^2 - 14x + 6 = 0$

 FURTHER PRACTICE

5. Solve the following equations using the completing the square method, giving your answers rounded to 3 significant figures.
   (a) $(x - 1)(x + 8) = 1 - 6x$
   (b) $(x - 4)^2 = 7x$
   (c) $6x^2 + 18x = 13$
   (d) $2x(x - 5) = 7(x + 1)$

 MATH@WORK

6. The cost of a square artwork of length x cm is $\$(x^2 + 4x)$. If one such artwork costs $300, what is its length?

 BRAIN WORKS

7. Find a quadratic equation whose roots are $2 - \sqrt{3}$ and $2 + \sqrt{3}$.

8. What can you say about the roots of the equation $(x - 1)^2 = -1$?

14.3 *Quadratic Formula*

We can use the completing the square method to derive a formula for the solution of any quadratic equation $ax^2 + bx + c = 0$, where a, b, and c are real numbers and $a \neq 0$.

$$ax^2 + bx + c = 0$$

$$x^2 + \frac{b}{a}x + \frac{c}{a} = 0 \qquad \text{Divide each term by } a \text{ so that the coefficient of } x^2 \text{ is 1.}$$

$$x^2 + \frac{b}{a}x = -\frac{c}{a} \qquad \text{Subtract } \frac{c}{a} \text{ from both sides.}$$

$$x^2 + \frac{b}{a}x + \left(\frac{b}{2a}\right)^2 = -\frac{c}{a} + \left(\frac{b}{2a}\right)^2 \qquad \text{Add } \left(\frac{b}{2a}\right)^2 \text{ to both sides.}$$

$$\left(x + \frac{b}{2a}\right)^2 = \frac{b^2 - 4ac}{4a^2} \qquad \text{Factorize the LHS and simplify the RHS.}$$

$$x + \frac{b}{2a} = \pm\sqrt{\frac{b^2 - 4ac}{4a^2}} \qquad \text{Take the square root of both sides.}$$

$$\therefore x = -\frac{b}{2a} - \frac{\sqrt{b^2 - 4ac}}{2a} \quad \text{or} \quad x = -\frac{b}{2a} + \frac{\sqrt{b^2 - 4ac}}{2a}$$

MATH WEB

Explore the applet on the quadratic formula at http://www.univie.ac.at/future.media/moe/galerie/gleich/gleich.html under Applet: Quadratic equations 1.

Thus, we have the **quadratic formula** as follows:

The roots of $ax^2 + bx + c = 0$ are $x = \dfrac{-b \pm \sqrt{b^2 - 4ac}}{2a}$, where a, b, and c are real numbers and $a \neq 0$.

Example 8

Solve the equation $3x^2 - 5x - 1 = 0$ using the quadratic formula, giving your answers rounded to 3 significant figures.

Solution

For the equation $3x^2 - 5x - 1 = 0$,

$a = 3$, $b = -5$, and $c = -1$.

$$\therefore \ x = \frac{-b \pm \sqrt{b^2 - 4ac}}{2a}$$

$$= \frac{-(-5) \pm \sqrt{(-5)^2 - 4(3)(-1)}}{2(3)}$$

Since $b = -5$, $-b = -(-5)$, and $b^2 = (-5)^2$ not -5^2.

$$= \frac{5 \pm \sqrt{37}}{6}$$

$\therefore \ x = 1.85$ or $x = -0.180$ (rounded to 3 sig. fig.)

Note: This quadratic equation has two **real and distinct roots**.

Try It! 8

Solve the equation $4x^2 + 7x - 3 = 0$, giving your answers rounded to 3 significant figures.

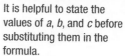
DISCUSS

What do you observe about the value of $b^2 - 4ac$, if the equation $ax^2 + bx + c = 0$ has real and equal roots?

Example 9

Solve the equation $(2x + 3)(2x + 9) = 2(2x + 1)$ using the quadratic formula.

Solution

We first convert the equation into the form $ax^2 + bx + c = 0$.

$(2x + 3)(2x + 9) = 2(2x + 1)$

$4x^2 + 24x + 27 = 4x + 2$

$4x^2 + 20x + 25 = 0$

Here, $a = 4$, $b = 20$ and $c = 25$.

$$\therefore \ x = \frac{-20 \pm \sqrt{20^2 - 4(4)(25)}}{2(4)}$$

$$= \frac{-20 \pm 0}{8}$$

$$= -\frac{5}{2}$$

$\therefore$ the equation has **equal or repeated roots** of $-2\frac{1}{2}$.

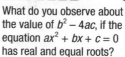

DISCUSS

What do you observe about the value of $b^2 - 4ac$, if the equation $ax^2 + bx + c = 0$ has real and equal roots?

Try It! 9

Solve the equation $(9x + 5)(x + 2) = -x - 6$ using the quadratic formula.

Example 10

Solve the equation $2x^2 + 7 = 3x$ using the quadratic formula.

Solution

$$2x^2 + 7 = 3x$$
$$2x^2 - 3x + 7 = 0$$

Here $a = 2$, $b = -3$, and $c = 7$.

$$\therefore\ x = \frac{-(-3) \pm \sqrt{(-3)^2 - 4(2)(7)}}{2(2)}$$

$$= \frac{3 \pm \sqrt{-47}}{4}$$

$\sqrt{-47}$ is not a real number.

$\therefore$ the equation has **no real roots**.

Note: When you enter $\sqrt{}$ $+/-$ 47 into your calculator and press $=$, you will get an error message.

DISCUSS

If an equation $ax^2 + bx + c = 0$ does not have real roots, what can you say about the value of $b^2 - 4ac$?

Try It! 10

Solve the equation $3x^2 + 11 = 5x$ using the quadratic formula.

Example 11

Solve the equation $\dfrac{3}{x-2} - \dfrac{x-3}{x+4} = 2$.

Solution

$$\frac{3}{x-2} - \frac{x-3}{x+4} = 2$$

Multiplying both sides by the common denominator the $(x-2)(x+4)$, we have

$$3(x + 4) - (x - 3)(x - 2) = 2(x - 2)(x + 4)$$
$$3x + 12 - x^2 + 5x - 6 = 2x^2 + 4x - 16$$
$$3x^2 - 4x - 22 = 0$$

Here, $a = 3$, $b = -4$ and $c = -22$.

$$\therefore\ x = \frac{-(-4) \pm \sqrt{(-4)^2 - 4(3)(-22)}}{2(3)}$$

$$= \frac{4 \pm \sqrt{280}}{6}$$

$\therefore\ x = 3.46$ or $x = -2.12$ (rounded to 3 sig. fig.)

Check:
When $x \approx 3.46$, the denominators
$x - 2 \approx 3.46 - 2 \neq 0$
$x + 4 \approx 3.46 + 4 \neq 0$.

When $x \approx -2.12$,
$x - 2 \approx -2.12 - 2 \neq 0$
$x + 4 \approx -2.12 + 4 \neq 0$
$\therefore$ the derived roots do not cause the 'division-by-zero' error.

Try It! 11

Solve the equation $\dfrac{x+2}{x} + \dfrac{1}{x+2} = 5$.

You have now learned four methods of solving quadratic equations. Which of these four methods can always be used to solve any quadratic equation?

EXERCISE 14.3

BASIC PRACTICE

1. Solve the following equations using the quadratic formula, giving your answers rounded to 2 decimal places.
   (a) $x^2 - 12x + 6 = 0$
   (b) $2x^2 + 6x + 1 = 0$
   (c) $3x^2 - 2x - 5 = 0$
   (d) $5x^2 - x + 4 = 0$
   (e) $7x^2 + x - 2 = 0$
   (f) $9 - 5x - 8x^2 = 0$

FURTHER PRACTICE

2. Solve the following equations using the quadratic formula, giving your answers rounded to 3 significant figures.
   (a) $2x(x - 2) = x + 8$
   (b) $(4x + 7)(x - 1) = 5x + 2$
   (c) $11 - (2x - 3)^2 = 0$
   (d) $x(1 - 2x) + 9 = 0$

3. Solve each of the following equations and state the type of roots it has.
   (a) $(x - 2)(x + 1) = 8$
   (b) $3x^2 - 4 = 7x$
   (c) $(x - 2)(x + 2) = 4(x - 2)$
   (d) $5x(x + 1) = 3(x - 2)$

4. Solve the following equations.
   (a) $\dfrac{4x - 1}{5} = \dfrac{x}{x + 3}$
   (b) $\dfrac{12}{x} - 4 = \dfrac{x}{2}$
   (c) $2 - \dfrac{x - 5}{x + 1} = \dfrac{2}{3x}$
   (d) $\dfrac{1}{x + 3} - \dfrac{4}{x - 3} = 5$

MATH@WORK

5. A ball is thrown from the top of a building. Its vertical distance, h metres, from the ground after time t seconds, is given by $h = 50 + 10t - 5t^2$.

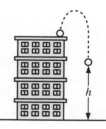

   (a) Find the height of the building.
   (b) When is the ball at the same level as the top of the building again?
   (c) When does the ball reach the ground?
   (d) When is the ball 30 m above the ground?

BRAIN WORKS

6. (a) Find the number of roots that can be obtained from the quadratic equation $ax^2 + bx + c = 0$.
   (b) How can you determine its number of roots without actually solving the equation?

14.4 Graphical Method

Some quadratic equations, such as $x^2 - x - 3 = 0$, cannot be solved by the factorization method. An alternative way is to solve these equations graphically, that is, by drawing their corresponding quadratic graphs.

Example 12 Solve the equation $x^2 - x - 3 = 0$ graphically, by drawing the graph of $y = x^2 - x - 3$ for $-3 \leqslant x \leqslant 3$.

Solution First, construct a table of values of $y = x^2 - x - 3$ for $-3 \leqslant x \leqslant 3$. Then draw the graph.

x	–3	–2	–1	0	1	2	3
y	9	3	–1	–3	–3	–1	3

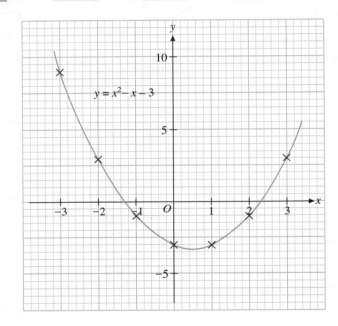

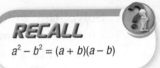

When the graph of $y = x^2 - x - 3$ **cuts the x-axis**, we have $y = 0$. That means $x^2 - x - 3 = 0$.

Therefore, the roots of the equation $x^2 - x - 3 = 0$ are the x-coordinates of the **points of intersection** of the graph of $y = x^2 - x - 3$ and the x-axis.

Hence, the required roots are

$$x \approx -1.3 \quad \text{or} \quad x \approx 2.3$$

Compare this solution with that in Example 6 for the same equation.

Note: When the graph of $y = ax^2 + bx + c$ cuts the x-axis at **two different points**, the equation $ax^2 + bx + c = 0$ is said to have two **distinct real roots**.

Solve the equation $x^2 + x - 4 = 0$ graphically for $-3 \leqslant x \leqslant 3$. Copy and complete the following table. Using a scale of 2 cm to 1 unit on the x-axis and 2 cm to 2 units on the y-axis, draw the graph of $y = x^2 + x - 4$.

x	−3	−2	−1	0	1	2	3
$y = x^2 + x - 4$							

Example 13

Solve the equation $x^2 - 2x + 1 = 0$ graphically, by drawing the graph of $y = x^2 - 2x + 1$ for $-2 \leqslant x \leqslant 4$.

Solution

Draw the graph of $y = x^2 - 2x + 1$.

x	−2	−1	0	1	2	3	4
y	9	4	1	0	1	4	9

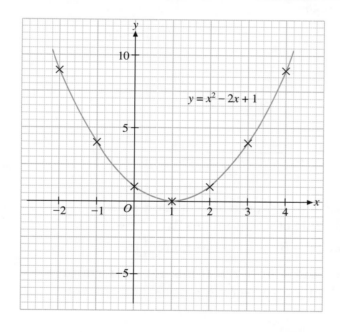

The graph of $y = x^2 - 2x + 1$ touches the x-axis at $x = 1$ only. Therefore, the root of the equation $x^2 - 2x + 1 = 0$ is

$$x = 1. \quad \longrightarrow \quad \text{The root is repeated.}$$

Note: When the graph of $y = ax^2 + bx + c$ **touches the** x**-axis** at one point only, the equation $ax^2 + bx + c = 0$ has **equal** or **repeated roots**.

Solve the equation $x^2 + 4x + 4 = 0$ graphically for $-5 \leqslant x \leqslant 1$. Copy and complete the following table. Draw the graph of $y = x^2 + 4x + 4$ using a scale of 2 cm to 1 unit on the x-axis and a scale of 2 cm to 2 units on the y-axis.

x	−5	−4	−3	−2	−1	0	1
$y = x^2 + 4x + 4$							

Example 14

Solve the equation $2x^2 - 5x + 7 = 0$ graphically, by drawing the graph of $y = 2x^2 - 5x + 7$ for $-1 \leqslant x \leqslant 4$.

Solution

x	−1	0	1	2	3	4
$y = 2x^2 - 5x + 7$	14	7	4	5	10	19

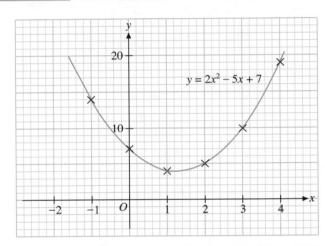

The graph of $y = 2x^2 - 5x + 7$ does not cut the x-axis.
∴ there is no real value of x that makes $2x^2 - 5x + 7 = 0$.
Thus, the equation $2x^2 - 5x + 7 = 0$ has no real roots.

We can also say, no real number x satisfies $2x^2 - 5x + 7 = 0$.

Note: An equation $ax^2 + bx + c = 0$ has **no real roots** if the graph of $y = ax^2 + bx + c$ **does not cut the** x**-axis.**

Try It! 14

Solve the equation $x^2 - x + 3 = 0$ graphically for $-2 \leqslant x \leqslant 3$. Copy and complete the following table. Draw the graph of $y = x^2 - x + 3$ using a scale of 2 cm to 1 unit on the x-axis and a scale of 2 cm to 2 units on the y-axis.

x	−2	−1	0	1	2	3
$y = x^2 - x + 3$						

BASIC PRACTICE

1. **(a)** Copy and complete the following table.

x	−3	−2	−1	0	1	2	3
$y = x^2 - 3$							

(b) Draw the graph of $y = x^2 - 3$ for $-3 \leqslant x \leqslant 3$.

(c) Hence solve the equation $x^2 - 3 = 0$ graphically.

2. **(a)** Copy and complete the following table.

x	−1	0	1	2	3	4	5
$y = x^2 - 4x + 4$							

(b) Draw the graph of $y = x^2 - 4x + 4$ for $-1 \leqslant x \leqslant 5$.

(c) Hence solve the equation $x^2 - 4x + 4 = 0$ graphically.

3. **(a)** Copy and complete the following table.

x	−3	−2	−1	0	1	2
$y = x^2 + x + 2$						

(b) Draw the graph of $y = x^2 + x + 2$ for $-3 \leqslant x \leqslant 2$.

(c) Hence solve the equation $x^2 + x + 2 = 0$ graphically.

 FURTHER PRACTICE

4. **(a)** Draw the graph of $y = x^2 - 2x - 3$ for $-2 \leqslant x \leqslant 4$.

(b) Hence, solve the equation $x^2 - 2x - 3 = 0$ graphically.

5. **(a)** Draw the graph of $y = 2x^2 + 5x - 1$ for $-3 \leqslant x \leqslant 2$.

(b) Hence, solve the equation $2x^2 + 5x - 1 = 0$ graphically.

6. **(a)** Draw the graph of $y = 3x^2 - 2x + 4$ for $-2 \leqslant x \leqslant 3$.

(b) Hence, solve the equation $3x^2 - 2x + 4 = 0$ graphically.

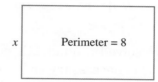 **MATH@WORK**

7. The length of one side of a rectangle is x units and the perimeter is 8 units.

x	Perimeter = 8

(a) Find the length of the other side of the rectangle.

(b) Show that the area, A square units, of the rectangle is $A = x(4 - x)$.

(c) Draw the graph of the function $A = x(4 - x)$ for $0 < x < 4$ on a sheet of graph paper.

(d) Hence, find the size of the rectangle when it has the largest area.

 BRAIN WORKS

8. Can the quadratic equation $6 - 2x - x^2 = 0$ be solved by the graphical method? If so, illustrate the steps and find the roots.

9. **(a)** Draw the graph of $y = x^2 - 3x$ for $-2 \leqslant x \leqslant 5$.

(b) Solve graphically the equation $x^2 - 3x = 0$.

(c) Can you use the graph in **(a)** to solve the equation $x^2 - 3x - 4 = 0$ without drawing another quadratic graph? If so, illustrate your method and find the roots of the equation.

(*Hint*: You may consider inserting the graph of a suitable straight line on the same grid.)

14.5 *Applications of Quadratic Equations*

Quadratic equations can be applied to solve real world problems. We can follow similar steps used to solve linear equation problems to solve quadratic equation problems.

- Identify and use a letter (e.g. x) to represent the unknown quantity to be found in a problem.
- Express other quantities in terms of this letters.
- Form the quadratic equation based on the given information.
- Solve the equation.
- Write the answer statement.

After we have solved a quadratic equation relating the unknown quantity of a problem, it is necesssary that we check if the two roots obtained satisfy the original problem. For example, if the original problem requires positive integer solutions, then we need to reject the negative roots and fractional roots.

Example 15

A rectangular cardboard measures 28 cm by 20 cm. A picture of area 300 cm^2 is pasted on the cardboard leaving a border of uniform width on all four sides. Find the width of the border.

Solution

Let x cm be the width of the border.

Then, length of the picture = $(28 - 2x)$ cm,
width of the picture = $(20 - 2x)$ cm.

As area of the picture = 300 cm^2,

we have $(28 - 2x)(20 - 2x) = 300$
$$560 - 96x + 4x^2 = 300$$
$$4x^2 - 96x + 260 = 0$$
$$x^2 - 24x + 65 = 0$$
$$x = \frac{-(-24) \pm \sqrt{(-24)^2 - 4(1)(65)}}{2(1)}$$
$$= \frac{24 \pm \sqrt{316}}{2}$$
$$= 3.11 \quad \text{or} \quad 20.9 \quad \text{(rejected)}$$
$$\therefore \ x = 3.11 \quad \text{(rounded to 3 sig. fig.)}$$

Hence, the width of the border is 3.11 cm.

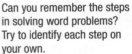

RECALL

Can you remember the steps in solving word problems? Try to identify each step on your own.

Note: The width of the border should be less than half of the width of the cardboard, i.e. 10 cm. Therefore, the root $x = 20.9$ is rejected.

Try It! 15

A rectangular swimming pool measures 20 m by 16 m. A path of uniform width is built around the pool. If the area of the path is 100 m², find the width of the path, giving your answer rounded to 3 significant figures.

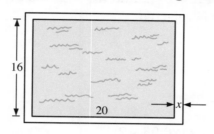

Example 16

PQR is a triangular plot of land in which angle PRQ is a right angle. The lengths of the three sides PQ, PR, and RQ, are $(2x + 1)$ meters, $(x - 2)$ meters, and $(2x - 5)$ meters respectively.

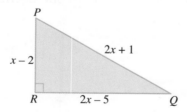

(a) Form an equation involving x and show that it reduces to $x^2 - 28x + 28 = 0$.

(b) Solve this equation, giving your answers rounded to one decimal place.

(c) Hence find the area of the triangular plot PQR.

Solution

(a) Applying Pythagorean Theorem to right-angled $\triangle PQR$, we have

$$PR^2 + RQ^2 = PQ^2.$$
$$(x - 2)^2 + (2x - 5) = (2x + 1)^2$$
$$x^2 - 4x + 4 + 4x^2 - 20x + 25 = 4x^2 + 4x + 1$$
$$x^2 - 28x + 28 = 0$$

Thus, we obtain the equation $x^2 - 28x + 28 = 0$.

RECALL

The longest side of a right-angled triangle is its hypotenuse.

(b) $x^2 - 28x + 28 = 0$

$$x = \frac{-(-28) \pm \sqrt{(-28)^2 - 4(1)(28)}}{2(1)}$$

$$= \frac{28 \pm \sqrt{672}}{2}$$

≈ 26.96 or   1.039

$= 27.0$ or   1.0   (correct to 1 d.p.)

(c) When $x = 1.0$, lengths $PR = x - 2$ and $RQ = 2x - 5$ are negative. Thus, $x = 1.0$ is rejected.

∴ Area of $\triangle PQR$

$= \frac{1}{2} \times RQ \times PR$

$= \frac{1}{2} \times (2x - 5) \times (x - 2)$

$= \frac{1}{2} \times (2 \times 26.96 - 5) \times (26.96 - 2)$ Substitute $x = 26.96$

$= 610.5 \text{ m}^2$ (correct to 1 d.p.)

Try It! **16**   The sides of a right-angled triangle are $(x - 4)$ cm, $(x - 2)$ cm, and $(x - 1)$ cm.

(a) Form an equation involving x and show that it simplifies to $x^2 - 10x + 19 = 0$.

(b) Solve this equation to find the perimeter of the triangle, giving your answers rounded to one decimal place.

EXERCISE 14.5

 BASICPRACTICE

1. The product of two consecutive positive integers is 1260. Find the integers.

2. The sum of the squares of two consecutive positive odd numbers is 650. Find the numbers.

3. The height of a triangle is 5 cm shorter than its base. The area of the triangle is 228 cm². Find the base of the triangle.

4. The perimeter of a rectangle is 68 cm and its area is 253 cm². Suppose the length of the rectangle is x cm,
   (a) express the width of the rectangle in terms of x,
   (b) find the dimensions of the rectangle.

5. The sides of a right-angled triangle are $3x$ cm, $(3x - 2)$ cm, and $(x - 5)$ cm.
   (a) Use Pythagorean Theorem to form an equation involving x.
   (b) Solve the equation, giving both answers rounded to two decimal places.
   (c) Hence find the area of the triangle.

6. The sum of Jack's and his father's ages is 34 years. In 4 years' time, the square of Jack's age will be equal to his father's age. Find Jack's present age.

7. A piece of wire is 76 in. long. It is cut into two pieces of different lengths and each piece is bent into a square. The sum of the areas of the two squares is 205 square inches. Find the length of the shorter piece of the wire.

FURTHER PRACTICE

8. The sum of the squares of three consecutive positive even numbers is 2360. Find the smallest number.

9. On a 21 cm by 29 cm rectangular sheet of paper, the typing area is a rectangle of area 380 cm². There are margins of equal width on all four sides of the paper. Find the width of each margin, giving your answer rounded to the nearest 0.1 cm.

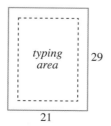

10. At noon, Ada left junction T and walked due north. At 1.00 p.m., Bob left junction T and walked due east. Both of them walked at a speed of 4 km/h. At what time would they be 10 km apart? Give your answer rounded to the nearest minute.

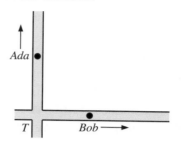

11. A pole AB, 65 feet long, leans against a vertical wall. Its lower end B is 25 feet from the wall. When it slides down to the position DE, it is found that $AD = BE$. Find the length of
   (a) AC,   (b) AD.

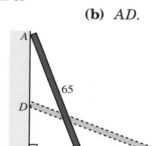

12. The distance between two stations, A and B, is 100 miles. If the average speed of a train is increased by 5 mph, the time taken by the train to travel from A to B would be 10 minutes less. Find the original average speed of the train, giving your answer rounded to 3 significant figures.

MATH @ WORK

13. The distance s metres traveled by a car in time t seconds is given by

$$s = 3t^2 + 4t.$$

Find the time taken for the car to travel 100 m, giving your answer rounded to 3 significant figures.

14.

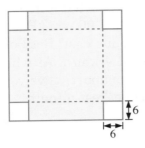

6

6

The figure shows a square cardboard. A 6-cm square is cut from each of its corners and the remaining figure is then folded along the dotted lines to form a square tray. If the volume of the tray is 2,000 cm^3, find the length of a side of the cardboard, rounded to 3 significant figures.

15. A tank holds 50 litres of water. Tap A can fill the tank with x liters of water per minute and tap B fills the tank with $(x + 0.5)$ liters per minute.

(a) Find, in terms of x, the number of minutes it takes
   (i) tap A to fill the tank completely,
   (ii) tap B to fill the tank completely.

(b) If it takes tap A four minutes longer than tap B to fill the tank, form an equation involving x.

(c) Solve the equation, giving your solutions rounded to 2 decimal places.

(d) Find the time taken, in minutes and seconds, rounded to the nearest second, for tap A to fill the tank completely.

16. A store owner has 80 copies of a computer game. Based on past experience, if the price is set at $60 per copy, all of them will be sold. For each $5 increase in price, an additional 4 copies of the game will be unsold.

(a) If the price is set at $70 per copy,
   (i) find the number of copies that will be sold,
   (ii) find the total sales amount.

(b) If the total sales amount is $5,100, find the price per copy of the game.

(c) What should the price per copy be in order to get the maximum total sales amount?

[Assume that the price per copy of the game is a multiple of 5 in (b) and (c).]

Solution of Quadratic Equations

(a) Factorization method

$$ax^2 + bx + c = 0$$

By factorization,

$$(px + q)(rx + s) = 0$$

$$x = -\frac{q}{p} \quad \text{or} \quad x = -\frac{s}{r}$$

(b) Completing the Square method

$$x^2 + bx + c = 0$$

By completing the square,

$$\left(x + \frac{b}{2}\right)^2 = q$$

$$x + \frac{b}{2} = \pm\sqrt{q}$$

$$\therefore \ x = -\frac{b}{2} \pm \sqrt{q}$$

When $q < 0$, there are no real roots.

(c) Quadratic formula

The roots of $ax^2 + bx + c = 0$ are:

$$x = \frac{-b \pm \sqrt{b^2 - 4ac}}{2a}$$

When $b^2 - 4ac < 0$, there are no real roots.

(d) Graphical method

By drawing the graph of $y = ax^2 + bx + c$.

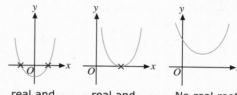

| real and different roots | real and equal roots | No real roots |

Fractional Equations

$$\frac{A}{x - p} + \frac{B}{x - q} = C$$

$$\left(\frac{A}{x - p} + \frac{B}{x - q}\right)(x - p)(x - q) = C(x - p)(x - q)$$

$$A(x - q) + B(x - p) = C(x - p)(x - q)$$

- Both sides of the fractional equation are multiplied by their common denominator.
- Fractional equations reducible to quadratic equations are rewritten in the form $ax^2 + bx + c = 0$.
- Ensure that the roots of the quadratic equation do not give rise to 'division-by-zero' error in the original equation. If this happens, we need to reject that value.

In this exercise, give your answers rounded to 3 significant figures where applicable.

1. Solve the following equations by factorization.
  (a) $2x^2 + x - 15 = 0$
  (b) $3x^2 - 20x - 7 = 0$
  (c) $9x^2 - 25 = 0$
  (d) $(x + 3)(x - 2) = 5x(x - 2)$

2. Solve the following equations by the method of completing the square.
  (a) $x^2 - 6x + 4 = 0$
  (b) $x^2 + 4x - 3 = 0$
  (c) $x^2 + 5x + 8 = 0$
  (d) $x^2 - 7x - 2 = 0$

3. **(a)** Draw the graph of $y = x^2 + 3x - 6$ for $-5 \leqslant x \leqslant 2$.
  (b) Use your graph to solve the equation $x^2 + 3x - 6 = 0$.

4. Solve the following equations using the quadratic formula.
  (a) $x^2 + 3x - 80 = 0$
  (b) $36x^2 + 12x - 1 = 0$
  (c) $4x^2 - 5x + 9 = 0$
  (d) $5x^2 - 8x - 2 = 0$

5. Solve the following fractional equations.
  (a) $\dfrac{x + 1}{2} = \dfrac{18}{x + 1}$
  (b) $10(x - 2) + \dfrac{10}{x - 2} = 29$
  (c) $\dfrac{x}{x + 1} + \dfrac{x + 1}{x} = 3$
  (d) $\dfrac{3}{7x - 2} - \dfrac{2}{7x + 3} = \dfrac{3}{4}$

6. Solve the following equations.
  (a) $3x^2 + 7x + 1 = 0$
  (b) $(2x - 1)^2 = (x + 1)^2$
  (c) $(x + 3)(2x - 9) = x(x + 2)$
  (d) $\dfrac{1}{3x} + \dfrac{2}{3x - 1} + \dfrac{3}{3x + 1} = 0$

7. A rectangular flower bed measures 30 m by 20 m. It is surrounded by a path of uniform width. The area of the path is $\frac{1}{3}$ of the area of the flower bed. Find the width of the path.

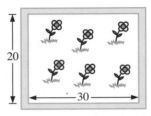

8. The distance traveled by a train is 180 miles. If the average speed of the train is increased by 10 mph, the time taken by the train would be 30 minutes less. Find the train's average speed.

9. **(a)** Factorize $6v^2 + 11v - 10$.
  (b) Hence, or otherwise, solve the equation $6(x + 4)^2 + 11(x + 4) - 10 = 0$.

10. A rectangle is 24 in. long and 17 in. wide. When its length decreases by x in. and its width increases by x in., its area is increased by 12 square inches.
  (a) Express, in terms of x,
    (i) the new length,
    (ii) the new width,
    (iii) the new area of the rectangle.
  (b) Find the value of x.

11. Two rectangular garden plots, A and B, each have an area of 16 m^2. The length of rectangle A is x m and that of rectangle B is 2 m more. If the width of rectangle A is 3 m more than the width of rectangle B,
  (a) find the width of rectangle B,
  (b) which garden plot has a greater perimeter?

12. (a) When a car is driven in town, it runs x miles on each gallon of gasoline.

    (i) Find, in terms of x, the number of gallons of gasoline used when the car is driven 200 miles in town.

    (ii) When driven out of town, the car runs $(x + 7)$ miles on each gallon of gasoline. It uses 2 gallons less gasoline to go 200 miles out of town than to go 200 miles in town. Use this information to form an equation involving x.

(b) Solve the equation, giving your answers correct to two decimal places.

(c) What is the total amount of gasoline used when the car is driven 30 miles in town and 270 miles out of town?

EXTEND YOUR LEARNING CURVE

Sum and Product of Roots

It is given that α and β are the roots of a quadratic equation $ax^2 + bx + c = 0$.

The sum of the roots, $\alpha + \beta$, and the product of the roots, $\alpha\beta$, can be expressed in terms of the coefficients a and b, and the constant c. Find the expressions for $\alpha + \beta$ and $\alpha\beta$ in terms of a, b and/or c.

WRITE IN YOUR JOURNAL

You have learned four methods of solving quadratic equations. Which method do you find easiest to use and which do you find most challenging? Write about the ease or difficulty that you encountered in using those methods.

ANSWERS

Chapter 8   Graphs of Linear and Quadratic Functions

Try It!

1. (a)

x	0	2	4	6
y	24	16	8	0

(c) $y = 24 - 4x$

2. (b) 50; speed in km/hr

(c) 0

(d) $y = 50x$

3. (a) −0.4 L/hr; 0.4 L of water leaves the container every hour.

(b) initial amount of water in the container

(c) 2.4 L

4. (b) 3 cm   **(c)** $x = 3$

(d) 1 cm

5. (a) 2 m   **(c)** 1.47 s

(d) 0.2 s, 1 s   **(e)** $t = 0.6$

(f) 3.8 m

Exercise 8.1

1. (a) (0, 3), (2, 5), (4, 7), (6, 9)

(c) $y = x + 3$

2. (a)

x	0	1	3	5
y	0	2	6	10

(c) $y = 2x$

3. (a)

x	−2	−1	0	1	2
y	2	1	0	−1	−2

(b) (−2, 2), (−1, 1), (0, 0), (1, −1), (2, −2)

(c) $y = -x$

4. (a)

x	−3	−1	0	3
y	−7	−3	−1	5

(b) (−3, 7), (−1, −3), (0, −1), (3, 5)

5. (a) (i) Yes; 50   **(ii)** No

(b) (i) No   **(ii)** Yes; 15

6. (a)

x	−4	−2	0	2
$y = -\frac{1}{2}x + 3$	5	4	3	2

(c) slope $= -\frac{1}{2}$; y-intercept $= 3$

(d) decreasing function

7. (a) $P = 4x$; linear function

(b) $A = x^2$; non-linear function

8. (b) non-linear function; rate of change is not constant

9. (b) \$4/km; Martin raised \$4 for every km ran.

(c) increasing function

(d) 0

(e) $y = 4x$

10. (b) −9 °C/hr; The temperature of the tea drops by −9 °C every hour.

(c) decreasing function

(d) 96

(e) $y = -9x + 96$

11. (b) same y-intercept; y-intercept $= 2$

12. (b) same slope; slope $= -2$

13. (a)

x	1	2	3	4
y	70	110	150	190

(b) $y = 40x + 30$

(d) \$130

14. (a)

x	1,000	1,300	1,600	2,000
y	1,000	700	400	0

(b) $y = 2,000 - x$

(c) decreasing function

15. (a)

x	0	1	3	5
y	400	320	160	0

(c) $y = -80x + 400$

(d) after 5 years

16. (a)

x	1	3	5	10
y	26,000	38,000	50,000	80,000

(b) $y = 6,000x + 20,000$

(d) 8,000

Exercise 8.2

1. (a)

x	−3	−2	−1	0	1	2	3
$y = x^2 - 4$	5	0	−3	−4	−3	0	5

(c) $x = 0$; (0, −4)

2. (a)

x	−4	−3	−2	−1	0	1	2
$y = x^2 + 2x + 1$	9	4	1	0	1	4	9

(c) $x = -1$; (−1, 0)

(d) (−1, 0); x-intercept

3. (a)

x	–1	0	1	2	3	4	5
$y = -\frac{1}{2}x^2 + 2x$	–2.5	0	1.5	2	1.5	0	–2.5

(c) $x = 2$; (2, 2)

(d) (0, 0), (4, 0)

4. (a)

x	–5	–4	–3	–2	–1	0	1
$y = -3x^2 - 18x - 32$	–17	–8	–5	–8	–17	–32	–53

(c) $x = -3$; (–3, –5)

(d) –32

(e) 0

5. (a) (i) $x = -2$

　　(ii) minimum point; (–2, 1)

　　(iii) –4, 0

　　(iv) 0

　(b) **(i)** $x = 1.5$

　　(ii) minimum point; (1.5, 2.5)

　　(iii) none

　　(iv) 7

　(c) **(i)** $x = -0.5$

　　(ii) maximum point; (–0.5, 6.25)

　　(iii) –3, 2

　　(iv) 6

　(d) **(i)** $x = 0.75$

　　(ii) maximum point; (0.75, –1.875)

　　(iii) none

　　(iv) –3

6. $\left(\frac{1}{2}, -1\right)$ is above the graph; $\left(\frac{3}{2}, -3\right)$ is on the graph

7. (a) $A = -x^2 + 4x + 21$　　(c) $x = 2$; 25 m²

8. (a) 3 s　　　　　　　　(c) 1.5 m

　(d) 0.694 s, 2.31 s

9. (b) 2 m　　　　　　　　(c) 3 m

　(d) $x = 1$

10. (b) 10 chairs

　(c) 7, 8, 9, 10, 11, 12, 13

11. (a) When $0 < |a| < 1$, the parabola appears wider. When $|a| > 1$, the parabola appears thinner. When a is positive, the parabola opens upwards. When a is negative, the parabola appears downward. Changing a affects the shape of the parabola.

　(b) Changing b affects the location of the minimum/maximum point with respect to the y-axis. When $b = 0$, the minimum/maximum point lies on the y-axis. Changing b does not affect the shape of the parabola. Making b positive or negative only reflects the parabola across the y-axis.

　(c) Changing c affects the vertical shift of the graph. When $c > 0$, the graph shifts up c units. When $c < 0$, the graph shifts down c units.

Review Exercise 8

1. (a) (i) (1, 1), (3, 5), (5, 9), (7, 13), (9, 17)

　　(ii) $y = 2x - 1$

　(b) slope = –2; y-intercept = –1

2. (b) 16 miles/hr

　(c) The cyclist covered 16 miles in an hour.

　(d) $y = \frac{8}{30}x$

3. (b) \$0.035/min; A one minute call costs \$0.035.

　(c) 13.5; cost to maintain cell phone plan

　(d) $y = 0.035x + 13.5$

4. (a) 12,000

　(b)

x	0	1	2	3	4	5
y	80,000	68,000	56,000	44,000	32,000	20,000

　(c) $y = -12,000x + 80,000$

5. (a) $m = 2.5$; $b = -100$　　(c) \$40

6. (b) (3, –2)　　　　　　　　(c) 1.2, 4.8

7. (b) $x = -1.5$, (–1.5, 0.5)

　(c) (–2.5, 2.5) lies on the graph; (0.5, 9.5) lies below the graph.

8. (b) (i) 60 m　　　　　　**(ii)** 80 m

　　(iii) 6 s

9. (a) $b = 3$; $c = -4$

　(c) **(i)** $x = -1.5$　　　　**(ii)** (–1.5, –6.25)

10. (b) 4

　(c) 65; The cost of the workmanship is \$65.

Chapter 9　Graphs in Practical Situations

Try It!

1. (a) (i) 2,170 mi　　　　**(ii)** 1,890 mi

　(b) 6 mi

2. (b) (i) 14.5 km　　　　**(ii)** 3 mi

　(c) 1.61

　(d) $y = 1.61x$

3. (a) 3 hr 45 min　　　　(b) 07:38

　(c) 10 km　　　　　　　　(d) 1 hr

　(e) 32 km/hr

　(f) 8.30 A.M. to 9.00 A.M.; 40 km/hr

　(g) 16 km/hr

4. (a) Jane traveled from P to Q at a uniform speed of 20 km/hr in the first hour, rested for the next 20 minutes and traveled from Q to P at a uniform speed of 30 km/hr for the next 40 minutes.

　(b) 20 km/hr

　(c) **(ii)** 10.40 A.M.

　　(iii) 10.26 A.M.; 16.5 km away from P

5. (a) 160 km

　(b) **(i)** 8 km/s　**(ii)** 16 km/s　**(iii)** $11\frac{3}{7}$ km/s

Exercise 9.1

1. **(b)** **(i)** 11 lb   **(ii)** 6.8 kg
2. **(a)** 0, 0, 0, 0
   (b) **(i)** 83 km   **(ii)** 114 km
   (iii) 46 km   **(iv)** 120 km
3. **(a)** $6.47, $6.38, $6.49, $6.38
   (b) Cliff
   (i) 32   **(ii)** 50   **(iii)** 26.6
4. **(c)** $y = 1.8x + 32$
5. **(b)** **(i)** $16   **(ii)** $3   **(iii)** $2
   (c) $y = 2x + 3$
6. **(a)** **(i)** $27,000   **(ii)** after 4 years
   (b) **(i)** 37%   **(ii)** 14%
   (c) 70%
7. **(b)** **(i)** US$44.20   **(ii)** 27.70 euros
   (c) $y = 1.26375x$
8. **(a)** **(i)** $20   **(ii)** $20   **(iii)** $23.20
9. **(a)**

Rack	Hammer	Chisel	Saw	Pliers	Total
A	4	12	5	2	23
B	9	6	8	11	34
C	10	7	14	12	43
Total	23	25	27	25	

   (b) 100

Exercise 9.2

1. **(a)** 42 km   **(b)** 9.00 A.M.; 30 min
   (c) 8.00 A.M. to 9.00 A.M.; 30 km/hr
2. **(a)** **(i)** 20 km/hr   **(ii)** 0 km/hr
   (iii) $13\frac{1}{3}$ km/hr
3. **(a)** **(i)** 5 km/hr   **(ii)** $3\frac{1}{3}$ km/hr
   (b) 4 km/hr
   (c) Mrs. Brown traveled from P to Q at a uniform speed of 5 km/hr and returned to P at a uniform speed of $3\frac{1}{3}$ km/hr.
4. **(a)** $\frac{1}{2}$ hr   **(b)** $45\frac{5}{7}$ km/hr
   (c) **(ii)** after 2 hr 21 min; 56 km away from P
5. **(a)** Clark was given a 50 m lead
   (b) $8\frac{1}{3}$ m/s
   (c) after 18 s; 150 m from the starting point
   (d) Jordan; 3 s
6. **(a)** 5 m/s
   (b) The speed of the cart is decreasing; 3 m/s
   (c) 4 m/s
7. **(a)** 20 min   **(c)** 75 km/hr

8. Ben left his office at 5 p.m. and drove at a uniform speed of 40 km/hr for 15 minutes to deliver a parcel. Then, he drove back to his office at a uniform speed of 40 km/hr for the next 15 minutes, fetched his colleague, and drove to the cinema in 15 minutes at a uniform speed of 100 km/hr. They spent the rest of the evening watching a show that lasted 1 hour and 15 minutes.

9. **(b)** **(i)** 2.5 m/s   **(ii)** 3.125 m/s

Review Exercise 9

1. **(a)** **(i)** S$46   **(ii)** US$39
   (b) US$1 = S$1.28
2. **(a)** 0.70, 1.1, 1.5, 1.7, 1.9. 2.4, 2.9
   (c) 14 min
3. **(a)** **(i)** Chicago, Honolulu, Seattle, Vancouver
   (ii) Sydney, Tokyo, Auckland
   (b) **(i)** 1 hour ahead   **(ii)** 9 hours behind
   (iii) 22 hours behind
   (c) 1 A.M., Tuesday
   (d) No, it will be 8 P.M. in Seattle.
4. **(a)** **(i)** 0 km/hr   **(ii)** $13\frac{1}{3}$ km/hr
   (b) $13\frac{1}{3}$ km/hr   **(c)** 9.5 km away
5. **(a)** **(i)** 150 m/min   **(ii)** 100 m/min
   (b) 125 m/min
   (c) 200 m
   (d) Peter
   (e) They met at time = 2 min, 300 m from Mary's home and again at time = 6.8 min, 880 m from Mary's home.
   (f) 200 m
6. **(a)** $t_1 = 10, t_2 = 25, t_3 = 45$
   (b) 25 km away
   (c) 45 min
   (d) 100 km/hr

Chapter 10   Pythagorean Theorem

Try It!

1. 13 in.
2. 15 cm
3. **(a)** 9.75 cm   **(b)** 20.5 cm
4. **(a)** No   **(b)** Yes
5. 5.83 cm
6. 2.28 m
7. 37.8 m
8. 2.23 in.

Exercise 10.1

1. (a) 10 cm   (b) 29 cm
   (c) 35 cm   (d) 10 cm
2. 41 in.
3. 60 cm
4. 6.32 ft
5. (a) 3.16 cm   (b) 3.74 cm
6. (a) 4 m   (b) 7.21 m
7. (a) 17.4 m   (b) 36.4 m
8. (a) 17 cm   (b) 34 cm
   (c) 38.0 cm
9. 18.4 cm
10. (a) 8.49 cm   (b) 72 cm^2
11. (b) $a - b$ (c) $0.5ab$
    (d) $a^2 + b^2$ (e) c^2
12. (a) $b_3 = 24$, $c_4 = 41$
    (b) $a_5 = 11$, $b_5 = 60$, $c_5 = 61$
    (c) $c_n = b_n + 1$
    (d) $a_n = 2n + 1$, $b_n = 2n^2 + 2n$, $c_n = 2n^2 + 2n + 1$

Exercise 10.2

1. (a) Yes; $\angle ABC$ (b) No
   (c) Yes; $\angle GHK$ (d) Yes; $\angle QPR$
2. (a) Yes   (b) No
   (c) Yes   (d) No
3. $\angle ABC$ and $\angle ADC$ are right angles.
4. (a) $PQ = 15$ cm, $RQ = 20$ cm
   (b) Yes
5. 12.5 ft
6. (a) (i) 13 cm   (ii) 19.5 cm
       (iii) 23.4 cm
   (b) Yes
7. (a) $z^2 = a^2 + b^2$
   (b) Yes
   (d) $\angle C = 90°$, $\triangle ABC$ is a right-angled triangle.
   (e) We can conclude that such a triangle is a right-angled triangle.
8. CA is not perpendicular to AB since $56^2 + 33^2 \neq 64^2$.
9. (a) Yes   (b) 630 m^2
   (c) 23.8 m
10. (b) $OC = 1\frac{2}{3}$ m, $OD = 3\frac{1}{3}$ m
    (c) 3.73 m
11. Point P is 4 cm to the right of point D.

Exercise 10.3

1. 3.06 m
2. 3.4 m
3. 2.39 cm
4. 14.1 cm
5. (a) 8.66 cm   (b) 43.4 cm^2

6. 2.24 m
7. (a) 12.7 cm   (b) 12 m
   (c) 114 m^2
8. 9.56 m
9. 22.9 m
10. (a) 2.77 m   (b) 0.99 m
11. Possible answers:
    $AC = 10\sqrt{2}$, $BC = 10\sqrt{2}$;
    $AC = 8\sqrt{5}$, $BC = 4\sqrt{5}$;
12. (a) Possible answers:
       $AP = 2$ cm, $PB = 14.9$ cm;
       $AP = 5$ cm, $PB = 14.1$ cm;
       $AP = 10$ cm, $PB = 11.2$ cm
    (c) Semicircle

Review Exercise 10

1. (a) 6.71 cm   (b) 18.3 cm
   (c) 24 cm   (d) 12.0 cm
2. (a) $x = 4$ ft, $y = 8.06$ ft
   (b) $x = 3.32$ ft, $y = 4.47$ ft
3. (a) 5.66 cm   (b) 4 cm
4. 84.9 ft
5. (a) Yes, $\angle C$ (b) No
6. (a) 8 cm
7. (a) 17.2 cm   (b) 9.00 cm
   (c) 19.4 cm
8. (a) 10   (b) 240 cm^2
   (c) 9.23 cm
9. (a) 17.9 miles   (b) 14.7 miles
   (c) 46.1 miles
10. (a) 8   (b) 56 cm
11. (a) 42 cm^2

Chapter 11   Coordinate Geometry
Try It!

1. (a) $PQ = \sqrt{13}$ units, $QR = \sqrt{52}$ units, $PR = \sqrt{117}$ units
2. (a) $PQ = \sqrt{40}$ units, $QR = \sqrt{50}$ units, $RP = \sqrt{10}$ units.
   (c) 16.6 units
   (d) 10 units^2
3. (a) -3 (b) $-\frac{1}{3}$
   (c) $1\frac{1}{2}$
4. (a) $-\frac{1}{2}$ (b) $T(4, 0)$
5. (a) 0   (b) undefined
6. (a) $y = \frac{2}{5}x$ (b) $y = -7x + 8$
   (c) $y = -\frac{1}{2}x + 3$

7. (a) $y = -x + 1$ (b) $y = 5$

8. (a) $y = \frac{2}{3}x + \frac{4}{3}$

   (b) slope $= \frac{2}{3}$, y-intercept $= \frac{4}{3}$

Exercise 11.1

1. (a) 4 units   (b) 8 units
   (c) 5 units   (d) 13 units
   (e) $\sqrt{26}$ units   (f) $\sqrt{41}$ units

2. (a) $\sqrt{50}$ units   (b) 10 units^2

3. (a) (i) $AB = \sqrt{5}$ units, $BC = \sqrt{5}$ units, $AC = \sqrt{20}$ units
      (ii) Points A, B and C lie on a straight line.
   (b) (i) $AB = \sqrt{17}$ units, $BC = \sqrt{5}$ units, $AC = \sqrt{40}$ units
      (ii) Points A, B and C do not lie on a straight line.

4. (a) $AB = 4$ units, $BC = \sqrt{17}$ units, $AC = 5$ units
   (b) 13.1 units
   (c) 8 units^2

5. (a) $PQ = \sqrt{85}$ units, $QR = \sqrt{17}$ units, $RP = \sqrt{68}$ units
   (b) 21.6 units
   (c) 17 units^2

6. $k = -1$, $k = 5$

7. $C(3, 1)$

8. (a) 10 units
   (b) circumference $= 20\pi$ units, area $= 100\pi$ units^2

9. (c) parallelogram
   (d) 26.7 units

10. Possible answers: $(-4, 2)$, $(-2, 6)$

Exercise 11.2

1. (a) 1   (b) -1
   (c) undefined   (d) 0
   (e) $\frac{4}{5}$ (f) -2
   (g) $-\frac{1}{4}$ (h) $\frac{3}{p+q}$

2. slope of $AB = \frac{1}{3}$, slope of $BC = -\frac{3}{5}$, slope of $AC = 1\frac{1}{2}$

3. slope of $AB = \frac{1}{6}$, slope of $CD = -1$, slope of EF is undefined, slope of $GH = 0$

4. 8

5. 5

6. -1

7. $R\left(0, 2\frac{1}{11}\right)$

8. $t = -1\frac{2}{3}$, $t = 2$

9. (a) slope of $AB = \frac{1}{4}$, slope of $BC = 3$, slope of $CD = \frac{1}{4}$, slope of $AD = 3$
   (b) The slopes of the opposite sides of a parallelogram are equal.

10. (a) slope of $PQ = \frac{1}{2}$, slope of $QR = -2$, slope of $RS = \frac{1}{2}$, slope of $PR = -2$
   (b) The product of the adjacent slopes of a rectangle is -1.

11. (a) $C(75, 0)$ (b) $A(0, 100)$
   (c) $-\frac{4}{3}$ (d) 250 units

12. Possible answers: $\left(0, \frac{2}{5}\right)$, $(-1, 1)$

Exercise 11.3

1. (a) slope $= 5$; y-intercept $= -8$
   (b) slope $= -3$; y-intercept $= 1$
   (c) slope $= \frac{4}{7}$; y-intercept $= 0$
   (d) slope $= 0$; y-intercept $= -9$

2. (a) $y = 2x + 3$ (b) $y = -\frac{2}{7}x + 7$
   (c) $y = -3x - 5$ (d) $y = \frac{4}{9}x$

3. (a) $y = 3x + 1$ (b) $y = -2x + 1$
   (c) $y = 4$ (d) $y = -\frac{4}{5}x - 8\frac{3}{5}$
   (e) $y = \frac{3}{4}x - 8$ (f) $y = -x - 8$

4. (a) $y = \frac{2}{3}x + 3$ (b) $y = -3x + \frac{5}{7}$
   (c) $x = 4$ (d) $y = -6$
   (e) $y = \frac{5}{4}x - 10$ (f) $y = -\frac{1}{5}x - 3\frac{1}{2}$

5. (a) (i) $y = -2x + 3$
      (ii) slope $= -2$, y-intercept $= 3$
   (b) (i) $y = \frac{1}{4}x - 2$
      (ii) slope $= \frac{1}{4}$, y-intercept $= -2$
   (c) (i) $y = -\frac{3}{7}x - \frac{6}{7}$
      (ii) slope $= -\frac{3}{7}$, y-intercept $= -\frac{6}{7}$
   (d) (i) $y = -\frac{3}{5}x + 3$
      (ii) slope $= -\frac{3}{5}$, y-intercept $= 3$

6. $L_1: y = x$, $L_2: y = \frac{1}{2}x + 3$, $L_3: y = -\frac{3}{2}x - 2$, $L_4: y = -2$, $L_5: x = 3$

7. (a) $\frac{3}{4}$ (b) $y = \frac{3}{4}x - 4$
   (c) 6 units^2 (d) 5 units
   (e) 2.4 units

8. (a) 8   (b) $-1\frac{1}{8}$

9. $y = -\frac{3}{7}x - 5\frac{6}{7}$

10. $y = -\frac{4}{5}x + 3$

11. (a) AB: $x = -4$; BC: $y = 1\frac{1}{6}x + 2\frac{2}{3}$; CA: $y = \frac{2}{3}x + 3\frac{2}{3}$

    (b) $\left(0, 3\frac{2}{3}\right)$

    (c) 9 units^2

    (d) 1.95 units

12. (a)

x	20	40	60	80	100
y	800	1,400	2,000	2,600	3,200

    (b) $y = 30x + 200$

    (c) (i) 30, cost per person in \$

        (ii) 200, basic charge for a party

13. $y = -x + 2$

Review Exercise 11

1. (a) $p = -3, p = 5$

    (b) $y = -1\frac{1}{2}x - 8$; $k = -2$

2. (a) $y = -\frac{2}{3}x + 6$

    (b) $R(-3, -4)$

    (c) 54 units^2

    (d) $PQ = \sqrt{117}$ units; 9.98 units

3. (a) $AB = \sqrt{13}$ units, $BC = \sqrt{13}$ units, $CA = \sqrt{26}$ units

    (c) right triangle

    (d) 2.55 units

    (e) $(4, 0)$

4. (a) $y = \frac{1}{2}x + 4$

    (b) 6

    (c) $OA = \sqrt{13}$ units, $OB = \sqrt{52}$ units

    (d) $\triangle OAB$ is not a right triangle.

5. (a) CD: $y = 6$, AC: $y = 2\frac{1}{2}x - 10$

    (b) $B(4, 0)$, $C(6.4, 6)$

    (c) 51.2 units^2

    (d) 25: 64

6. (a) $AG = \sqrt{20}$ units, $BG = \sqrt{10}$ units, $CG = \sqrt{20}$ units, $DG = \sqrt{10}$ units

    (d) G is the point of intersection of diagonals AC and BD.

    (e) parallelogram

7. (a) $y = -\frac{2}{3}x + 4$

    (b) $B(0, 4)$

    (c) $y = 2x + 4$

    (d) $\triangle ABC$ is not a right triangle.

    (e) 16 units^2

8. (a) $\frac{3}{4}$

    (b) $P(-4, 0)$, $Q(0, 3)$, $R(4, 0)$, $S(0, -3)$

    (c) $-\frac{3}{4}$

    (d) QR: $y = -\frac{3}{4}x + 3$, RS: $y = \frac{3}{4}x - 3$, PS: $y = -\frac{3}{4}x - 3$

9. (a) $y = -\frac{1}{7}x + 9$

    (b) $AB = \sqrt{160}$ units, $AD = \sqrt{160}$ units

    (d) 80 units^2

10. (a) $B(a, a)$, $C(0, a)$, $P(0, 1)$, $Q(a, 1)$, $R(a - 1, a)$, $S(0, a - 1)$

    (b) $PQ = \sqrt{a^2 - 2a + 2}$ units, $QR = \sqrt{a^2 - 2a + 2}$ units

    (d) square

Chapter 12   Mensuration of Pyramids, Cylinders, Cones and Spheres

Try It!

1. 14.0 ft^2

2. (a) $VA = 5$ cm, $VB = 5$ cm, $AB = 4.24$ cm

    (b) 26.1 cm^2

3. 126 cm^3

4. (a) 896 cm^2 **(b)** 569 cm^3

5. (a) 28π in.^{3} **(b)** 36π in.^{2}

6. 4.89 cm

7. (a) 8 cm   **(b)** 40 : 33

8. (a) 226 cm^3 **(b)** 1,140 cm^2

    (c) 2,410 cm^3

9. (a) 60π in.^{2} **(b)** 96π in.^{2}

10. 3 cm

11. (a) 84π cm^3 **(b)** 42π cm^3

12. (a) 4.15 cm   **(b)** 203 cm^2

13. 88.0 cm^3

14. 2 : 1

15. 256 cm^3

16. 50.3 cm^2

17. 6.91 cm

18. (a) 94.2 cm^3 **(b)** 104 cm^2

Exercise 12.1

1. (a) 15.6 cm^2 **(b)** 31.2 cm^2

2. (a) 70 in.^{3} **(b)** 297 in.^{3}

    (c) 168 in.^{3} **(d)** 150 in.^{3}

3. 51.6 ft^2

4. 140 cm^3

5. 210 m^3

6. (a) 400 cm^3 **(b)** 360 cm^2

7. (a) 223 in.^{2} **(b)** 192 in.^{3}

8. 6 cm

9. 15 ft

10. (a) 10.4 cm^2 **(b)** 17.3 cm^3

    (c) 5.39 cm

11. 6,240 in.^{3}

12. 9.16×10^7 ft^3

13. (a) 2,000 cm^2 (b) 6,520 cm^3

14. 20 cm

15. Height = 4 cm, Length = 9 cm;
     Height = 9 cm, Length = 6 cm

Exercise 12.2

1. (a) Volume = 1470 in.^{3}, Surface area = 716 in.^{2}
     (b) Volume = 7630 in.^{3}, Surface area = 2210 in.^{2}

2. Volume = 34.6 in.^{3}, Surface area = 75.4 in.^{2}

3. Volume = 462 cm^3, Surface area = 440 cm^2

4. (a) 452 cm^3 (b) 276 cm^2

5. (a) 7 in.   (b) 7.96 in.

6. (a) 5 cm   (b) 3.99 cm

7. (a) 66 cm   (b) 80 cm

8. (a) 45 in.   (b) 33 : 47

9. (a) 689 cm^3 (b) 674 cm^2

10. (a) 1,780 in.^{3} (b) 1,020 in.^{2}

11. 12.4 cm

12. (a) 3,930 mm^3 (c) 1,600 mm^2

13. (a) 58.9 cm^3 (b) 47.1 cm^2

14. (a) 5,650 cm^3 (b) 97,200 cm^3
     (c) 14.7 cm   (d) 18

15. (a) 2.5 cm   (b) 1,410 cm^3
     (c) 5,670 cm^2 (d) 11,300 cm^3

16. (a) *B*   (b) No

Exercise 12.3

1. (a) 245 cm^2 (b) 1,370 cm^2

2. (a) 25,10 in.^{2} (b) 393 in.^{2}

3. (a) 2,710 cm^3 (b) 1,280 cm^3

4. (a) 1,820 cm^2 (b) 8,800 cm^3

5. (a) 5 in.   (b) 227 in.^{3}
     (c) 157 in.^{2}

6. (a) 13 cm   (b) 12 cm
     (c) 314 cm^3

7. (a) 4 cm   (b) 5 cm
     (c) 75.4 cm^2

8. 3.69 cm

9. (a) 1,060 in.^{3} (b) 28.6 in.
     (c) 540 in.^{2}

10. (a) 679 cm^3 (b) 509 g

11. 36

12. (a) 436 mm^3 (b) 486 mm^2

13. (a) 6 cm   (b) 188 cm^2
     (c) 302 cm^3

14. (a) $h = 8$, $v = 7$, volume = $\frac{392}{3}\pi$ cm^3; $h = 9$, $r = 6$,
     volume = 108π cm^3
     (b) $r = 10$

Exercise 12.4

1. (a) Surface area = 452 cm^2, Volume = 905 cm^3
     (b) Surface area = 28.3 m^2, Volume = 14.1 m^3
     (c) Surface area = 1020 mm^2, Volume = 3050 mm^3

2. (a) Surface area = 531 cm^2, Volume = 1150 cm^3
     (b) Surface area = 0.503 ft^2, Volume = 0.0335 ft^3
     (c) Surface area = 154 mm^2, Volume = 180 mm^3

3. (a) 281 in.^{2} (b) 42 in.^{3}

4. (a) 55.4 cm^2 (b) 38.8 cm^3

5. (a) 1,140 cm^2 (b) 2,790 cm^3

6. (a) 3 : 4   (b) 9 : 16
     (c) 27 : 64

7. 7.5 cm

8. (a) 3 cm   (b) 113 cm^2

9. (a) 254 cm^2 (b) 316 cm^3

10. (a) 6 cm   (b) 452 cm^2

11. (a) 565 in.^{3} (b) $\frac{8}{27}$ in.

12. (a) 6 cm   (b) 176 cm^2

13. (a) 5 cm   (b) 576 cm^3
     (c) 361 cm^2

14. (a) 718 in.^{3} (b) 354 in.^{3}
     (c) 757 in.^{2}

15. (a) 576 mm^3 (b) 550 mm^2

16. (a) 8 cm by 8 cm by 8 cm
     (b) 244 cm^3

Review Exercise 12

1. (a) 80 in.^{3} (b) $13\frac{1}{3}$ in.^{3}
     (c) 36.1 in.^{2}

2. (a) 324 cm^3 (b) 19.5 cm
     (d) 489 cm^2

3. (a) 8,704 cm^3 (b) 2,624 cm^2

4. (a) 2,640 cm^3 (b) 1,340 cm^2

5. (a) 5.64 cm   (b) 284 cm^2

6. (a) 10.3 cm   (b) Rotate about *BC*
     (c) 546 cm^2

7. (a) 874 cm^2 (b) 1560 cm^3
     (c) 7.19 cm

8. (a) 1,750 cm^3 (b) 833 cm^2

9. (a) 5 in.   (b) 32 : 125

10. (a) 0.226 m^3 (b) 0.9 m

11. (a) (i) 4.02 m^3 (ii) 4,020,000 cm^3
     (b) (i) 9,420 cm^3 (ii) 0.00942 m^3
     (c) 426

12. (a) 3,370 cm^2
     (b) 18,300 cm^3
     (c) 12.1 cm

13. (a) 16 in.   (b) 8,550 in.^{2}
     (c) 27,100 in.^{3} (d) 7,580 lb

14. (a) 660 cm³   **(b)** 2,650 cm²
(c) 10,600 cm³   **(d)** 7.36 cm
15. (b) 793 cm², 1,330 cm³   **(c)** 10.3 cm
(d) 2 bottles

Chapter 13   Data Analysis
Try It!

1.

Grades	Tally	Frequency
A	//// ////	9
B	//// //// /	11
C	//// ////	10
D	////	4
E	//	2
	Total	**36**

2. (a)

Prices ($)	Tally	Frequency
$10 < x \leqslant 20$	////	5
$20 < x \leqslant 30$	//// ///	8
$30 < x \leqslant 40$	//// ///	8
$40 < x \leqslant 50$	///	3
	Total	**24**

(b) 45.8%

3. (a)

Kinds of Movies	Sixth Graders	Eight Graders	Total
Action (A)	10	8	18
Comedy (C)	10	5	15
Romance (R)	5	12	17
Total	**25**	**25**	**50**

(b) A: 36%, C: 30%, R: 34%
(c) A: 40%, C: 40%, R: 20%
(d) A: 32%, C: 20%, R: 48%
(e) Although almost equal percentages of students like each of the three kinds of movies, the sixth graders like action and comedy movies much more than romance movies. Almost half of the eight graders like romance movies and the percentage is more than twice that of the sixth graders.

4. (a) 36 kg   **(c)** A
5. (a) The sales of coffee dropped over the first 3 hours, from 8 A.M. to 10 A.M., and then increased slightly at 11 A.M.

(b) 10 A.M.
(c) 94
6. (b) The histogram shows that most of the students took between 50 and 70 minutes to complete the assignment. There are more students in the highest class than in the lowest class.
7. (b) Except for a slight increase in 1990, the crude birth rate decreased from 1970 to 2010. The drop in 1980 was the greatest and the drop from 1990 to 2010 was smaller.
(c) 11.6 to 12.0
8. (a) The Consumer Price Index increased over the years from 2005 to 2011, although there is a big drop in 2007. The increase in the later years was greater than that in the earlier years.
(b) 89
(c) Year 2008; 10 points
9. (b) Most of the data points are clustered in the shape of a straight line, except for the points (2, 6) and (6, 1).
(d) The line which runs through the data points has a negative slope. Thus, there is a negative correlation between the number of hours spent watching TV per night and the number of A's scored.

Exercise 13.1

1.

Ages	Tally	Frequency
12	//// /	6
13	//// //// ////	14
14	//// ////	9
15	///	3
	Total	**32**

2. (a)

Candidates	Tally	Frequency
Alan	//// ////	10
Ben	//// //// //// /	16
Cliff	//// //// ////	14
	Total	**40**

(b) Ben

3. (a)

Study Preference	Women	Men	Total
Approved	98	21	119
Disapproved	37	74	111
Total	**135**	**95**	**230**

(i) 111   **(ii)** 21

(b)

Study Preference	Seventh grades	Eighth grades	Nineth grades	Total
Eat breakfast regularly	53	80	22	155
Do not eat breakfast regularly	9	40	30	79
Total	**62**	**120**	**52**	**234**

(i) 234   **(ii)** 80   **(iii)** 155

4. (a)

Study Preference	Boys	Girls	Total
Study alone	8%	18.7%	26.7%
Study in pairs	53%	26.4%	32%
Study in a group	20%	21.3%	41.3%
Total	**33.3%**	**66.7%**	**100%**

(b) The boys distinctly prefer to study in a group, as evident by a high percentage of 60. The percentage of boys who prefer to study in a group is twice that of the girls. The preference to study in pairs seems more for the girls; 40% of them prefer to study in pairs. This is also twice that of the boys who prefer to study in pairs.

5. (a)

Grades	Tally	Frequency
A	////	5
B	//// ///	8
C	//// //// /	12
D	//// ////	9
F	//// /	6
Total		**40**

(b) Grade C   **(c)** 32.5%

6. (a)

Distances (in km)	Tally	Frequency
$0 < x \leqslant 2$	///	3
$2 < x \leqslant 4$	//// /	6
$4 < x \leqslant 6$	//// ////	9
$6 < x \leqslant 8$	//// //	7
$8 < x \leqslant 10$	////	5
Total		**30**

(b) 40%

7. (a)

Study Preference	Seventh graders	Eighth graders	Total
Country (C)	4	2	6
Hip Hip (H)	5	7	12
Jazz (J)	2	5	7
Rock (R)	9	6	15
Total	**20**	**20**	**40**

(b) 35%

(d) Overall, the preference of the students for Rock music is the greatest with 37.5% of all students liking Rock music. This is clearly the case for the 7th graders; 45% of the 7th graders like Rock music. The 8th graders (35%) like Hip Hop music more.

8. (a)

Study Preference	Male	Female	Total
Drama Club	8	14	22
Math Club	8	4	12
Chess Club	8	12	20
Literary Club	4	6	10
Total	**28**	**36**	**64**

(b)

Study Preference	Male	Female	Total
Drama Club	28.6	38.9	34.4.
Math Club	28.6	11.1	18.8
Chess Club	28.6	33.3	31.3
Literary Club	14.8	16.7	15.6
Total	**100**	**100**	**100**

(c) The Drama Club has the highest percentage of involvement (34.4%) from the students. 38.9% of the female students are involved in its activities. However, it is not true for the male students as an equal percentage of only 28.6 each are involved in Drama, Math and Chess Clubs.

9. (a)

	Men	Women	Children	Total
Shopping	0.04	0.26	0	0.3
Sports	0.24	0.1	0.14	0.48
Watching TV	0.12	0.04	0.06	0.22
Total	**0.4**	**0.4**	**0.2**	**1.0**

(b)

	Men	Women	Children	Total
Shopping	0.13	0.87	0	1.0
Sports	0.5	0.21	0.29	1.0
Watching TV	0.12	0.18	0.27	1.0
Total	**0.4**	**0.4**	**0.2**	**1.0**

(c) Almost half (0.48) of the group of people surveyed preferred sports as their weekend activities and of which 0.24 of these people are male. Children also form a high ratio of those who preferred sports. 0.26 out of 0.30 of the people who preferred shopping are women. Only 0.22 of the people preferred watching TV.

(d) Table 3 shows the proportion of men, women and children in each activity. Women constitute 0.87 of those who preferred shopping as a weekend activity, men forms 0.5 of those who preferred sports and 0.55 of those who preferred watching TV.

10. (a)

Number of defective vases	Tally	Frequency
0	### ///	8
1	### ###	10
2	###	5
3	////	4
4	///	3
	Total	**30**

(b) 60%

11. (a)

Number of hours	Tally	Frequency
$0 < x \leqslant 3$	### ### ///	13
$3 < x \leqslant 6$	### ///	8
$6 < x \leqslant 9$	///	3
$9 < x \leqslant 12$	///	3
	Total	**27**

(b) 40.7%

12. (a)

Lifetime of batteries (in hours)	Tally	Frequency
$0 < x \leqslant 2$		0
$2 < x \leqslant 4$	////	3
$4 < x \leqslant 6$	### /	6
$6 < x \leqslant 8$	### ### //	12
$8 < x \leqslant 10$	### ////	9
	Total	**30**

Exercise 13.2

1. (a) chips **(b)** 210
   (c) candy and popcorn
   (d) chips, chocolate bars and fruit
2. (a) May **(b)** 1 : 2
   (c) 6.5
3. (b) bar graph
4. (a) 2 km **(b)** 12.5%
   (c) The histogram shows that the number of students who stayed within 2 km from the school is the highest and the number who stayed 6 to 8 km from school is the least. The histogram is tallest at the left end and lowest on the right end.
5. (a) 25
   (b) The distribution is symmetrical about the middle class interval "85–90", which has the highest frequency.
6. (a) Andrew's monthly income increased steadily from January to March.
   (b) January; $500
   (c) His total income was greater than this total expenditure.
7. (a) 5 : 8 **(b)** Company D
   (c) 3
8. (b) 18%
   (c) The distribution is not symmetrical. It has a long tail on the right. The peak is at the interval "$50 < A \leqslant 70$".
9. (a) $35 < t \leqslant 40$; 10 **(c)** 62.5%
   (d) $45 < t \leqslant 70$
10. (b) Candy, cookies, fruit and ice cream.
   (c) Chips
   (d) Popcorn
11. (b) 60%
   (c) The shape of the new histogram is the same as the original one. However, the new histogram shifts $5 to the right as a result of the change in class intervals. The new class intervals are $35 < x \leqslant 45, 45 < x \leqslant 55$ etc.
12. (c) 9
14. (a) (i) 1 year **(ii)** 5 years

Exercise 13.3

1. (a) 40° C; 9 P.M. **(b)** 3
2. (a) The mobile phone subscription has an increasing trend. The increase is greatest from 2006 to 2008 but subscriptions grew at a slower rate after 2010.
   (b) 7.8 millions
3. (b) The closing price of the stock decreases steadily, except for a slight increase in price between Tuesday and Wednesday before it decreases again.

4. (a) high negative linear correlation
   (b) moderate positive linear correlation
   (c) high non-linear correlation
   (d) no correlation
5. (a) −0.07
   (b) negative
   (c) high
   (d) There is a high negative correlation between the number of hours the students spent on online activities and their academic performances that is the fewer the number of hours the students spent on online activities, the better/higher are their grade point averages.
6. (b) The boy's height increase by 7 cm each year from age 8 to 10 and by 6 cm each year from age 10 to 12. From age 12 to 13, he grows by 5 cm and from age 13 to 14, his growth slows down to 2 cm.
   (c) (i) At age 15, he is likely to be still growing by 2 cm each year. His height is probably about 171 cm.
   (ii) At age 24, he is likely to have stopped growing. His height is probably about 171 to 173 cm.
7. (b) (i) 1.77%   (ii) 1.19%
   (c) The trend of the population is increasing. However, the population grows at a much slower rate from 2003 to 2012.
   (d) 4.29 millions
8. (b) The data points are clustered in a way that closely resembles a rising straight line, except for one point (2, 2).
   (c) The line of best fit has a positive slope. Thus, there is a positive correlation between the amount of sunlight exposure per day and plant growth.
9. (b) The data points seem to cluster roughly in the shape of a curve, but the point (16, 85) deviates from the other points.
   (c) There is a low non-linear correlation between age and pulse rate of the group of young people.
10. (b) The unemployment rate dropped gradually from 2004 to 2007. The trend of the unemployment from 2007 to 2010 is an increasing one. The greatest increase was from 2008 to 2009. However, the unemployment rate dropped again in 2011.
    (c) 8.1%
11. (a) one hour after drinking, 0.08%
    (b) 0.02%
    (c) at least 2.5 hours
12. (b) Most of the data points roughly clustered in a way that resembles a straight line. Since the line of best fit has a positive slope, there is a low positive correlation between the total fat and the total calories in fast food.

(c) (i) 10.833
    (ii) $y = \dfrac{65}{6}x + 205$
(d) 422 calories

Review Exercise 13

1. (a) 29   (b) basketball, soccer
2. (a) 3:1   (b) Choir
   (c) Dance   (d) 39
3. (b) The growth in height is greatest from age 11 to 12, and then slows down in the next four years. Her height remains the same from age 16 to 17, which shows that she has probably stopped growing in height.
   (c) 169 cm
   (d) (i) 67.2   (ii) $163\dfrac{1}{3}$
4. (c) $8\dfrac{1}{3}\%$
5. (b) The SGD per USD exchange rate is decreasing steadily over the years from 2005 to 2012, except in 2009 when there is a slight increase. The decrease in the rate slowed down in 2012.
   (c) 1.20
6. (b) 3
   (c) 2nd day; 5° F
7. (b) There is a high positive correlation between the number of people going to the beach and the average daily temperature.
8. (a) (ii) There is no correlation between the number of hours spent in the mall and the number of dollars spent, as shown by the random scattering of the data points.
   (d) Overall, 56% of people have shopping as the main intention of going to the shopping mall. However, this is not true for the group of age 29 years and below. Only 24% goes to the shopping mall to shop. 88% of the 30 to 50 years old and 56% of the 51 years and above have shopping as their main intention of going to the shopping mall.

Chapter 14   More About Quadratic Equations
Try It!

1. $x = -\dfrac{7}{5}, x = 3$
2. $x = \dfrac{2}{3}$
3. $x = -\dfrac{3}{5}, x = \dfrac{9}{2}$
4. (a) $x = -5, x = 7$
   (b) $x = -8.80, x = 0.796$
5. (a) $\left(-\dfrac{1}{2}\right)^2$ (b) $\left(\dfrac{4}{5}\right)^2$

6. $x = -1.19, x = 4.19$
7. $x = 0.814, x = 3.69$
8. $x = -2.11, x = 0.356$
9. $x = -\dfrac{4}{3}$
10. no real roots
11. $x = -1.80, x = 0.554$

12.

x	–3	–2	–1	0	1	2	3
$y = x^2 + x - 4$	2	–2	–4	–4	2	2	8

13.

x	–5	–4	–3	–2	–1	0	1
$y = x^2 + 4x + 4$	9	4	1	0	1	4	9

14.

x	–2	–1	0	1	2	3
$y = x^2 - x + 3$	9	5	3	3	5	9

15. 1.30 m
16. $x = 7.54$; 15.4 cm

Exercise 14.1

1. **(a)** $x = 2, x = 12$
   (b) $x = -15, x = 2$
   (c) $x = -\dfrac{1}{2}, x = 7$
   (d) $x = \dfrac{4}{3}, x = 2$
   (e) $x = -2, x = \dfrac{3}{5}$
   (f) $x = -\dfrac{3}{4}, x = -\dfrac{1}{2}$
   (g) $x = -\dfrac{1}{5}, x = \dfrac{1}{3}$
   (h) $x = -\dfrac{3}{7}, x = \dfrac{5}{2}$
   (i) $x = -\dfrac{7}{9}, x = 0$
   (j) $x = -\dfrac{5}{4}$

2. **(a)** $\dfrac{7}{2}$
   (b) $x = -10, x = 1$
   (c) $x = -\dfrac{5}{2}, x = \dfrac{4}{3}$
   (d) $x = -\dfrac{6}{5}, x = \dfrac{6}{5}$
   (e) $x = 0, x = \dfrac{11}{7}$
   (f) $x = -1, x = 8$
   (g) $x = 0, x = 3$
   (h) $x = -\dfrac{5}{6}, x = -1$
   (i) $y = -15, y = \dfrac{7}{5}$
   (j) $y = -\dfrac{5}{4}$

3. 10 cm
4. 6
5. No

Exercise 14.2

1. **(a)** 1^2 **(b)** $(-2)^2$
   (c) $(-4)^2$ **(d)** $\left(\dfrac{7}{2}\right)^2$
   (e) $\left(-\dfrac{1}{2}\right)^2$ **(f)** $\left(-\dfrac{11}{2}\right)^2$

2. **(a)** $x = -10, x = 4$
   (b) $x = 1, x = 4$
   (c) $x = -6.65, x = -1.35$
   (d) $x = -0.162, x = 6.16$
3. **(a)** $x = -10.3, x = 0.292$
   (b) $x = -0.348, x = 14.3$
   (c) $x = -3.19, x = -0.314$
   (d) $x = 0.584, x = 11.4$
4. **(a)** $x = -7.65, x = 0.65$
   (b) $x = -0.618, x = 1.62$
   (c) $x = -6.55, x = 0.550$
   (d) $x = 0.477, x = 4.19$
5. **(a)** $x = -13.7, x = 0.659$
   (b) $x = 1.16, x = 13.8$
   (c) $x = -3.60, x = 0.602$
   (d) $x = -0.394, x = 8.89$
6. 15.4 cm
7. $x^2 - 4x + 1$
8. no real roots

Exercise 14.3

1. **(a)** $x = 0.523, x = 11.5$
   (b) $x = -0.177, x = -2.82$
   (c) $x = -1, x = 1.67$
   (d) no real roots
   (e) $x = -0.611, x = 0.468$
   (f) $x = -1.42, x = 0.793$
2. **(a)** $x = -1.11, x = 3.61$
   (b) $x = -1.27, x = 1.77$
   (c) $x = -0.158, x = 3.16$
   (d) $x = -0.189, x = 2.39$
3. **(a)** real and distinct; $x = -2.70, x = 3.70$
   (b) real and distinct; $x = -0.475, x = 2.81$
   (c) real and equal; $x = 2$
   (d) no real roots; no solution

4. (a) $x = -1.90$, $x = 0.396$
  (b) $x = -10.3$, $x = 2.32$
  (c) $x = -6.44$, $x = 0.104$
  (d) $x = -2.77$, $x = 2.17$

5. (a) 50 m
  (c) 4.32 s
  (b) 2 s
  (d) 3.24 s

6. (a) 0, 1 or 2
  (b) find the value of $b^2 - 4ac$

Exercise 14.4

1. (a)

x	–3	–2	–1	0	1	2	3
$y = x^2 - 3$	6	1	–2	–3	–2	1	6

  (c) $x = -1.73$, $x = 1.73$

2. (a)

x	–1	0	1	2	3	4	5
$y = x^2 - 4x + 4$	9	4	1	0	1	4	9

  (c) $x = 2$

3. (a)

x	–3	–2	–1	0	1	2
$y = x^2 + x + 2$	8	4	2	2	4	8

  (c) no real roots

4. (b) $x = -1$, $x = 3$

5. (b) $x = -2.69$, $x = 0.186$

6. (b) no real roots

7. (a) $(4 - x)$ units
  (d) 2 units by 2 units

8. $x = -3.65$, $x = 1.65$

9. (b) $x = 0$, $x = 3$
  (c) Draw the line $y = 4$; $x = -1$, $x = 4$

Exercise 14.5

1. 35, 36
2. 17, 19
3. 24 cm
4. (a) $34 - x$
  (b) 11 cm by 23 cm
5. (a) $x^2 - 22x + 29 = 0$
  (b) $x = 1.41$, $x = 20.6$
  (c) 466 cm^2
6. 2 years old
7. 24 in.
8. 26
9. 2.6 cm
10. 2 min
11. (a) 60 ft
  (b) 35 ft
12. 52.3 mph
13. 5.15 s
14. 30.3 cm
15. (a) (i) $\dfrac{50}{x}$
  (ii) $\dfrac{50}{x + 0.5}$

(b) $4x^2 + 2x - 25 = 0$
  (c) $x = -2.76$, $x = 2.26$
  (d) 22 min 6 s

16. (a) (i) 72
  (ii) $5,040
  (b) $75
  (c) $80

Review Exercise 14

1. (a) $x = -3$, $x = 2.5$
  (b) $x = -\dfrac{1}{3}$, $x = 7$
  (c) $x = -1\dfrac{2}{3}$, $x = 1\dfrac{2}{3}$
  (d) $x = \dfrac{3}{4}$, $x = 2$

2. (a) $x = 0.764$, $x = 5.24$
  (b) $x = -4.65$, $x = 0.646$
  (c) no real roots
  (d) $x = -0.275$, $x = 7.27$

3. (b) $x = -4.37$, $x = 1.37$

4. (a) $x = -10.6$, $x = 7.57$
  (b) $x = -0.402$, $x = 0.0690$
  (c) no real roots
  (d) $x = -0.220$, $x = 1.82$

5. (a) $x = -7$, $x = 5$
  (b) $x = 2.4$, $x = 4.5$
  (c) $x = -1.62$, $x = 0.618$
  (d) $x = -\dfrac{2}{3}$, $x = \dfrac{5}{7}$

6. (a) $x = -0.153$, $x = -2.18$
  (b) $x = 0$, $x = 2$
  (c) $x = -3.27$, $x = 8.27$
  (d) $x = -\dfrac{1}{9}$, $x = \dfrac{1}{6}$

7. 1.86 m

8. 55.2 mph

9. (a) $(3v - 2)(2v + 5)$
  (b) $x = -6\dfrac{1}{2}$, $x = -3\dfrac{1}{3}$

10. (a) (i) $24 - x$
  (ii) $x + 17$
  (iii) $-x^2 + 7x + 408$
  (b) $x = 3$, $x = 4$

11. (a) 3.62 m
  (b) garden plot A

12. (a) (i) $\dfrac{200}{x}$ gallons
  (ii) $x^2 + 7x - 700 = 0$
  (b) $x = -30.19$, $x = 23.19$
  (c) 10.3 gallons